SHIP MODELS
FROM THE AGE OF SAIL

SHIP MODELS
FROM THE AGE OF SAIL
Building and Enhancing Commercial Kits

KERRY JANG

Seaforth
PUBLISHING

Copyright © Kerry Jang 2022

First published in Great Britain in 2022 by
Seaforth Publishing
An imprint of Pen & Sword Books Ltd
47 Church Street, Barnsley
S Yorkshire S70 2AS

www.seaforthpublishing.com
Email info@seaforthpublishing.com

British Library Cataloguing in Publication Data
A CIP data record for this book is available from the British Library

ISBN 978-1-5267-7753-9 (Hardback)

ISBN 978-1-5267-7754-6 (ePub)

ISBN 978-1-5267-7755-3 (Kindle)

All rights reserved. No part of this publication may be reproduced or transmitted in any form or by any means, electronic or mechanical, including photocopying, recording, or any information storage and retrieval system, without prior permission in writing of both the copyright owner and the above publisher.

The right of Kerry Jang to be identified as the author of this work has been asserted in accordance with the Copyright, Designs and Patents Act 1988

Pen & Sword Books Limited incorporates the imprints of Atlas, Archaeology, Aviation, Discovery, Family History, Fiction, History, Maritime, Military, Military Classics, Politics, Select, Transport, True Crime, Air World, Frontline Publishing, Leo Cooper, Remember When, Seaforth Publishing, The Praetorian Press, Wharncliffe Local History, Wharncliffe Transport, Wharncliffe True Crime and White Owl.

Typeset and designed by Neil Sayer
Printed and bound in India by Replika Press Pvt Ltd

Contents

Preface — 6
Acknowledgments — 6
1 The Fun of Ship Models — 7
2 Resources - Research, Kits, Semi-kits, Timbering Sets and More — 13
3 Essential Tools — 21
4 Solid Hull Modelling – United States Ship *Perry* — 29
5 Single Plank-on-Bulkhead Modelling – *Cutty Sark* — 43
6 Double Plank-on-Bulkhead Modelling – HM Brig *Speedy* — 71
7 Semi-Scratch Double Plank-on-Bulkhead – The 74-Gun *Vanguard* — 85
8 Plank-on-Frame Modelling – French Naval Lugger *Le Coureur* — 121
9 Masts and Yards — 133
10 Standing Rigging — 145
11 Running Rigging — 155
12 Finishing Up and Inspiration — 165
Recommended References and Sources — 176

Preface

Those who make model sailing ships have long been considered amongst the most patient of all model makers. Whether the ship was made from a kit or was scratch-built requires the same fundamental skills and an understanding of nautical history and ship design. Acquiring and developing these skills and knowledge often takes years and has discouraged many modellers from having a go. Happily, advances in research and design, along with advanced prefabrication methods like laser cutting, resin casting, Computer Numerically Controlled (CNC) carving, 3D design, and chemical milling have now made building a model sailing ship accessible to a wide range of hobbyists with different skills and experience.

Despite these advances, successful completion of a ship from the age of sail still requires developing new modelling skills, a working knowledge of ships and the sea, and vocabulary that must be learned and practised. This volume presents a range of construction projects that will help you acquire these new skills and use them to build your model. Building a model ship requires a lot of problem solving and forethought and I hope my approach assists you in developing the confidence and skills to see a model to completion or going it alone to build one from scratch. In many ways, this book is really more about mistakes – how to avoid making them, but when they happen, how to recover from them.

Kerry Jang
Vancouver, Canada, June, 2021.

Acknowledgements

Special thanks to my son and daughter whose young and nimble fingers completed the most tedious tasks such as cutting and laying of thousands of copper hull plates to stropping hundreds of rigging blocks that I just didn't feel like doing some days. And most especially to my wife who never complained when I called her at the most inopportune moments to come down to the workshop to hold up photographic equipment; or to crawl around on the floor looking for that part I dropped and couldn't find. She always found them.

1: The Fun of Ship Models

'Would all the boys and girls aged 8 years old please come up to the front of the stage and get your present from Santa!' was the beginning of my interest in sailing ship models. In the late 1960s our family went to the annual Christmas pageant held by my father's labour union where hundreds of families gathered for a day of holiday cheer with magicians and sing-alongs accompanied with plenty of sugary drinks, candy and high sodium snacks. That year all the boys my age received a plastic model of the *Sovereign of the Seas* by the Aurora Plastics Corporation (Figure 1). I was mesmerized by the box top painting, and to my sugar addled mind it captured all the majesty and grace of King Charles I's most decorated vessel. I was fascinated by the instruction sheet's potted history and the strange words that was said to be inscribed on both sides of her rudder:

'Qui mare, qui fluctus, ventos, navesque, gubernat, Sospitet Hanc arcen, Carole magne tuam.'

It turns out these words were Latin and translated to 'May He whom sea, land and tides obey, and the winds that blow the ships, Guard this, great Charles, thy man-of-war with sustenance Divine...' and the history ended with, '...she was never defeated in battle although she saw a great deal of action. Then, in 1696 an overturned candle caused her to go up in flames, an ignominious end to a glorious ship.'

What were these sailing ships that on the one hand epitomized power and strength, but on the other hand were so fragile? From that day on I was hooked and scoured the local library shelves for books about sailing ships and the famous naval exploits of their crews both real and fictional.

The *Sovereign of Seas* model occupied a place of honour on our fireplace mantle. For years afterwards my parents and doting relatives

1

Aurora's 1967 *Sovereign of the Seas* plastic kit began my fascination with sailing ships. That spark must still be burning strong to make me purchase the kit again over 50 years later at an over-inflated collector's price.

2

Plastic sailing ship models come in many different scales. Pictured are Airfix's 1/180 HMS *Victory* and in 1/130 the clipper *Cutty Sark*. From Heller is the magnificent 1/75 scale galley *La Reale de France* and the 1/200 *La Belle Poule* made famous for bringing home to France Napoleon's ashes from Saint Helena, and the 1/200 scale model of King Louis XV's 116-gun *Royal Louis*. The 1/350 *Chinese Junk* is from Imai and Rod Langton's 1/300 scale 32-gun *Amazon* class frigate *Juno* is cast in resin for use in naval wargaming or display. Sailing ships of all types and nationalities can be found as plastic and card kits ready for assembly.

gifted several plastic sailing ship kits. Soon Airfix's *Victory*, *Cutty Sark*, and *Endeavour* joined the fireplace mantle fleet. Pride of place – my Mum's sideboard – was reserved for Revell's 1/96 scale *Thermopylae* built with a full set of billowing vacformed plastic sails and rigged with sewing thread. Plastic kits hit their zenith with Heller's large and detailed offerings of *Le Soleil Royal*, *Victory*, *Pamir*, *Passat* and my favourite, the galley *Reale de France*. Building these kits taught me the basic anatomy of sailing ships, introduced basic nautical vocabulary, and taught the practical aspects of rigging in which every line had a definite purpose (Figure 2).

At some point in the late 1980s I came to the realization that models of sailing ships should be made of wood just like the real thing. I started to subscribe to *Model Shipwright* and *Ships in Scale*, magazines that provided in-depth articles on how models were built from plans or how to modify a wooden kit to be more accurate. Being a university student with very limited means meant that a small kit was the best option for me. All of the wood, plans, fittings and instructions would be conveniently contained in one box. The local model shop carried several kits from the Danish company Billings and the Spanish makers Artesania Latina and Dikar. I purchased the Dikar kit of the Canadian fishing schooner *Bluenose* given its modest price and the box top claim it contained easy to follow instructions.

Quite a shock awaited me upon opening the box. Bundles of wood strips labelled as 'tanganyika', 'sapele' and 'mazonia' – what the

3

All that remains of my first attempt at a wooden model ship, Dikar's 1/88 scale kit of the Canadian fishing schooner *Bluenose*, are a few untouched cast metal fittings and now rusted wire. I abandoned the model over 30 years ago because I neither had the skills nor knowledge to successfully complete the model.

heck is that? Several walnut dowels, some die-cut plywood hull formers, and a couple of bundles of string. Only the bag of white metal fittings was something that resembled the plastic models I was used to. Instructions were multilingual in something resembling English (though I imagine the Spanish instructions were perfect) and a set of 1:1 scale drawings to show how the wood was to be cut, shaped and worked to get the model together. Despite my best attempt the model was a disaster. I didn't really know how to bend wood or shape a plank to fit the curved shape of a hull properly. The exotic woods defied bending, especially the mazonia that snapped before it bent. Moreover, the model was clearly designed to be a decorative item that instructed you to polish the brass fittings, gild any carvings in gold paint, and to varnish all of the natural woodwork despite the fact that *Bluenose* was painted black with a red lead bottom. In total frustration the model was thrown away and the cast metal parts and a few fittings remain in my scrap box over 30 years later (Figure 3).

Several years passed before I took another look at wooden ships again when I turned to scratch-building scenic waterline models after being inspired by the no nonsense approach of the famed miniaturist Donald McNarry. He built magnificent models using little more than scraps of wood and items scavenged around the house (Figure 4). In the past decade, I have had a second look at kits because a revolution was taking place in wooden ship kit design. Talented designers who were model makers themselves began creating kits that took advantage of computer aided design (CAD) and 3D modelling to ensure more accurate and realistic models. The wooden parts were now precisely cut with a laser, chemical milling or 'photo-etching' created delicate fittings and fully round CNC carved parts such as figureheads and bas relief decoration that just a few years earlier were unheard of in wooden ship kits. Recently, new highs have been achieved with fully shaped hull planks, assembly jigs and aids to ensure all of the thousands of parts that comprises a sailing ship are constructed accurately. The gap between what a model kit and a scratch-builder can produce is shrinking rapidly. The kit builder is only limited by what ships are kitted, while the scratch-builder is free to build whatever ship is desired.

Does this mean that wooden ship kits can be easily assembled like a plastic kit? Does this mean that traditional woodworking skills aren't required? The answer is a definite no! Despite extensive prefabrication these models still require you to learn how wood – a natural material – behaves. It's not a matter of sticking part #32 to part #33: you still have to learn how to bend, taper and bevel a plank so it lies properly on a curved surface. The parts are not assembled but fitted. Beyond the hull there is the matter of rigging and sails and it is not good enough to string a line between two points and call it done. At the very least the correct scale weight of line must be used and when the rigging is completed, anyone should be able to a pick out a line and understand its purpose by tracing its run. Sail making is yet another skill to master. In addition to learning how to stitch and sew, there is

4

A miniature (1/192) scenic model of the French schooner *La Jacinthe* built to the drawings by Jean Boudriot. The model was constructed using the methods described in Donald McNarry's *Ship Models in Miniature* (background). The hull and ship's boat were carved from scrap pieces of wood and the deck planking was cut from a piece of holly salvaged from a cabinet making shop. The sails are typing paper and the rigging painted copper wire stripped from old loudspeaker cables. The seascape was the most expensive item being a textured plastic sheet designed to resemble water. A few N scale figures taken from my model railway layout (that never seems to get finished) populate the deck and were painted to resemble French matelots.

the additional challenge of making sails that look like sails and not over-scale baggy pieces of cloth hung on a yardarm.

Building a sailing ship model is a satisfying experience. Understanding how a real ship is built and the materials used in its construction is key to creating a realistic model that breathes life. The purpose of this book is to help you gain this experience whether you are building one of the latest kits, a second-hand one found at a jumble sale, or thinking about scratch-building. There are a multitude of ways a model can be built, and understanding some basic kit designs and the techniques to get the best from them will ensure that the model gets finished – and proudly displayed on your Mum's sideboard!

THE SOLID HULL MODEL

The solid hull model is the oldest way to make a model ship. In its simplest form the hull is carved from a block of wood. With the help of templates that give the shape of the hull at points along its length (called *station lines*) the hull is shaped using gouges and rasps. The wood can be a single block, or the hull can be carved from two blocks that are joined together after carving. Another variation is that the block of wood is made up of several horizontal slices of wood (called *lifts*) that represents the horizontal cross sections of the ship's hull (called *waterlines*). Each lift is cut to shape and glued on top each other (known as the *bread and butter method*) and the edges are smoothed down to produce the hull. Virtually all solid hull kits provide a roughly shaped block of wood to be worked down to the final hull shape (Figure 5).

Carving wood and making the chips fly is a deeply satisfying activity as something beautiful slowly emerges from a formless block of wood. Solid hull models are typically full hull models and the interior of a ship cannot be shown unless the block of wood is hollowed out. Solid hull models are usually painted and do not require any hull planking, making them easier to build. However, a solid hull can be planked over with your own wood stock if the hull has a varnished natural wood finish (called *bright* finished). If you go this route it is important to adjust your templates so that the carved hull's dimensions are slightly smaller to accommodate the thickness of the planks. Solid hull models are perfectly suited for miniature and waterline model ships because there is no need to find or glue up large blocks of wood. How to build a solid hull model is shown in Chapter 4 with the brig USS *Perry* from the American company Bluejacket Shipcrafters of Maine.

5

Most solid hull kits available today are manufactured in the United States and provide the hull as a roughly shaped block of wood. The pilot boat *Phantom* by Model Shipways is a popular introductory model (bottom left). The hull of the *Bounty* (top) is from the now defunct Model Ship Company whose kits are readily found from online retailers and auction sites. In some kits the block covers the hull to the level of the main deck. In contrast, as shown on the two hulls pictured, the hull including the bulwarks are pre-carved as part of the block. John McKay's 'Anatomy of the Ship' book on the *Bounty* will provide a lot of information to fully detail the model.

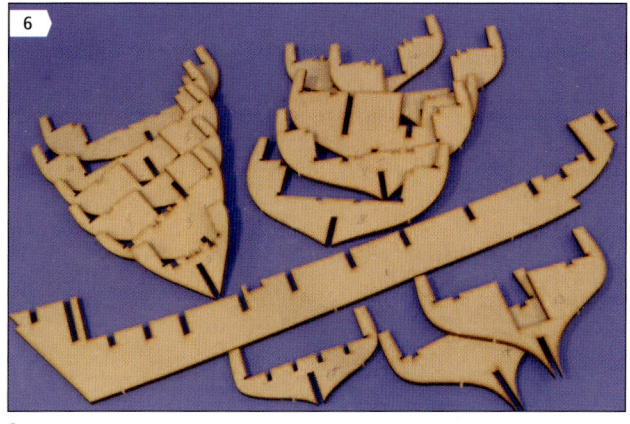

6

False keel and bulkheads characteristic of plank-on-bulkhead kits. Pictured are laser-cut parts from Vanguard Models 1/64 scale *Speedy* kit. Scratch-builders using this method will use plans obtained from a museum to trace out the ship's profile to create a false keel with the bulkheads traced from the 'body plan'.

PLANK-ON-BULKHEAD

Plank-on-bulkhead construction is the most common method found in kits and extensively used by scratch-builders as well. This method creates a skeleton of the hull that is planked over with strips of wood to sheath the framework like a skin. The backbone of the ship is called the *false keel* that represents the side profile of the ship that is slotted to take the *bulkheads* that form the ribs of the ship. The bulkheads are vertical cross sections that correspond to the shape of the ship at specific points along its length. A typical false keel and bulkhead system is shown in Figure 6.

There are many variations of this design. For example, if we look at the false keel, this part may incorporate the ship's stem, keel, and rudder post as one unit. Alternatively, the stem, keel and rudder post can be added as separate parts after the hull is planked, and each variation has implications for how the hull framework is planked over. The number of bulkheads also varies across kits with some providing relatively few widely spaced bulkheads whilst others provide several that are set closely together. Some designs only provide closely spaced bulkheads in strategic areas like the bow and stern to provide support for planks that have to go around extreme curves. A careful examination of the spacing and hull curves often suggests areas where filling the space between bulkheads with scrap

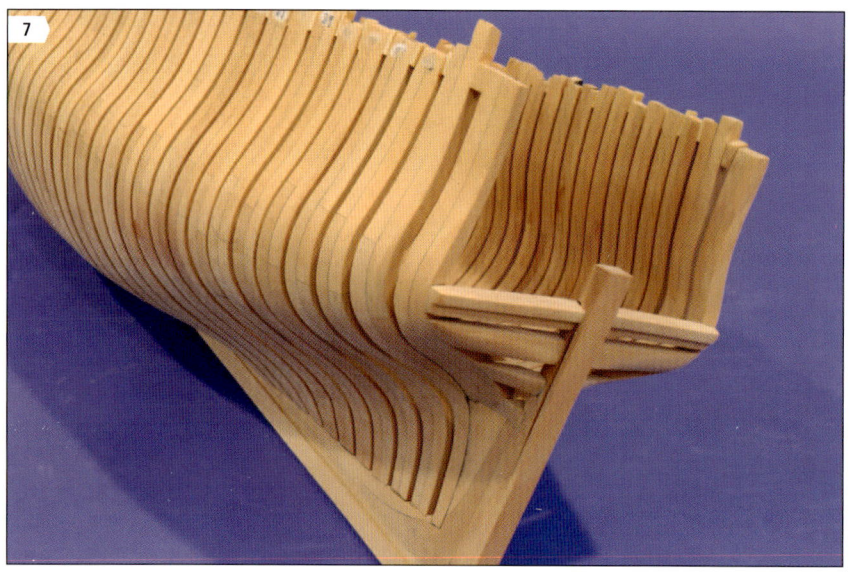

7 The stern timbers of the bomb vessel *Le Salamandre* to 1/48 scale. The framing is based on the drawings by Jean Boudriot and Hubert Berti. Each of the frame timbers was cut from pear wood planks that had been seasoned for a year. A band saw fitted with a fine blade roughly cut out each of the ship's timbers with the final shape worked in using a bench mounted power disc and spindle sanders, and finished with fine cut needle files powered by a lot of elbow grease. All the proper scarf joins were used and mistakes were plenty. In some cases it took three or four attempts to get the shapes correct. I started this model over 20 years ago and it remains unfinished.

wood is a wise precaution to support the planking. This is important because how the hull framework is planked also differs between kits. Some are 'single planked', meaning that only one layer of planks is applied to the framework, whereas others are 'double planked' in which the hull framework is planked twice – the first time with a softer wood, such as lime or basswood with the aim of getting the hull shape established in all three dimensions. None of this first layer of planking will be visible because it is covered by the second layer of planking that now has a firm base to adhere to. Unlike a double planked hull, a single planked model has to be done perfectly (or painted over) because there are no second chances – everything will show.

It is possible to turn a single planked hull into a double planked one by using the kit-supplied wood for the first layer and planking over that with your own wood stock. This will incur extra expense, and the finished hull will be oversized by the thickness of the second layer multiplied by two. You can reduce the thickness of the first planking by the thickness of the second, but that will mean finding a thickness sander or buying all new wood for the first planking.

Alternatively, the dimensions of the bulkheads themselves can be reduced but that's risky because it is very easy to inadvertently change the shape of the bulkhead. The variations of plank-on-bulkhead design and the techniques to tackle them are demonstrated with the build of the single planked clipper *Cutty Sark* (Chapter 5); the double planked with separate stem, keel, and rudder post design of the brig *Speedy* (Chapter 6); and the double planked integrated stem, keel and rudder post model of the 74-gun *Vanguard* (Chapter 7).

Framed Models

Framed models are the epitome of the model ship art. It is a form of model that seeks to represent if not reproduce exactly the way actual ships were built. A keel is laid, typically composed of many parts, followed by erecting the stem and rudder posts whose parts are all properly joined together with the correct *scarphs* or *scarfs* (eg, plain scarfs, hook scarfs, lock scarfs, etc). The ship's ribs are exact representations of a ship's frame, again made up of specific pieces of wood called *futtocks, floors,* and *top timbers* (Figure 7). The frames are built to reflect the national differences, such as French or English

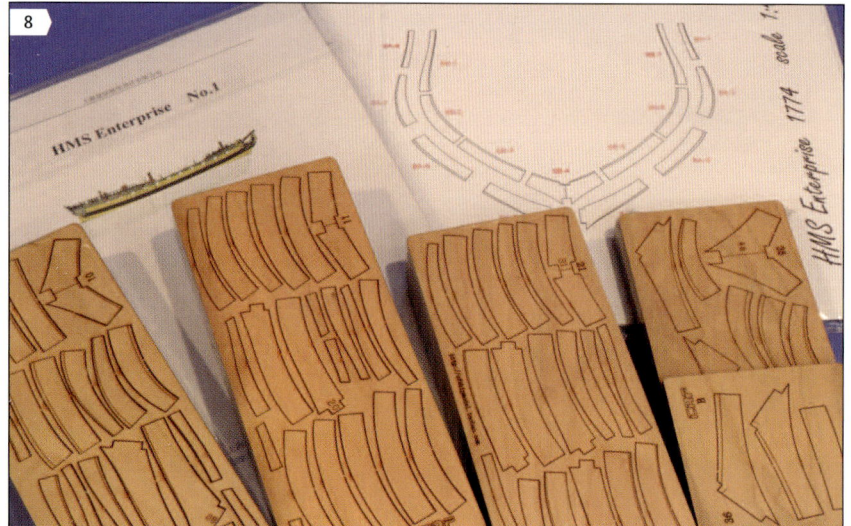

8 CAF Models has produced an impressive kit of the 28-gun frigate *Enterprize* (1774) in 1/48 scale. Every timber is laser- or CNC-cut and features laser etched markings to guide the bevelling of the frames after assembly. Pictured are just a few of the frame parts (futtocks and floors) and drawings. The kit is produced in North American cherry wood and weighed in at over 10 kgs.

9

Harold Hahn's stylized method of building ship's frames and building jig. Pictured are the frame blanks and jig for the schooner *Le Chaleur*. The Hahn method is described in his book *Ships of the American Revolution and their Models*.

10

The frame and keel under construction for the 16-gun brig-sloop *Pelican* using the Hahn method. Note how the tops of the frames have been extended so that the model lies in a perfect horizontal plane. The model is made from boxwood that has a creamy yellow colour.

practice in how the futtocks are cut, shaped and scarfed together. All of the planking applied to the inside (*ceiling planks*) and outside the hull are made to scale lengths and widths and fixed to the frames using the correct *shift of the butts* to ensure that the plank ends between rows are properly staggered. Each plank is fastened with miniature pegs or bolts called *trennels*. The same attention to detail is applied to all aspects of the model, from the laying of decks to all the fittings, masting, and rigging. No detail is too small to reproduce in miniature.

Framed models are often built from copies of the actual ship's draughts purchased from a museum. It is quite a thrill to build your model from the actual plans used to build the actual ship. With the plan in hand, the modeller would have to plot and draw (called *lofting*) out each frame and then apply the practice of the time to determine how large each futtock should be and what scarf joint to use to put them all together. There are several sets of commercially available plan sets that have done all the lofting for you and serve as the true scale patterns to cut your wood. Framed models permit the interior of the ship to be shown by leaving some or all of the planking off. Just like a dockyard administrator, supplies of wood would have to be procured and models in frame must use tight grained hardwoods such as box, pear, holly, and cherry. The models are built in purpose-made jigs that resemble a dockyard slipway to erect each part onto the keel. Thanks to 3D modelling and CAD design, fully detailed framed model kits cut from fine hardwoods are now available (Figure 8).

There are other types of framed model that show all of the ship's frames but in a more stylized and modeller-friendly way. One popular method is called the 'Hahn Method' after Mr Harold Hahn who developed the technique. Instead of piecing together each frame from individual futtocks and floor timbers, each frame is cut out of a generic 'frame blank' (Figure 9). The frame blank is made up of

11

Admiralty style framing on a 1/60 model of the *Royal William* being scratch-built by Mr Katsuji Tsuchiya. (Photo courtesy of Mr Katsuji Tsuchiya)

lengths of wood that are pieced together to approximate the shape of the frames. The joins between the lengths of wood do not correspond to the location of scarfs found on a real ship, but are an approximation to show the viewer that the frames are made up of several pieces of wood. Although the keel, stem, and rudder post are assembled together from individual parts, these parts incorporate several smaller constituent pieces that normally would have been shaped and pieced together individually. A second innovation is that the tops of the frames are extended so that the hull, when placed upside down on a flat surface is perfectly horizontal. In this way, the ability to mark the waterline, gunports, and decks is simplified because the flat surface serves as a consistent datum to take all measurements along the length of the hull. A third innovation is that the hull frames are fitted into a jig that holds the frames in the correct position and spacing, and that the jig has a hole cut out of its bottom to allow access into the interior. Hahn developed a large range of plans for British, French, and American ships from the American War of Independence. Each plan set provides the frame blank patterns and jig (Figure 10). Although the frames are simplified the finished product is impressive.

Navy Board or Admiralty Framing

Navy Board framing is the most stylized of all frames and was developed by model makers in Britain working to official Admiralty or Navy Board commissions. Such models were not designed to accurately show how a ship was built *per se*, but to illustrate the shape and volume of the hulls being built or proposed for the Navy. These models were essentially display pieces and the style of framing was more of an art form, evolving into a model making convention that makes use of 'single foothooks' [or 'futtocks'] for the frames. A real ship's frame is typically made of two layers of wood. The joins between the futtocks making up each slice are staggered so the joins do not overlap. The single foothook design leaves a few futtocks out on one of the slices, and where they are left out is carefully planned so that the gaps correspond to the sweep of the hull lines (Figure 11). An Admiralty style model is beautiful but, in reality, it is a model of a period model.

This short sampling of the different types of sailing ship models illustrates the wide variety of models that can be built. There are, of course, models that incorporate constructional and design elements from across the spectrum that is only limited by the ingenuity of the designer or the whim, skills, inclination, and resources of the builder. Beautiful model ships can be built from kits that have incorporated all of the latest innovations or from the meanest and most humble materials found around the house. All one really needs is a good set of plans to work from, a knowledge of how real ships were built, a few basic tools, some wood, and – most of all – the right attitude.

2: Resources
Research, Kits, Semi-kits, Timbering Sets and More

It is tempting to head out and buy a ship model kit after seeing an exciting new advertisement or review. It looks on paper to be just what you are looking for – the subject appeals, the construction appears straightforward, and the price is right. After that first flush of excitement and exchange of money, you have a closer look and more often than not experience a little buyer's remorse. The model may not get started or, as I have learned the hard way, started and then discarded or put away. A little research can save you a lot of heartache and this chapter is to point you to key references on how ships were built and some classic model making treatises to help you along the way. We will also have a look at some kits, semi-kits, and timbering sets to suit your skill and inclination. In this way, you will be well armed to spend your money and time not only wisely, but in a way to get the most enjoyment and satisfaction out of model shipbuilding.

THE RESEARCH PATHWAY

When picking a ship to model, there is a sequence of unconscious considerations that influences the ultimate decision. The first step is the type of ship. Did you want to build a ship of the line, a dashing little brig, maybe a gunboat or an exotic xebec? Were you were taken by Henry VIII's *Mary Rose* after a visit to Portsmouth or an elegant tea clipper? A little pilot boat perhaps, a lugger like *Le Coureur* or a rotund collier like Captain Cook's *Endeavour* in which Australia, New Zealand and much of the south Pacific was first charted. After a few candidates are selected, it is time to consider the nationality of the ships on the short list. Nationality is important because shipbuilding practices differ between countries. Part of the reason why is that a country's resources place limits on what and how a ship is made in order to get the best use of timber and cordage supplies. For example, the size and shape of futtocks differ between France and England in part due to the availability of large pieces of oak for frames. English construction made extensive use of wood offcuts, used to make angled *chocks* to help fasten the shorter pieces of wood together that are much less common in France (Figure 12). If you were considering a fully framed model, these constructional differences are centrally important. Such national differences are quite visible even on the fully planked hull. For example, take the main *wale* – a thick plank of wood fastened to the side of the ship to provide longitudinal stiffness to the hull. English practice was to plank the wale out of angled pieces of wood whereas the French used straight planks (Figure 13).

Model makers and scholars are well served by books on these very topics. English practices are extensively covered by Peter Goodwin's *The Construction and Fitting of the English Man of War 1650-1850*, Brian Lavery's *The Arming and Fitting of English Ships of War 1600-1815*, and James Lees' T*he Masting and Rigging of English Ships of War 1625-1860* (Figure 14). French practice is covered by Jean Boudriot and Hubert Berti in their seminal four-volume *Le Vasseu de 74 Canons (The 74 Gun Ship)* that describes in intimate detail the selection of timbers, construction of each frame, the fitting out, rigging and operation of a typical French 74-gun ship of the line (Figure 15). Indeed, their publishing company ANCRE continues to regularly release books on ships that served in the French sailing

12

Differences in French and English frame construction are highlighted when comparing Jean Boudriot's *The Seventy Four Gun Ship* and Peter Goodwin's *The Construction and Fitting of the English Man of War 1650-1850*.

13

English and French differences in how the main wale is planked are shown in Goodwin's *The Construction and Fitting of the English Man of War 1650-1850* and Jean Boudriot and Hubert Berti's *Le Salamandre*. British methods use angularly shaped planks compared to straight planking typical of French practice. Replicating national differences in planking and framing practice is key to authenticity and moves the model from a decorative item to a truly authentic replica.

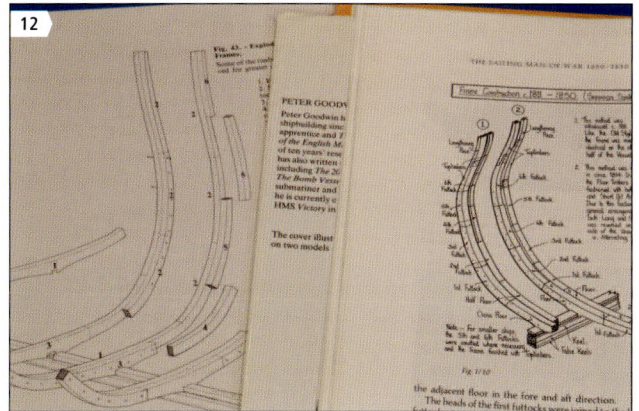

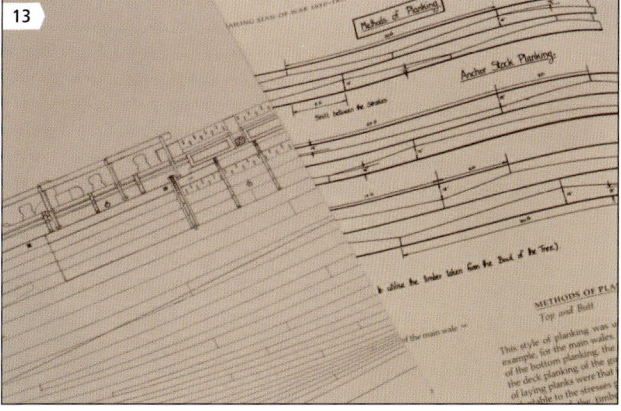

14

Three key references on English warships: Peter Goodwin's *The Construction and Fitting of the English Man of War 1650-1850*; James Lees' *The Masting and Rigging of English Ships of War 1625-1860*; and Brian Lavery's *The Arming and Fitting of English Ships of War 1600-1815*.

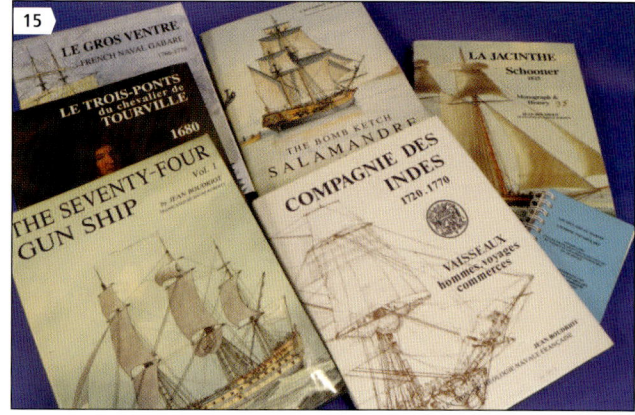

15

A small selection of the vast range of books published by ANCRE that covers ships from all periods of French naval history. The monographs contain detailed scale drawings of all of the ship's timbers, fittings from windlasses to buckets to hooks, the rigging, and even the fastenings that hold the ship together. Many of the books are available in English, Italian and Spanish language editions. The standard of the English translations from French is excellent.

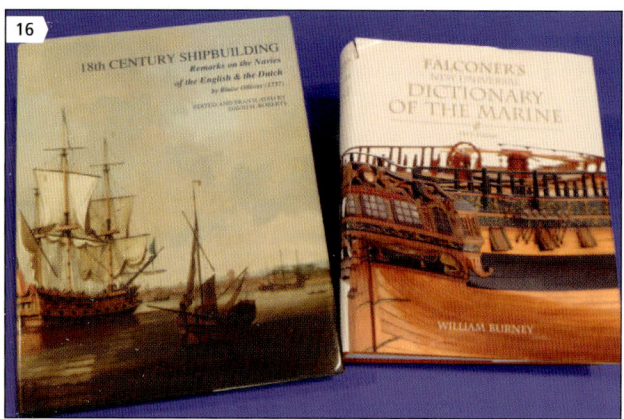

16

Two first-hand period books that are very helpful to the model maker are Blaise Ollivier's *Remarks on the Navies of the English and Dutch made in their Dockyards in 1737 by Mr Ollivier shipwright to the King* (left) and *Falconer's New Universal Dictionary of the Marine* from 1815 (right). The prose these books were written in is delightful and really conveys the time and character for ships of this period.

navy including facsimile reprints of period naval treatises. Karl Heinz Marquardt's *Eighteenth-century Rigs & Rigging* illustrates the rigging practices of different nations and the anatomy of sail plans ranging from lug sails and lateens to square sails and how each is rigged.

A book that deserves special mention is *Remarques sur la Marine des Anglois et des Hollandoise faites sur le lieux en l'annee 1737 by le Sr Ollivier constructeur des vaisseux de Roi* (Remarks on the Navies of the English and Dutch made in their Dockyards in 1737 by Mr Ollivier shipwright to the King) shown in Figure 16. Blaise Ollivier was a master shipwright stationed in Brest who was ordered by Compte de Maurepas, Minister of the Navy to visit England and Holland on an 'espionage' mission to learn all he could about shipbuilding in comparison to French practices. His travels lasted nearly five months and resulted in a 360-page treatise that describes the minutiae of differences in shipbuilding and dockyard practice between the three countries. Opening up the book at a random page, you will find a description such as this:

> XX. The beams of the gundeck in English ships are joined to the sides of the vessel each by four wooden knees, two at each end, of which one is a hanging knee and the other is a lodging knee. These knees are fastened to the sides of the ship and the beam with iron bolts; these are the same size as in our own ships. By this method the English shipwrights fit four knees where we only place two, but their ships need this extra strength since the waterways are not scored down over the beams, as I shall explain in the following Remark. (p51)

The book contains thousands of these first-hand observations and getting to know the characteristic national practices is a means for you to determine if a kit designer has accurately captured characteristically French, English or Dutch features; or help you determine if the parts are accurate in shape and use.

Maritime Dictionaries

An excellent source of information are contemporaneous maritime dictionaries, many of which are available in modern reprints (Figure 16). Shipbuilding and ships have their own special vocabulary. In the passage from Blaise Ollivier he describes wooden *knees*, both *hanging* and *lodging* which to us land dwellers means very little. Maritime dictionaries not only provide a definition that is helpful in deciphering plans and instructions, but period dictionaries also provide a detailed description of where the part comes from and how its shape is calculated. One of the finest is *Falconer's New Universal Dictionary of the Marine (1815 edition)* edited by William Burney. Looking up *knees* in the dictionary provides this definition:

> KNEES, (*courbes*, Fr,) are crooked pieces of timber, having two branches or arms, and are generally used to connect the beams of a ship with her sides or timbers. (p211)

However, the entry describes several versions of knees (*eg*, dagger knees, knee of the head, iron knee, iron plate knees) and then comments on a then new method by Mr Robert Thomas of the Navy Office on how to secure knees to their beams and sides without the need for standards, top and breadth riders. His idea was considered so innovative he was awarded a cash prize and a silver medal from the Society of Arts by the King. This information may appear superfluous to a model builder but that is hardly the case. These dictionaries illustrate the evolution of shipbuilding practice that can be incorporated in your model, greatly enhancing its accuracy and authenticity. Period marine dictionaries are available for several navies, sometimes in translation, but if not, a translation application on your smart phone provides the gist of an entry by simply pointing and shooting.

Books on Seamanship

Some of the most useful books for modellers are those on how to sail. D'Arcy Lever's *The Young Sea Officer's Sheet Anchor: Or a Key to the Leading of Rigging and to Practical Seamanship* was first published in 1808 and became a standard guide throughout nineteenth century England (and the United States) for young officers in the Royal Navy and East India Company (Figure 17). The book covers the principles of rigging, the effect of wind on sails, the use of a compass, raising a ship's anchor, how ropes were spliced and knots tied among other useful things. This book is also profusely illustrated and shows all of the major fittings of a ship and how they are used. Dr John Harland's *Seamanship in the Age of Sail* is a comprehensive treatise, beautifully illustrated by Mark Myers, detailing how square-rigged ships are sailed in different wind conditions and is used today as a textbook for those learning how to sail square-riggers. When the modeller knows the basic principles of seamanship and ship handling – even in just a theoretical sense – it will result in better models because you will intuitively understand what each part of the ship does and why it must be shaped a particular way; and where each rigging line should go as opposed to blindly following a kit instruction that may be incorrect or over-generalized.

Museums

All of the major – and not so major – maritime countries have a naval museum. Many of these institutions publish large and glossy picture books of the most notable models and significant drawings in their collection (Figure 18). The pictures are often captioned in multiple languages and it is a great way to view the museum's collection without having to travel there. Many museums can supply copies of the actual ship's draughts and these are helpful if you want to build the ship from scratch, or are really unsure of a kit's design. Copies of these draughts can be expensive but many can be found in books that reproduce ship draughts to illustrate the evolution of design, such as David Lyon's *The Sailing Navy List* and Jean Boudriot's *History of the French Sailing Frigate 1650-1850*. Madrid's Museo Maritim offer scaled reconstructions of significant ships like *San Juan de Nepomunceno* or the massive four-decked *Santissima Trinidad* that were part of the Spanish line at the Battle of Trafalgar. These highly detailed reconstructions provide full sail and rigging plans and any national peculiarities are highlighted.

17

Books on rigging, sailing, and general seamanship are very helpful for the modeller to understand not just what a thing is and how it looks, but also what it does, and how to use it. Having this knowledge helps you build a better model and to spot and correct errors in a kit or set of drawings.

18

The books pictured here show models from the Musée National de la Marine in Paris, The Museo Naval in Madrid, and the National Maritime Museum, Greenwich in London. All the books include curated notes on the models. The Smithsonian Institution in Washington, DC is another wonderful source and are very helpful to modellers. I was able to obtain copies of original ship draughts and detailed reconstructions of US naval ships such as the *Chesapeake* which was captured by *Shannon* during the War of 1812. I obtained drawings for *Shannon* from the National Maritime Museum in Greenwich to build the pair one day.

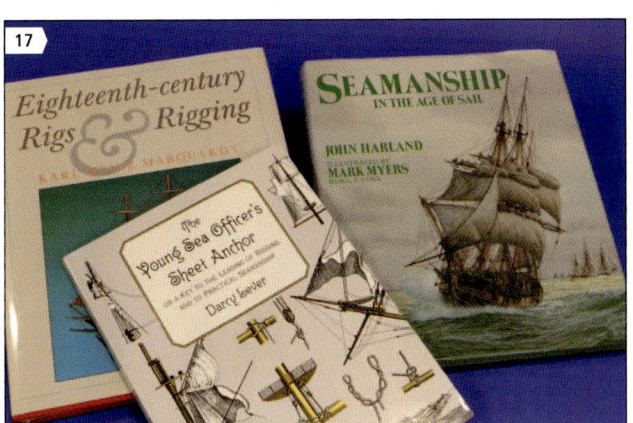

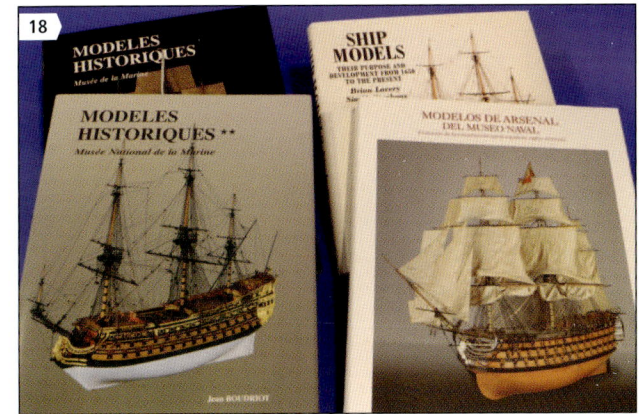

Books on Ship Modelling

There are probably items in your kit that you want to make more accurate, or if scratch-building, items you need to figure out how best to make with the tools and materials to hand (Figure 19). Two of the best model making manuals were penned by C Nepean Longridge who built a single plank-on-bulkhead model of *Victory*, and a solid hull model of *Cutty Sark*. Both of these books hail from the late 1950s and some of the techniques and products are a little dated, but the thinking process and how he approached each subject remains relevant today. Virtually every aspect of his models is built from fairly basic materials with the simplest of hand and power tools. Longridge chronicles everything from making decorative shaped mouldings, planking rules for the deck and hull, rigging a gun carriage to turning all the masts and yards. The books are beautifully illustrated with drawings by George F Campbell supplemented by photographs of the model and the actual ships. There are a few techniques he recommends that are a product of post-war austerity in the UK that need not be followed, such as using black shoe polish to colour wood black for his model of *Victory*. I did try it once to see if it worked and it does, but today's hobby paints are much easier to use and don't smudge so easily!

The *Swan Class sloops (1767-1780)* by David Antscherl is a five-volume odyssey that covers everything from setting up the workshop through picking wood to making each part of the sloop the way the actual ships were built. The books are profusely illustrated with drawings showing the shape of each item, suggestions on how to make them, including cutting a scarf joint, all demonstrated with photographs of his model under construction. The series is really a *practicum* because it is a step-by-step guide to building a specific model, but even if you are not going to build the *Swan*, having everything on a single ship dissected is a great guide to scratch-building or improving kit parts.

A final book that deserves space on your shelf is *Modelling Sailing Men-of-War* by the miniaturist Phillip Reed. Reed's book describes

Lennarth Petersson's *Rigging Period Ship Models* provides the modeller step by step instructions on how to rig a model ship. He has one book devoted to square rigs and another on rigging fore and aft sails. Phillip Reed has two books devoted to building carved full hull and framed miniature ships. David Antscherl has a five-volume set describing and demonstrating the construction of the *Swan* class of sloops complete with plans, and has recently written a book for the first-time scratch-builder with the *Hayling Hoy*. Bernard Frolich's demonstrates the construction of fully framed models of French ships. It is interesting to contrast the approaches, techniques, and styles of these different modellers. Finally, a delightful book that has been around for many years is George F Campbell's *The Neophyte Shipmodeller's Jackstay*. This timeless book is beautifully illustrated with his line drawings and shows how to make models and fittings in a simple and effective way. It features modelling techniques and materials of an earlier time by making parts from bits of wood, glue, talcum powder, wire and paper that are as effective today as any machine-made part designed by CAD.

19

20

Miniature model techniques are ideal for use on small-scale plastic kits. Heller's 1/200 *La Belle Poule*'s plastic deck was moulded with over-scale planks, cleats and eyebolts. This was replaced with a scale deck made from scribed basswood sheet. The new eyebolts were made from fine brass wire and the hull bottom sanded smooth of its heavily moulded and unrealistic copper plate detail to be replaced with copper painted paper or self-adhesive copper plate cut to the correct scale sizes.

in depth a how to build highly realistic miniature ship models at 1/16in = 1ft (1/192 scale). His general approach is to carve solid wooden hulls, plank them, and set his models in realistic seascapes. Miniature methods focus on scale fidelity and to achieve this delicacy, hull planking is not just wood veneer, but wood shavings glued to tissue paper. The methods used by miniaturists are readily adapted to larger scale models to produce much more delicate fittings. I have built a few miniature models using his methods and they are extremely effective and quite easy to master. Many plastic kits are in the miniature scale of 1/192 or less and the techniques he describes are directly applicable to improving over-scale kit parts (Figure 20). Of particular note is how he finishes the models. He provides tips on how to achieve the most authentic paintwork to their smallest detail like fluttering flags and the *catenary* (or sag) of the rigging lines under their own weight for a hyper-realistic effect.

SIZE, COMPLEXITY, PERSONAL CONFIDENCE AND SKILL

Size of the model, *complexity*, and *personal skill* are the last three considerations. Do you have the space to store the finished model? By the time masts and rigging are installed in addition to the plinths used to hold the hull, the overall dimensions of the displayed model will be greatly increased. How are you planning to protect the model from dust, pets, and little inquisitive fingers? If a case is contemplated at least an additional 2in is required to be added all around the inside dimensions. When it comes to *complexity*, this is really a personal examination of whether or not you have the patience to carry out a lot of repetitive functions. A complex model of a man of war means that there are a lot of repetitive tasks to do. For example, tying hundreds of knots to rig one mast is trebled in a large warship with three of them to do. Planking a large deck will take a lot more time than a smaller ship. Fitting out three decks is much more work than one or two decks and an assessment of a model's complexity is really a function of your patience.

Personal confidence and skill is a self-examination of what you think you can do. Think of it as a variation of the old saying 'Are your eyes bigger than your stomach?' If the ship is one you are really passionate about that will no doubt provide the intrinsic motivation to learn the skills to do it justice much more so than one that caught your eye in a glossy new catalogue or purchased at a bargain sale price. Model ships are many small projects amalgamated into a whole. Each frame you make, each gun you build, and each deck you lay is a mini project unto itself. Confidence is built if you are able to take joy in the completion of each of the smaller projects. Confidence grows like a snowball, the skills and confidence you gain on one aspect of the project readily transfer to the next and continues to grow with each subsequent completion. What is key is your willingness to understand the model as a *process*. Each one builds upon the next, and the workmanship of each project improves over time and with each project.

THE MODEL MAKING COMMUNITY – THE NAUTICAL RESEARCH GUILD

Whether you are starting out or are an experienced modeller, having a community of fellow travellers is vitally important to provide support, constructive criticism, or simply to answer questions. In larger cities there may be a club, typically composed of plastic model makers, but there are often members who cross over to wooden shipbuilding. Modellers are modellers whatever the material and hearing about a new technique that is focused on plastic kit construction and finishing may well have an application in the wooden ship model world that you have never considered. In today's interconnected world you can correspond with some of the finest international model makers, researchers, and historians within seconds. The long-established website *Model Ship World* (www.modelshipworld.com) is devoted to model shipbuilding in all its forms – whether they are made from wood, plastic, tinplate or card, and from any point in history, they are all discussed. The site hosts several build logs of all the popular kits and scratch-built subjects, and has separate forums for framing, planking, masting, rigging, sails, metal work and soldering, and how to select wood, among others. There are regular reviews of books, kits, and tools, and you can correspond directly with some kit designers and authors. The members are very supportive of model makers of any skill level and are quick to help you finish your model.

This site is run by the *Nautical Research Guild* (NRG). The NRG was established in 1946 and is the oldest organization in the world devoted to model ships. It is highly recommended that you take out a membership, which comes with a subscription to the quarterly *Nautical Research Journal* that contains historical articles covering ships and shipyards, model building features, tips and tricks and they host an annual conference and exhibition. The guild takes an active hand in model ship development by supporting high quality research and production for kits and materials. Most recently, the guild has been battling unscrupulous practices of some model kit companies that make inexpensive unauthorized copies of existing kits or reproduce copyrighted research materials in their products. Beyond pointing out who not to purchase from, the NRG has taken it a step further to work directly with some of these kit producers to produce original quality kits and accessories. This experience has been a positive for these manufacturers thanks to the constructive feedback they receive from the members on their new products, and input as to what ships might be commercially viable. Much of the growth in the hobby and the adoption of new technologies is due to the input and support of the NRG community.

WOODEN SHIP MODEL KITS

The most accessible way to build a wooden sailing ship model is to start from a kit. A kit has the advantage of having all of the wood, fittings, cordage, and plans conveniently packaged in one box. *Billings Boats, Artesania Latina* (see Chapter 5), *OcCre, Amati* (see Chapter 7), *Bluejacket Shipcrafters* (see Chapter 4), *and Model Shipways* kits are readily available worldwide in shops and from on-line retailers. Many of the venerable brands like *Mantua Model, Sergal*, and *Mamoli* from Italy have been taken over by companies like *Dusek* who have worked to update the kits with better research, redesign of parts and the inclusion of true scale fittings. One of the oldest brands, *Euromodel* continues to offer magnificent kits of ships like the sumptuously decorated *Royal William* (see Figure 21). New manufacturers like *Vanguard Models* (see Chapter 7) bring accuracy and modeller-friendly design to very high standards. The *Nelson's Navy Series* by *Jotika (Caldercraft)* has one of the largest ranges of well-designed and accurate British warships kits available (Figure 22). The Spanish manufacturer OcCre offers several kits of Spanish ships like the four-decked *Santissima Trinidad* and the frigate

21

Euromodel's *Royal William* is a magnificent model that sports a full suite of detailed white metal castings to replicate the rich bas relief carvings that adorn the hull. The wooden parts are laser-cut and the hull is double planked. The kit is based on the *Royal William* model held at the National Maritime Museum, Greenwich.

22

Caldercraft's HMS *Victory* model in 1/72 scale is one the largest and most complex on the market today. The model was designed to portray *Victory* in her 1805 appearance with high bulwarks above the upper decks but these bulwarks are open to question as other experts claim the ship resembles her current appearance in Portsmouth. The box is filled to the brim with wood stock, CNC-cut wooden sheets, fittings cast in white metal, several sheets of photo-etched brass details, a huge set of plans and three instruction booklets. The hull is first planked in lime, and over that in walnut.

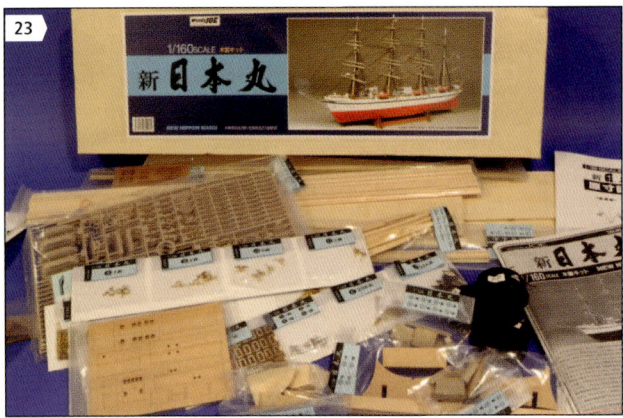

23

Woody Joe's *Nippon Maru* is a single-planked model that is intended to be painted. The wooden parts are a mix of die- and laser-cut pieces, and pre-shaped blocks of wood. It is a truly multi-media model with fittings in brass, wood, photo-etched brass and injected moulded plastic. The instructions are in Japanese but are fully illustrated so if your Japanese language skills are limited to ordering a draft beer at a sushi bar you will not be handicapped in any way.

Mercedes that were present at Trafalgar, to the *Nuestra Señora del Pilar*, whose lost treasure can be viewed in the naval museum in Cartegena, Spain.

Model ship kits come from all over the world, and the Russian *Master Korabel* line offers highly detailed ships from that country. Their choice of model is refreshing in that each ship has a unique story that is not always about its role in a historic naval action. For example, the tender *Avos* is tied to a tragic love story. In 1807 Captain Nikolai Rezanov sailed to California in *Avos* to purchase supplies for the starving settlements in Alaska. There he met the teenage Maria de la Concepcion Arguello, daughter of a Spanish diplomat. They fell deeply in love but could not marry because she was a Catholic and he belonged to the Eastern Orthodox Church. Rezanov needed the Emperor's permission to marry and quickly sailed *Avos* back to Alaska and from there intended to ride horseback across Russia to St Petersburg. Tragically, he died en route and Maria refused to believe the news of his death for 25 years. In 1842 she received confirmation of his death from a British diplomat and, in her grief, she took a vow of silence and retired to a monastery in Monterey, California until her death in 1857.

China's *CAF Models* produces accurate and highly detailed models of ships in frame including an Admiralty Board style model of the frigate *Enterprize* and a fully rigged model of the French lugger *Le Coureur* (see Chapter 8). Japan's *Woody Joe* offers kits of modern square-riggers like the *Nippon Maru* (Figure 23) and her sister the *Kaiwo Maru*; the latter still sails around the world and can be visited in person. Most interesting are their kits of notable Japanese square-riggers like the *Kanrin Maru*, the first Japanese ship (she had an auxiliary steam engine) to sail from Japan to the United States; or the traditional sailing craft like the *Higaki Kaisen* or *Kitamae Bune*.

It would be impossible to review all of the major kit lines and it would not be long before that list was out of date because new manufacturers continually come into the market. If you have a kit in mind, most are fully reviewed on the Model Ship World website, and if not, you can ask questions and seek opinions there before making a decision. With kits it is important to keep in mind that not all are created equal. Kits will vary in historical accuracy depending on the designer or what research material they relied upon. Most will be a form of single or double plank-on-bulkhead design and vary in the species and quality of wood provided. Is the wood sawn-cut or die-cut? Are the edges straight or ragged? Will the plywood delaminate? Is the wood brittle or pliable? Fittings can be cast in white metal, brass, resin, printed 3D plastic, pressed sawdust, injection moulded plastic or a mix. Fittings such as anchors, belaying pins, wooden rigging blocks, and windlasses can be generic parts that are just nominally suitable for several different kits in a manufacturer's line. Some kits contain a high degree of prefabricated parts and others do not and only provide blocks and strips of wood stock to fashion the part from a plan.

Most kits are laser-cut today and that entails cleaning off the wood burn or char left on the parts. In some kits the laser cutting is very fine and there is little char to remove whereas others provide parts that are heavily burned to the point you can smell it when you open the box. Manufacturers such as the Caldercraft's (Jotika) *Nelson's Navy* line CNC mill their parts out of wood sheet to avoid charring altogether. Some kits will contain sails and good quality rigging threads, and others will not. How fuzzy is the thread? Will the thread have to be dyed or is it pre-coloured? Is the thread cotton or cotton/polyester or top-quality linen? Kits in the past used to contain scale plans and maybe some generic construction advice whereas some manufacturers today no longer include scale plans at all. Construction is detailed in glossy multilingual illustrated instruction booklets similar as those found in conventional plastic kits. In contrast, the plans in the *Euromodel* line of kits actually encourage and show you how to build upon what they provide in the box to make a more detailed model. As you research a kit, ask these questions and answer if that is acceptable to you; if the answer is no, are you willing to make the investment of time and resources to make it right?

Another very important consideration is 'what kind of model did the designer intend?' Was the model designed to be *decorative* or *authentic*? A decorative model is one that looks like it could have been purchased from a seaside gift shop somewhere in Southeast Asia. These models have the appearance of home décor, and if you mounted a clock in the hull no one would be the wiser. The dead giveaway for this kind of kit is when the metal work is polished and different wood species are used to colour the model. This does not mean that the model is inaccurate, but instead the primary design goal is to show off the natural beauty of the materials used in its construction. In contrast, an authentic model attempts to replicate the actual finish of the ship by blackening all of the metalwork and instructing you to paint the hull in the correct colours. Many models fall in between, painting some parts but carefully selecting species of wood to represent the different colours on the ship. For example, ebony for the black painted main wale or boxwood or Alaskan cedar to plank the hull and represent the yellow ochre paint used to paint the hull sides. Holly is used for the decks for its whitish grey colour that looks like the deck has been 'holystoned' clean. This practice is called 'painting with wood' and is an accepted model making convention that emulates the style of the Navy Board model. It is on the one hand authentic and on the other hand artistic. Some kits even provide marquetry veneers in different species of wood to recreate a design on the hull sides. Decorative models can be made authentic often with just a coat of paint and remaking simplified parts. The primary consideration for you is does the kit provide enough of the materials to obtain the type of model you envision?

One final thought about kits. There are kits of ships that never really existed. A prime example is HMS *Surprise* based on the ship made famous by the fictional novels by Patrick O'Brian which in turn formed the basis for the motion picture *Master and Commander*. The real *Surprise* was the French corvette *Unité* captured in 1796 whereas the kits are based on the 1970s sailing replica HMS *Rose* (that itself was loosely based on the Admiralty draughts of the 20-gun *Rose*) used in the filming of the motion picture. There are a number of kits based on more authoritative sources such as the *Architectura Navalis Mercatoria* written in 1768 by the Swedish naval architect Fredrik Henrik af Chapman. This book contains detailed drawings of general ship designs to classify and categorize the many different types of ships that existed during his time. All of his plans are available from the Stockholm Maritime Museum (Sjöhistoriska Museet). A kit may be based in one of these drawings and given a fictional name. It is important to know the provenance of the kit's design so you are investing the time and effort in the ship you actually want.

Semi-kits and Timbering Sets

Semi-kits are usually produced for fully framed models. They are an option that gives the model maker a lot of freedom by providing a range of items for a particular ship and the builder is free to pick and choose what to purchase depending on skill and inclination. For example, these sets can provide a pre-cut keel and stem, carvings and decoration, fittings, windlasses, gratings and hatches, or guns and carriages (Figure 24). Hull planking and wood for the frames can be purchased as correctly sized strips or as baulks of timber to cut down if you have the tools. The *Syren Model Company* in New Jersey produces highly detailed and accurate semi-kits for the 32-gun *Winchelsea* from 1764 (Figure 25) and a plank-on-bulkhead model of the British Revenue cutter *Cheerful* from 1806 (Figure 26). Each project is accompanied by fully illustrated step-by-step instructions and there is much to learn from them regardless of experience level. Samples of these instructions can be found on the Syren website.

Timbering sets on the other hand provide all the milled wood stock for a model but that is about it (Figure 27). Some timbering sets may include a few laser-cut items such as window frames or laser-

24

The Syren Model Company offers an extensive line of parts that can be used on your own projects. They are highly detailed and beautifully produced. Pictured are a set of ship's lanterns (left) and a ship's wheel (right) to 1/48 scale. The range is extensive, offering capstans, blocks, carvings, boats, and chemically milled hull fittings like horseshoe and butterfly plates for use in a number of scales.

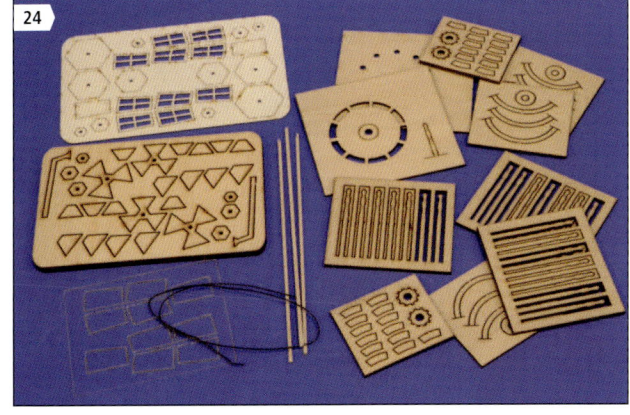

25 The stern of the *Winchelsea* semi-kit produced by the Syren Model Company. The carvings are cast in resin carefully coloured to look like the Alaskan cedar used to build the model. The ship is offered in 'chapters' that comprises step-by-step instructions and the requisite parts. The modeller can purchase some or all of the chapters as desired. (Photo courtesy of Charles Passaro)

26 The British cutter *Cheerful* is a single plank-on-bulkhead semi-kit. The sweet lines of this hull, modeller friendly design, and detailed construction manual make it suitable for the ambitious newcomer to the hobby. (Photo courtesy of Charles Passaro)

etch a design into a piece of wood to assist carving. These sets are a convenient and economical way of obtaining all of the wood required for a model because it is often difficult to source sufficient quantities of quality hardwood on your own, and having a workshop full of stationary power tools such as table saws, planers and thickness sanders (and knowing how to use them) to cut it down. The Lumberyard of Brecksville, Ohio produces timbering sets for many of the Harold Hahn designs which come with a copy of Hahn's plans, a laser-cut building jig, and a choice of woods that are matched for colour and grain. Ships available include the *Bounty* of Bligh fame, *Confederacy*, *Druid* and *Raleigh* among others.

A little research and time to muse on your strengths and weaknesses goes a long way towards picking the right project and seeing it through to completion. Choosing the project that best suits you at this time in your model making career is half the battle. Whether your research endeavours focus on the minutiae of ship construction in the Netherlands or the contents of a kit will help you come to know your ship better, result in a better model, but most of all, make your build that much more enjoyable and satisfying.

27 Timbering sets provide just the raw materials to build a ship. Pictured is set to build the 74-gun ship *Alfred* using the Hahn method offered by The Lumberyard. Included are bundles of strip wood and stock all cut to the correct nominal sizes, a few laser-cut parts (keel, stem and stern, deck beams), and the notched building jig. The modeller has a choice of woods, and this set has been milled from boxwood. All carvings and fittings are left to you.

3: Essential Tools

Your workbench probably already holds many of the tools required to build a wooden model ship. There are a few tools, both hand and power, that have been designed specifically for this branch of model making, but how essential they are remains to be seen – in my experience they do not always make the job that much easier.

The illustrations in this chapter show a selection of commonly used tools, but you should not assume you need all of them to get started. As you work on your model you will soon know what you need and where you can make do. The primary requirement of any tool is that they are kept in good condition, and that all cutting edges are kept sharp. This is especially true when working with wood because you have to saw, cut and pare through fibres. If your tool is dull it will more than likely slip off or get stuck into the work. You will compensate by applying more brute strength to force your way through the material and that just increases the risk of a slip and an injury. Blood was never designed to be used as a wood stain.

Useless and Useful Tools

Model shops market many tools to wooden ship modellers. The usefulness of many of them is doubtful. For example, a couple of manufacturers offer spring loaded 'pin pushers'. These tools hold a tiny brass nail to temporarily fix planks to a bulkhead. A pin is inserted into the hollow tube and its end is placed against the wood – press down and, presto, the spring action pushes it into the wood. This is all good in theory but in reality the spring is not strong enough to push the pin through the wood leaving you to hammer it home anyways. To make matters worse, the gauge of the nails provided in kits will differ, or the pins included may have larger heads so they cannot fit into the pin pusher's barrel. Clever manufacturers have solved this problem by creating pushers with interchangeable heads but that means added expense for you. Save your money because any pin can be set into the wood with a pair of ordinary needle-nosed pliers. The pin is gripped laterally, set in place and pushed into the wood and tapped home with a little hammer.

The 'keel clamper' shown in Figure 31 can be a helpful tool when used intelligently. There is no doubt it is a handy clamp and that the hull can be set to any position required. However, this is only the case when the tool is clamped to the false keel. If used to hold a keel that is pinned to the false keel and hull rotated to one side, the keel can snap off. Alternatively, a better way to hold the model is to use a soft towel laid on the work bench. The hull is cushioned, no stress

28
Cutting tools. A selection of hobby knives with different blades, a utility cutter best for heavy duty cutting, and some razor saws. In the top right is an 'Easy Cutter' which is a hand-held shear used to cut softer strip woods like lime or bass. It has a graduated base so precise angles can be cut. Two guillotine cutters with bases allow you to cut identical lengths of wood. Top left is from Amati and it has a hard plastic base. 'The Chopper' shown bottom right has a self-healing cutting mat under the blade. Both cut wood well, but on some thin materials like copper tape the hard base of the Amati tool cuts cleaner. The scissors shown are very sharp and have little cutting points critical for the precision cutting of rigging lines. A pair of small scissors should be kept and not used for anything but rigging to preserve its sharp edge.

29
Sanding tools. Sanding blocks are the maids of all work. They are used to fair frames and bulkheads, hull lines and finishing wood in preparation for paint and stain. Garnet sandpaper can be wrapped around different shapes of scrap wooden blocks to sand in the simplest to the most complex curves. Used sandpaper should be saved because its worn grit remains useful for finer sanding jobs. Tungsten carbide sanding blocks (Perma-Grit shown top left) are excellent ergonomically shaped tools that carry a fine and a coarse grit on each side. The tungsten carbide grit is extremely strong and does not wear down like sandpaper, and can be cleaned by flushing with water. On the right is a 'True Sander' that sands an edge square or at specific angle for perfect joints required for hatchways and coamings. This tool also comes with a protractor guide to sand in or true up specific angles.

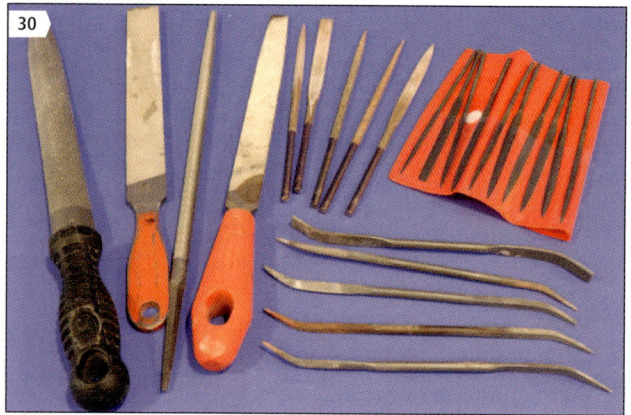

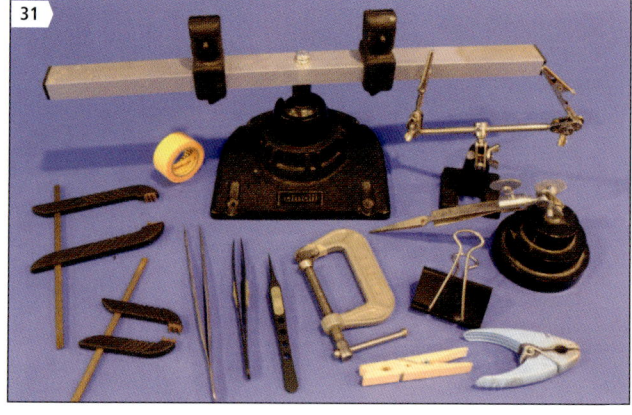

30

Filing tools. Wood rasps (left) are essential for shaping a solid wood hull. Rasps easily cut through end grain on a block of wood the way a carving tool cannot. Rasps leave a rough finish on the wood that must be smoothed off with sandpaper or multipurpose files (centre left). The most useful shapes of rasp and file are half rounds. The round side allows pinpoint smoothing whereas the flat side allows greater areas to be cut at once. Heavy duty tungsten carbide needle files (centre top) are useful for a number of jobs and their coarse grit cuts wood very easily. Many model boat fittings are made of brass, white metal, plastic or resin and a set of good quality #2 and #3 cut files cleans up seams without scarring (top right). To keep files from clogging up with swarf (white metal is the worst offender) rub a piece of chalk on the file before use to keep the metal from sticking into the grooves. At the bottom right are riffler files of different shapes. The curved neck of rifflers can access areas where a straight file cannot. Wood rasps are also available as rifflers which are useful for hollowing out carved wooden hulls.

31

Holding tools. Besides bench mounted woodworking and metalworking vices, a handy tool is a 'keel clamper' seen at the top of the photo. This clamp has adjustable sliding plastic jaws that hold the false keel firmly and the locking ball joint allows the hull to be swivelled into any position. Also shown are a variety of cam action clamps (left), tweezers (centre) and office butterfly clips, C clamps, and clothes pegs. Top right are two types of 'third hand' tools. The top one is mounted to a heavy metal base with two adjustable arms fitted with alligator clips. The one just below has a single arm that holds a cross action tweezer. These clamps are great for holding rigging blocks steady while you *strop* (wrap and tie rigging line) around them.

32

Drilling tools. Have on hand a pin chuck and sets of drill bits. High speed steel bits are preferable to diamond coated or tungsten carbide grit because the former cuts whereas the latter tends tear or grind through the wood. Several bits will break over a course of model, especially the smaller ones so having spares on hand saves a lot of time and frustration. Also shown are finger drills. These are drill bits set into short knurled knobs that allow drilling in confined spaces. Before drilling any hole in wood or white metal, it is recommended that the hole is marked by making a slight indentation (divot) using a sharp awl. The indentation will keep the drill bit from wandering, ensuring an accurately placed hole.

33

Measuring tools. Accurate measuring is essential and investing in quality dividers, callipers, and rulers will pay dividends. Of particular note are the three 'Incra rulers' that have slots milled into them for a pencil lead to ensure accurate and reproducible markings. These rules come in standard lengths, but also a T-square format and an angle. The 90° angle version marks two sides of a piece of stock simultaneously. Sharp pencils are a must because a dull pencil will produce a wide and sloppy line. It's then a bit of a guessing game to know what part of the mark to use – the right side of the line, the left side, or the centre? A sharp pencil will produce a thin line leaving no room for error. Keep a pencil sharpener to hand all the time. Remember, always measure twice, cut once!

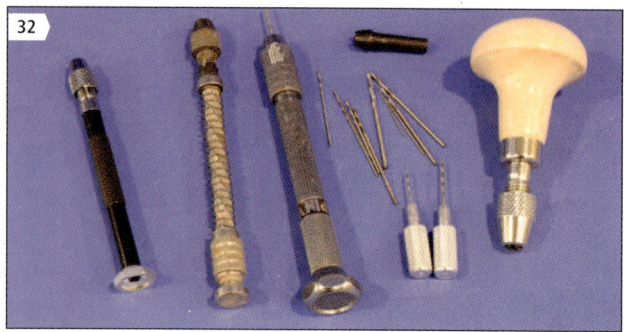

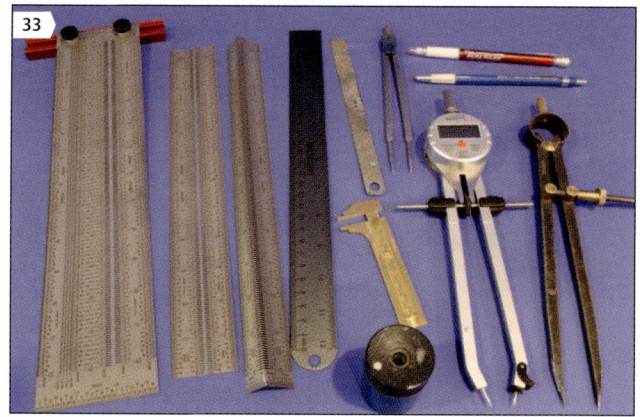

ESSENTIAL TOOLS

34

Carving tools. Carving tools are essential for solid hull models. Curved gouges are particularly suitable for wooden hulls before finishing off with a rasp and sandpaper. Flat chisels cut recesses and skew chisels for cleaning up and shaping corners. A mallet is sometimes helpful to push the blade along. The blades of Japanese chisels are much more acutely angled and the narrow ones are extremely useful for cutting slots. Learning how to sharpen and hone a chisel is an essential skill. Keeping them razor sharp allows them to cut wood like butter whereas a dull one will only tear through the wood, putting it at greater risk of slipping and causing grave injury. A brush keeps your work area clean.

35

Other useful tools. On the left is a set of centre-finding rules. These rules effortlessly find the exact centre of decks, transoms, mast tops and so on. The rulers pictured are etched steel versions made by Hasegawa Model Company in Japan, but centre-finding rulers are available from any good woodworking shop. A little hobby hammer gets a lot of use tapping in pins to hold parts together, and a few set squares ensure angles of assembled parts are 90° and handy for marking out wood. Jeweller's pliers have a multitude of uses from shaping brass rod to holding or pushing brass nails into wood during planking. The most useful are the needle nose, round, and wide flat jawed pliers and they will soon become extensions of your hands. Dust masks protect your lungs, and let's not forget eye protection. Ordinary glasses do not confer much protection and safety goggles or face shields are mandatory. Model making ceases to be fun when you lose sight in an eye or develop chronic obstructive pulmonary disease (COPD).

is imparted on any of the parts, and the towel keeps it from rolling onto the floor. A related tool is the extravagant building slip designed to hold the hull upright during construction. These tools have fancy cam action clamps and adjustable stops to hold the model upright and keep it straight. This is a luxury tool at best and does not offer anything more than what can be cobbled together with inexpensive DIY materials. A building slip is little more than two strips of wood screwed to a flat board (*eg*, shelf) that traps the keel along its length. Two aluminium or steel 'L' brackets on each side of the stem and rudder post will hold the model upright. All this can be had for less than a quarter of the cost of a commercial building slip.

Truly essential tools are electric and manual plank-benders shown in Figure 36. The electric plank-bender (also called a planking iron) is a soldering iron with a shaped aluminium head. The soldering iron heats the metal head over which the wood is bent. There are two shapes available, the kidney-shaped head and the round head. When you first purchase the kidney-shaped bender, the head is fitted with one or two spring loaded clamps. The purpose of these clamps is to hold the plank against the curved head to heat the wood and set the bend. These clamps have never really worked for me so I removed them and hold the plank-bender upright in a bench vice. This leaves both my hands free to hold and bend the plank over the curved head. With the clamps removed it's much easier to induce the bend when the wood strip can be moved around freely to apply heat and pressure wherever required. This freedom of movement also helps induce any twist and a curve to the plank simultaneously. Bending in two dimensions is necessary around the bow and stern areas where planks must also sweep upwards to follow the sheer of the hull.

The round-headed plank-bender comes with a wooden form. The idea is that the plank is placed on the former and the plank-bender's head is used to press down the wood into the former to induce the bend. This works well if you only need to bend the plank in one dimension, but it is impossible to induce the twist that will eventually be required. To simultaneously induce a twist and a curve with this tool, mount the plank-bender into the bench vice and rub the wood back and forth against the heated shank of the soldering iron. The round head does not work well because its surface area is very small and the round head renders it difficult to keep the wood in contact with it for the efficient transfer of heat. Both kidney and round-headed plank-benders work well on dry and damp wood. On wet or damp wood the heat will create steam that helps form far more acute curves and twists in a strip of wood. The heat from the planking iron also evaporates excess water and minimizes shrinkage as the wood strip dries out naturally. If you bend dry wood the natural spring of the wood will remain and the curve will spring back a bit whereas bending wet wood will have little or no spring back. Treat these tools with care because they generate a lot of heat and you can easily scorch the wood or worse yet, start a fire in your home.

Manual plank-benders work by scoring the backside of a plank to induce a curve. A razor blade is held in one jaw and the other is flat. The plank is placed in the jaw and the jaws *gently* closed – just enough for the blade to score the plank. The wood is moved on a bit and scored again. The closer the scores the tighter the bend. If

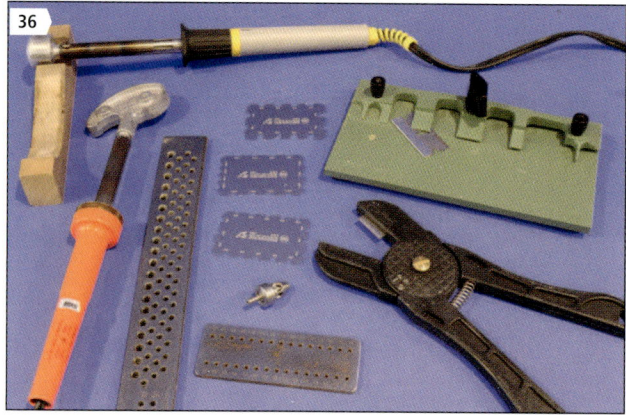

36

Special tools for model shipwrightry. Electric plank benders or planking irons (left) are shaped aluminium heads screwed into a soldering iron. The solid metal pieces with holes are drawplates used to make thin wooden pegs (trennals) to permanently fix wooden parts together. The drawplate is held in a bench vice and split bamboo kebab skewers are pulled through the holes with a pair of pliers. Each hole shaves off a little of the wood until the desired diameter is obtained. Drawplates can also be used to resize soft wire but instead of cutting away metal, they compress it. Using a drawplate can be very tedious work and trennal cutters (centre) that fit into a rotary tool make pegs in a fraction of the time. A thin piece of wood is fed into the spinning head that cuts it round, but you are limited to certain diameters only. These are luxury tools because a trennal can be made by shaving down the humble toothpick with a hobby knife. Period ships have a lot of shaped mouldings that decorate the hull and these can be made with profile scrapers (centre). Scraping them over a length of wood until the profile is cut takes practice. On the far right is a photo-etched part bending and folding tool. The razor blade is slipped under the part held in the jaws and lifted upwards to make the fold.

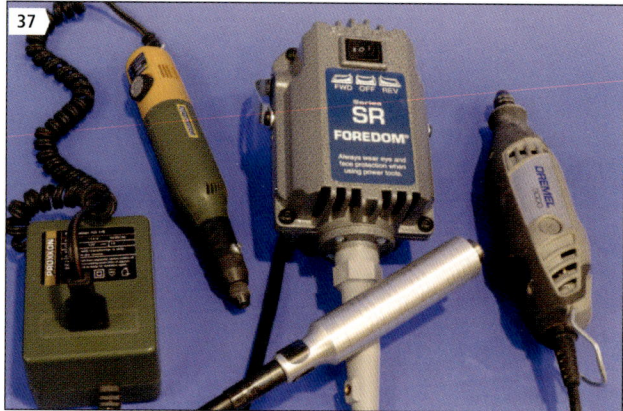

37

Rotary tools. Dremel, Proxxon, and Foredom rotary tools. When using a rotary tool, let the speed of the tool do the work and don't be tempted to push hard on the bit.

you close the jaws too far you can cut the wood strip in two. Your fingers are also an excellent set of manual plank-benders. Gentle curves are made by running the plank between your thumb and forefinger as you bend the plank. A little more of a curve is induced to the wooden strip with each pass.

Power Tools

Power tools provide freedom to model makers not possible with any other tool. They allow you to mill and cut your own wood stock, freeing you from what is supplied in a kit or can be profitably used to resize kit-supplied wood to scale dimensions. They also remove a lot of the effort of using hand tools, with cuts accomplished in a fraction of the time. Power tools make more precise and square cuts, drill perfectly straight holes, and generally speed up construction that feeds the enthusiasm for the project. Model makers are blessed with access to a wide variety of tools to suit all budgets. Many of them are multipurpose and are readily converted from a table saw to a disc sander in a few minutes. The choice of a tool really depends on what your needs are and whether the capacity of the machine is sufficient. If you plan on building kits, most of your needs will be resizing kit materials, making a few slots, cutting thin sheet stock, and truing up some edges, so a light duty, multi-purpose machine is sufficient. If you intend to replace the kit planking with hardwoods then a dedicated heavier duty tool with variable speed capacity is a better buy. If you are intent on scratch-building then several dedicated machines, such as a thickness sander and pillar drill will need a place in your workshop.

All modellers should have a hand-held rotary tool (Figure 37). Popular brands are offered by Proxxon or Dremel. Both integrate the motor into the handpiece that can be tiring to hold because of the added weight and girth. Proxxon hand pieces are lighter and slimmer, but are attached to the transformer via a cord that often gets in the way. The Dremel has greater torque, but the transformer is attached to the hand piece as well, making it the heaviest and the most awkward to use. Avoid any rechargeable battery models because as the battery diminishes so does torque and speed. Jewellers prefer the Foredom because the hand piece is attached to a flexible shaft. The hand pieces are ergonomically designed and lightweight, and because the flexible shaft and motor is hung from a hook there is little weight transferred to the hand piece. Power is controlled by a foot pedal and the choice of bits is endless. All of these rotary tools can drill, sand, grind and cut with a quick change of accessory. The primary consideration is how well the tool feels in your hand. Most hobby grade rotary tools have dedicated accessories that hold them vertically so they can be used as a pillar drill, light duty mill, or router, rendering them very versatile.

A modeller's table saw is indispensable for its ability to rip strips of wood for planking; and cross cuts are clean and square. Used with a mitre gauge any angle can be cut to make neat joints. It is probably the most used tool in my shop. The light duty variable speed Proxxon machine can be fitted with fine slitting saws to cut thin woods and veneers. When a carbide blade is mounted, thin hardwood sheets of box or pear can be cut. If you intend on cutting a lot of hardwoods and the sheets are ¼in thick or more, then investing in a powerful machine such as those made by Model Machines is a worthwhile investment (Figure 38). It has a high torque, single speed motor set

ESSENTIAL TOOLS

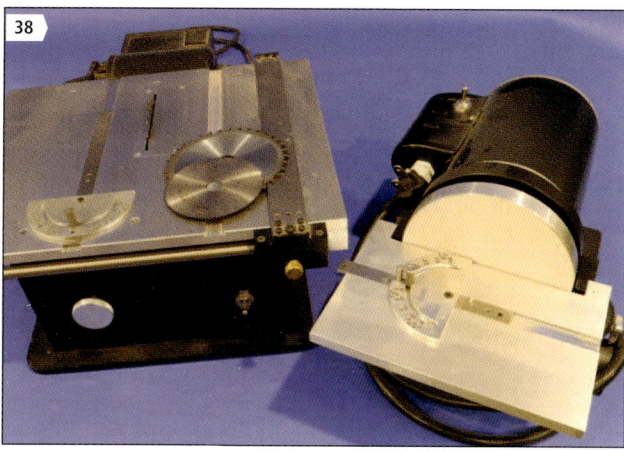

38

A miniature table saw coupled with the disc sander will become amongst the most used tools in your workshop. The saw frees you from having to source pre-cut strips and is great for cutting down or cleaning up the edges of strip wood found in kits. The blade guard has been removed for clarity but must be in place when used. The disc sander quickly squares up edges, removing laser char, and shaping woods. Tools shown are made by Model Machines and are constantly being upgraded with new features in response to modeller's demands.

into a base that is so stable that a coin can be balanced on its edge while running. This stability allows very precise cuts to be made, and with the correct blade any wood to quite a sizeable thickness can be cut without taxing the saw. The saw is continuously upgraded and can be had with tilting tables to allow angled edge cuts.

The next most used tool is a dedicated disc sander (Figure 38) that is invaluable for squaring edges, sanding in angles and mitres, general shaping tasks, and preparing laser-cut parts for assembly. Given the popularity of laser cutting, it should be noted that the edges of a laser-cut part are not 90°. Lasers cannot cut square because the beam gets deflected while burning through the wood. The thicker the wood, the more angled the edge. This is particularly evident when two laser-cut edges are offered up – on one side the seam is tight, but on the other side there is a gap. A disc sander will true up the edges far better than using a hand-held sanding stick or

file that is impossible to hold square to the edge. The Proxxon saw converts to a robust disc sander and because this machine has variable speed control, changing the speed of the disc prevents the wood from friction-scorching caused when the disc is run at too high a speed. The best sanding discs to purchase are the ones that are dead flat on one side and slightly convex on the other. The convex side allows pinpoint sanding and ends of long pieces of wood don't get gouged by hitting the outside edges of the disc as you move it around. The dead flat side is best used for sanding flat edges or shaping parts.

Thickness sanders reduce strips of wood to any desired thickness. There are dedicated heavy duty machines (Figure 39) and lighter duty machines that are powered by attaching an ordinary electric hand drill to turn the sanding drum. The best sanders have dual drums where coarse sandpaper is mounted on one side and a finer grit on the other so you can size and then finish the wood without having to stop and change the paper. A machine that can use standard garnet sandpaper is preferable to one that only mounts manufacturer supplied sleeves. Being able to cut and mount standard sandpaper is not only much more economical, but also allows you to choose the right grit for the job at hand, reducing the chance of burning the wood or sanding in gouges. Besides sizing strip woods, thickness sanders can also reduce any over-thick kit-supplied parts. For example, an over-thick keel piece can be held down onto a flat board with double sided tape and run through the machine. Light passes that just takes a little stock off at a time produces the best results. As with all power tools, thickness sanders must be used with care. The spinning drum can spit the wood back towards you like a bullet if you try to take too much off in one pass.

A specialist tool worth mentioning is the ropewalk to make your own scale rope. The rigging of a ship is just as much a part of the model as the hull. Kits provide a range of sewing threads to represent the many different sizes of rope carried aloft. By and large sewing threads work well, especially in the smaller scales. However, there are times when you need a particular style or thickness of rope not provided in the kit. A trip to the local model or sewing shop, or a visit to a specialist manufacturer who makes model rope usually resolves the problem. The alternative is to spin proper rope yourself and in this way you have control over the type of thread (*eg*, cotton, linen), hardness, and style of rope (*eg*, three strand *plain-* or *hawser-*laid rope, four-strand rope called *shroud-laid rope*, or larger rope *cable-laid* formed by counter-twisting three or more multi-strand ropes together).

39

This thickness sander is made by Model Machines and features a heavy duty motor and two sanding drums. Different grits of standard sandpaper can be mounted to each drum or a single grit along both drums to sand wider pieces of wood. A calliper is used to measure thickness and to the top right is an adaptor that allows the sander to be attached to a shop vacuum to take away the sanding dust. The adaptor can be found in any DIY centre. All machine tools have a dust port to be attached to a dust extraction system.

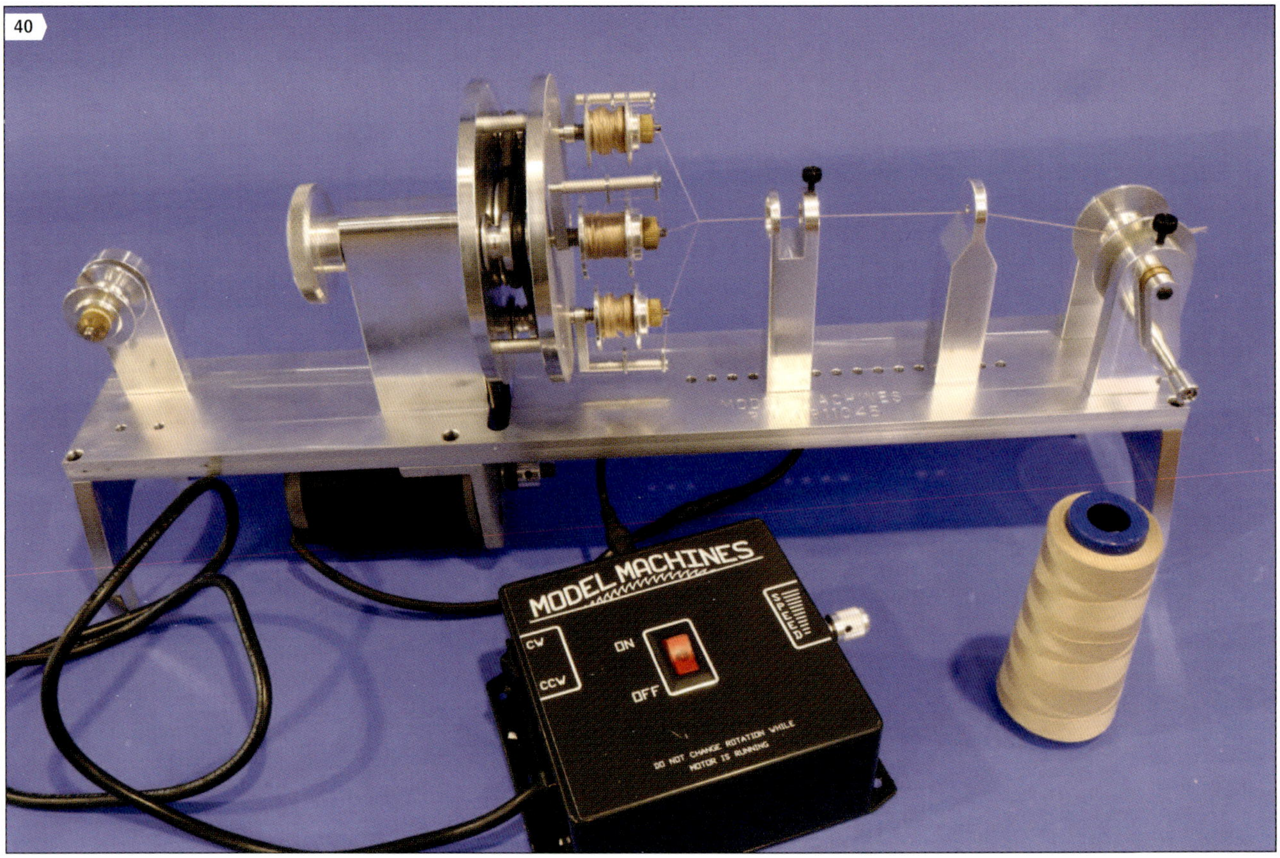

40

The electric ropewalk by Model Machines. This tool was an extravagance but liberating. The motor is variable speed to help you control the winding of the thread. The tool takes some practice and experimentation to get the best results but it can produce quite a quantity of rope very quickly.

41

A close up of the spindles that wind the thread and brings them together to form the rope. Very thin sewing thread is being spun to make a thin rope. Other sizes of thread can be easily mounted and wound to make any thickness and type of rope required. The finished rope can be coloured with fabric dye before any sizing is applied.

All ropewalks work on the principle that when strands of threads twisted (called *laid*) in opposite directions are allowed to come together, the tension caused by the twisting causes the strands to wrap around each other to form rope. You can demonstrate the principle yourself by taking a length of thread and hold one end in your left hand. The other end is twisted tight between the fingers of the right hand. Bring the two ends together and they will wrap around each other forming a length of rope. Ropewalks for model makers power the twisting of thread using motors, hand drills, lathes or a gearbox powered with a hand crank. In this way, two, three or four stands can be twisted at once to the same tensions before being brought together. You can easily make your own ropewalk with children's building blocks and gear sets, and several different models are available from specialist tool companies like Domanoff Model Workshops, Syren Ship Model Company or Model Shipways. Figure 40 shows a powered ropewalk from Model Machines. Model rope, like real rope must be stretched out or *hardened* by hanging it up with a weight suspended on the end. The rope can unravel a little when cut (like real rope) so any cut ends must be fixed with glue or a sizing, which is no more than white glue thinned with water applied along its length. Simply dip your thumb and forefinger into the sizing and run the rope through them. I also find that linen thread does not unravel as much as smoother threads made of polyester/cotton blends.

Adhesives

Polyvinyl acetate (PVA) glue, known as wood or white glue is the stuff that keeps your model together. Wood glues are typically a creamy yellow in colour and cure relatively clear, and some are tinted a light brown colour that leaves a visible line when cured so you are able to see where the join is. Wood glues vary in viscosity and are marketed as 'no run' that stays where you put it, and others that are thinner so they are more easily spread over wide surfaces, and now 'quick grab' with shortened open working times. White PVA glues can be used on wood, but their formulation does not yield as strong a joint as those formulated for wood whose joints are stronger than the wood itself. PVA glues are generally water-resistant but are not water-proof. Should you ever need to break a PVA joint the best way is to soak a cloth in isopropyl alcohol (rubbing alcohol) and wrap it around the faulty joint. Cling film is wrapped around the cloth to prevent the alcohol from evaporating and leave overnight. In the morning the joint will easily part and the softened glue can be scraped away.

Cyanoacrylate (CA) or 'super glue' has become an essential adhesive. All kits are multimedia in nature with parts supplied in wood, resin, brass, paper and this glue effectively joins these dissimilar materials. CA comes in different consistencies and each has a place in construction. The thin water-like CA easily runs into joints and soaks into wood that makes it ideal for repairing broken parts. It can be sanded and painted, and if the part is to be left in a natural finish, a coat of tung oil will blend the repair into the rest of the wood. Medium consistency CA is an all-purpose adhesive ideal for assembling metal parts or fixing items such as cleats or eyebolts into holes in the deck. Thick gel type CA has become the planking clamp of the 21st century. A dot of gel type CA on the bulkheads replaces the old-fashioned screw clamps that held the plank tight by screwing into the edge of the bulkhead. For the second layer of planking, a few dots on the back of a plank will fix it to the first planking with absolutely no damage to the face of the plank. Moreover, gel type CA provides time to position that plank, and can be instantly set with the application of a little accelerator dabbed into the joint with an old brush.

Acetate glue or 'balsa cement' is a fast-drying cement used to assemble flying model aircraft. Its value in ship modelling is that it contains no water and will not induce a warp or curve to the wood and is thus perfect for fixing scribed basswood sheet decking to a model. The water in PVA glue will immediately cause this decking material to roll up. *Two-part epoxy* can also be used to glue down scribed deck sheets and is useful for many assembly tasks. This epoxy is available in many different formulations that cure in 5 minutes to 24 hours. The quick set 5-minute type is the most useful for our purposes. Any excess catalyzed glue that squeezes out from a joint can be removed with a cloth dampened with methyl hydrate before it cures.

Fillers

The type of filler you use will depend on the flaw and how you intend on finishing the model. On a model that will be painted, almost any kind of filler can be used. For example, if you have to fill a deep gouge, two-part automotive repair putty, sold under the brand names 'Isopon', 'Bondo' or 'Plastic Padding' can be used. This material cures quickly and can be carved and sanded without crumbling. This same filler is sold to woodworkers under the label of 'Premium Wood Filler' and the only difference with the automotive type is that it is tinted a light tan colour instead of pink or blue (and it is more expensive given its 'premium-ness'). Under a coat of paint no-one would be the wiser. Small flaws between planks or other flaws can be filled with automotive glaze and spot putty, or ordinary plastic model putties by Tamiya or Humbrol for example. These putties all stick well to wood, metal, and resins and are easily sanded smooth. Ordinary wall spackling ('Polyfilla' would be a UK equivalent) can be used for minor cracks and is easily sanded.

If the model is to be bright finished then the specialist wood fillers found in home DIY centres can be pressed into service. These wood fillers come in a range of different colours to match the wood and are latex based so they dry quickly and sand out smoothly. On bright finished models the goal is to avoid using any filler at all because filler just looks like filler. A filler that creates the least obtrusive repair is one you make yourself. Create a pile of sawdust by sanding down some of the wood you are building the model from and mix into it a little thinned PVA to form a paste. The paste is pressed into the crack or flaw and is sanded smooth when dry. The filler is quite visible until a coat of tung oil or varnish is applied that helps blends it in with the rest of the wood. Finally, a superfine heavy bodied white PVA glue, sold under the brand names 'Micro Krystal Kleer' or Deluxe Materials 'Glue and Glaze' is an excellent gap filler. It is especially useful to fill gaps between two painted parts. The glue is put into the joint and the excess is wiped off with a damp cloth or cotton bud causing no damage. The glue dries absolutely clear and can be painted over, but because it dries clear the painted part's colour shows through the glue and the filler blends in neatly with the rest of the paintwork. This material was originally designed to glaze windows on model airliners and is perfectly suitable for cabin windows, port holes, and stern lanterns. A coat of gloss varnish will waterproof the window and impart a sparkle.

Paints

The colour and painting of sailing warships is largely a matter of educated guesses and the exact shades are subject to debate. Paint was made from ground earth colours (minerals), such as red oxide, yellow ochre, and lead oxide and mixed with linseed oil as a binder and turpentine as a dryer. The shade depended on the quality of the earth colours, how accurately they were measured out before mixing (paint did not come in premixed tins ready for application), and the natural amber colour of the binder and driers will cause an additional tonal shift. My point is that it is a colossal waste of time to get pedantic about the exact shade of paint on these ships. New research is showing that colours we accepted as standard are not, such as the research on *Victory* whose yellow ochre was found to have a distinct pinkish tone in 1805 when they peeled back the paint layers and matched each to a dockyard work order.

On sailing ships, there are only general rules on shades so there is a lot of latitude. Many shades are taken from paintings of ships, but these paintings were most often done long after the ship was out of service or were embellished for artistic and romantic reasons. Contemporary descriptions are also vague, and recipes are imprecise (*eg*, mix two pounds of red ochre with a quart of linseed oil and pint of turpentine …) and red ochre is a natural pigment that will be either more reddish or brownish depending on where it was mined – certainly, no BS, FS, or Munsell paint numbers to guide us! Moreover, daily wear and tear, and battle damage will have repairs painted in whatever supplies were in the Bosun's store.

Paint designed for model kits, such as enamels by Humbrol or Revell, or acrylics by Tamiya or Vallejo are excellent choices. Finding some colours that resemble 'red ochre' or 'yellow ochre' is a matter of mixing the colour yourself or finding a premixed tint that looks correct to your eye. The tintlet may read 'British 8th Army Yellow', 'NATO Black' or 'Russian Deck Red' but the colour is likely near enough to yellow ochre, lamp black and red ochre of Nelson's day. Caldercraft produces a line of high-quality acrylic paints suitable for the age of sail, all matched to samples used in *Victory* for her first restoration. A good source for shades suitable for sailing ships are those mixed to match the colours of railway rolling stock. On a recent trip to a model train shop I found that 'Canadian National Yellow' was the ochre shade that had the tan undertone I was looking for.

Artist's oil paints find extensive use in ship modelling. They are not for general painting but rather best used for repairing existing paintwork and creating special effects such as woodgrain, the effects of weathering, or shading to create depth. The paints by Windsor and Newton are very finely ground and a word of warning not to be tempted by the inexpensive 'student' lines of paints because the pigments in these are more coarsely ground. When student grade paints are mixed with white spirit to create a wash or glaze, large grains of pigment can be seen, destroying the transparency of the wash and leaving a sludgy discolouration instead. Student grade oil colours do not brush out as well, making it more difficult to blend and feather the paintwork. Artist's oils should not be used right out of the tube but a medium like Windsor and Newton's 'Liquin' mixed in. Oil paint mediums speed drying, and thins them to a smooth and creamy consistency ideal for blending and brushing out. Paint mixed with a medium like Liquin will dry in a day to an eggshell sheen whereas those mixed with turpentine will dry quite quickly to a dead matt finish. Paints mixed with linseed oil greatly extends the time for the paint to dry (sometimes weeks) and gives a glossy finish. When a model is complete, a consistent sheen is accomplished with a clear matt, satin or gloss topcoat as required. Clear topcoats also have the property of deepening out the colour, and in particular the effect of washes.

Any item that is to be painted needs to be primed. For white metal, brass or resin parts a good primer to use is Tamiya's white or light grey aerosol. These paints are a lacquer acrylic that adheres to all surfaces, are sandable, and produces a smooth matt surface. Wooden parts require a little more work, and how much depends on the grain of the wood. Wood grain is filled with a sanding sealer. The most common are latex based and contains a filler (*eg*, talc) to fill the grain. The sealer is brushed or sprayed on, allowed to dry and sanded back with fine garnet paper. Typically, two or sometimes three coats are required. The other type of sanding sealer just hardens the surface of the wood and does not fill the grain nearly as much. This sealer is used when you want some of the wood grain to show through. Personally, I like to have a little wood grain show through my paintwork. I realize that real ships didn't show any wood grain under the paint, but on a model, too perfect a finish gives it a toy-like quality to my eye. The choice is yours.

Wargame figure painters have blessed us ship modellers with an amazing product called the 'Army Painter Quickshade' that instantly shades carvings and decorations. Army Painter is a dark brown coloured solvent-based polyurethane varnish (three tones are available ranging from light brown to almost black) that can be brushed over a painted surface and flows into the creases and folds. It is left on for a second where it pools up and this excess is removed with a brush. The remaining varnish settles into the recesses and cures leaving beautifully shaded paintwork. Its brown colour also adds a very pleasant patina that looks just right on a period warship. The use of this product is demonstrated in Chapter 7. A DIY water-based acrylic version called 'The Dip' in wargaming circles can be made by tinting acrylic floor wax (*eg*, 'Pledge Revive It' in the UK or 'Pledge Revive' in North America) with brown acrylic hobby paint, or speciality paints called 'inks' made for shading wargame figures. It is a matter of trial and error to get the proportions correct but wargame miniatures painting techniques really bring to life the ship's carvings and decorations.

SAFETY

There are undoubtedly other tools, adhesives and paints that can be used on model sailing ships and more will be introduced throughout the book. Whatever tools you use, using them safely remains paramount. Knives are sharp and power tools kick back. Even the smallest light duty tools can cause blood to flow. Paints, thinners, and adhesives emit noxious fumes and can stick to and burn skin. It cannot be stressed enough the importance of eye protection. I inculcated this into my son when he was a very young lad. Whenever he came to visit me in the workshop I made him put on safety equipment. I am sure he thought it fun dressing up in all the gear looking like a spaceman exploring the Fifth Dimension of outer space. Something must have taken root, and soon whenever he heard me head to the shop he would pop down and hold up my safety glasses and dust mask as a reminder to wear them. It may seem like a hassle to put on the gear, but you will find after time that it becomes so automatic that you feel naked and vulnerable without it. It is also important to also train family members to wait until a power tool is switched off before calling you for dinner so as not to cause startle with a whirring blade near your fingers. Ask me how I know.

Woodworking creates a lot of dust and some species of wood have oils or resins that can cause allergic reactions or respiratory irritations. Wear a dust mask properly rated for filtering out wood particles and always sweep or vacuum your workshop after each use. Wood particles are a fire hazard so keeping the shop clean reduces that risk. Earplugs muffle the noise to non-harmful decibel levels; rings and jewellery should be removed, and long sleeves rolled up so they do not get caught in the spinning parts of a power tool. Be sensible and don't operate tools under the influence of alcohol, medications that can make you drowsy, or other substances. Nagging runs in my family.

4: Solid Hull Modelling
United States Ship *Perry*

Carving a hull from a solid piece of wood is one of the best ways to really come to understand the complex shape of a ship's hull and how this affects its performance through the water. There are a few model companies, mainly in the United States, that offer solid hull kits and the skills learned on these readily transfer to making your own hulls from scratch. The solid hull approach is an ideal place to start wooden ship modelling because the kits provide a roughly pre-shaped hull and carving to templates bring the hull down to its final lines. Moreover, there is typically no planking to do, and keel, stem and rudder posts are separate parts that are easily pinned in place. Finishing is usually no more complicated than a coat of paint in authentic colours.

The model chosen for this build is the 1/96 scale (⅛in = 1ft) American brig USS *Perry* (Figure 42). She was launched in May 1843 and commissioned into the United States Navy at the Norfolk Navy Yard. She was called the 'fastest ship in the Navy' and served during the American Civil War, the Mexican–American War, and when there were tensions with Paraguay. What attracted me to her was her role in combatting slavery in the United States. Her rig is from the 1850s making for some interesting model making. The kit is by *Bluejacket Shipcrafters* of Maine that has been producing model kits since 1905. The interesting thing about this company is that virtually all of the fittings, including the rigging blocks, are cast in pewter (Figure 43). Before the advent of modern CNC milling and laser cutting, kit-supplied wood blocks were just that – blocks of wood with holes drilled (often not evenly) through them. The pewter blocks were a revelation because they actually look like real ship's blocks with proper *sheave* (the pulley) detail, *beckets* (short length of rope wrapped around a rigging block that has an eye at one end), and *scores* (a groove cut along the side of a rigging block to hold rope) moulded in. The cast deadeyes were also highly detailed with proper scores for the lanyards and ropes, and they could be purchased in many different sizes and types. Most importantly, the pewter parts were in scale. Cast parts such as these require some clean-up of mould lines, clearing holes with a fine drill, and painting, but this extra work is of no consequence compared to the realism these items offer.

Shaping the Hull

The preparation of templates is fundamental to carving an accurate hull. The hull sections and the deck outlines are cut from the plans and glued to some stiff card using spray glue. It is really important to cut them out accurately (Figure 44). Pay attention to the top and bottom of the templates because these points locate the position of the templates when offered up to the hull. The kit's roughly shaped hull blank is shown in Figure 42. Although shaped, it still requires a great deal of carving. This hull blank includes the hull up to the various deck levels, and the hull above the deck (the *bulwarks*) are added from wood sheet later. It pays dividends to spend time examining the hull blank by turning it around and upside down and in your mind's eye visualizing what the finished hull will look like.

42

The *Perry* kit's wooden parts include a roughly shaped solid hull, laser-cut parts, and scribed wooden deck sheet. Several spools of high-quality threads of different diameters are included for the rigging. Several full-size plan sheets are also included and an illustrated instruction manual (not shown). The overall dimensions are approximately 21.5in (tip of bowsprit to end of spanker boom), 15in tall (top of main mast), and 6.5in wide (width of main yard).

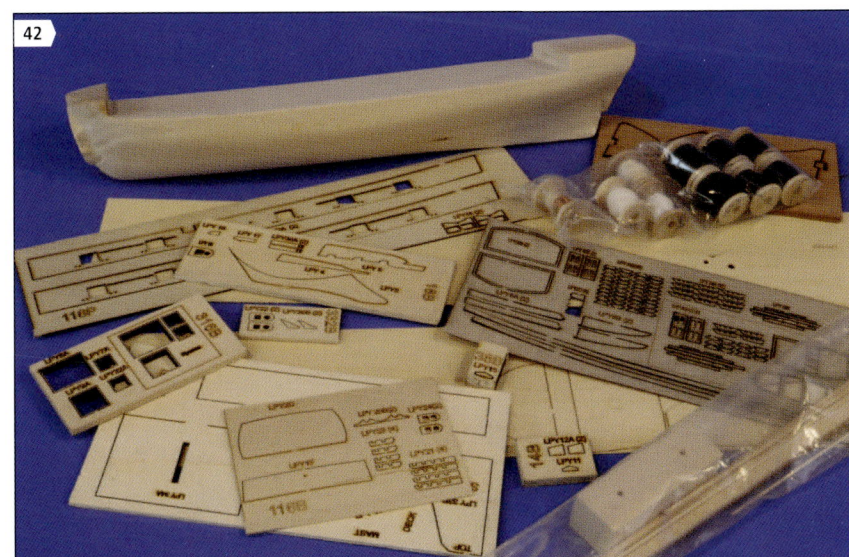

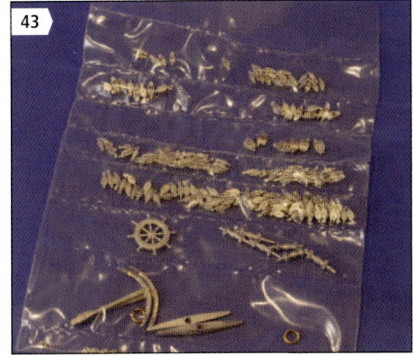

43

All *Bluejacket Shipcrafters* kits contain a large array of cast pewter parts, in particular the rigging blocks that are finely detailed. Shown is a small selection of items from the kit.

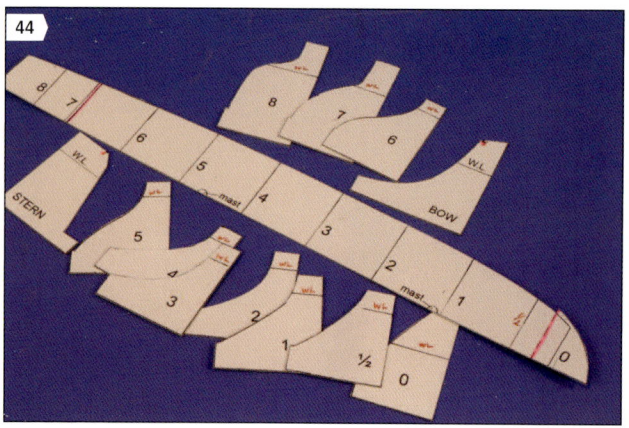

44

The carving templates were glued to stiff card and cut out. There are templates to shape the body of the hull, profile of the hull, and decks.

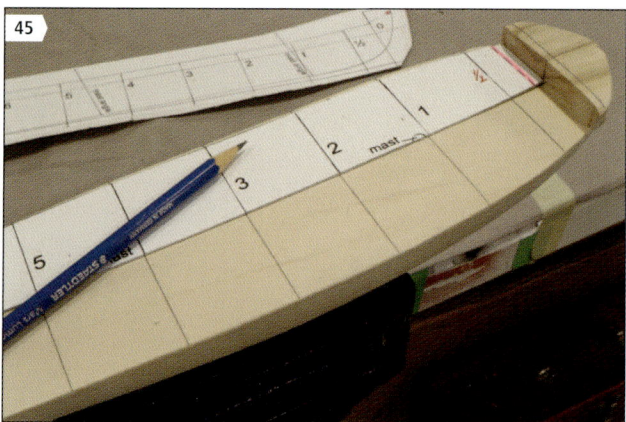

45

The hull blank is marked with centre and station lines.

This will help you come to know where most of the wood will have to be removed.

On the hull pick a datum point from where all the measurements for carving will be taken. I chose the break between the *quarterdeck*, the raised deck behind the main mast, and the *main deck*, the deck that runs from the quarterdeck to the *forecastle deck* (the raised deck forward of the foremast). The break corresponds to point #7 on the deck template. A centreline is drawn along the top and bottom of the hull blank from the forecastle, along the main deck and over the quarterdeck (Figure 45). It's difficult to say where the centre is on a rough carved hull blank so pick a point where the wood on both sides is at least the same size. The centreline is taken down and drawn along the bottom of the hull. The bottom centreline will be approximate but will still serve as a handy guide to locate templates during carving. Along the top centreline mark the locations of the hull templates.

Fixing the hull blank to a bench vice is essential because it leaves both hands free to carve. Wood screws and a scrap of wood is fixed to the hull bottom to form a handle. Bluejacket Shipcrafters thoughtfully provided these items in the kit (Figure 46). The first templates placed on the hull are the deck templates. Once in place trace onto the hull blank the shape of the main, forecastle and quarterdeck deck (Figure 47). This outline gives you a visual reference for the shape of the hull blank at each deck level. I usually start shaping the hull from about midships and work forwards and backwards from that point. The first hull template is put up against the hull blank and where it touches is where you want to remove wood. I usually place three templates on the hull blank and mark where they touch the hull to define a broad area to remove wood. I work on both sides in turn to ensure symmetry. The closer you get to the correct shape of the hull, little by little more of the template will touch the hull. It takes some time and several passes to begin to get the hull matching the shape of the templates. Areas at the bow and stern (Figures 48 to 55) require a lot more wood taken off but in time you will get there. The location of the centreline on the bottom may shift a little and will naturally come to the correct location as carving progresses. Carving and shaping will also remove some of the marks you used to locate the template and these lines

46

The hull blank is fitted with a block of wood to act as a handle, leaving both hands free to carve.

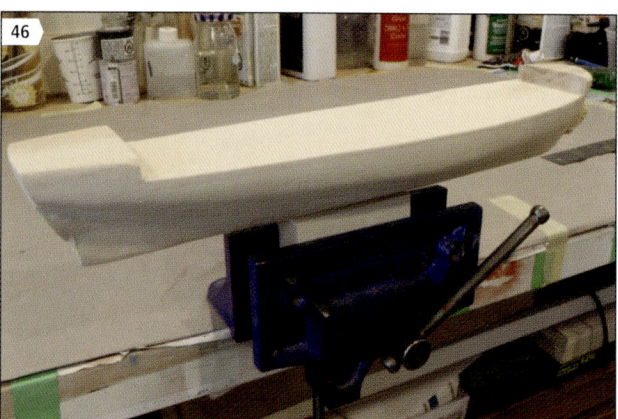

47

Carving begins by cutting down the edges to the marked deck outline.

48
Offer up the templates to the hull and mark with pencil the areas where the wood needs to be removed and repeat. Note that a piece of yellow tape has been laid along the hull bottom. The tape is a visual reminder of where a flat is required to attach the keel, stem and sternpost. The tape is cut to the width of these items (1/8in).

49
Carving underway. Note that shallow cuts were taken to remove unwanted wood to better control the shaping process. It is important to work on one side of the hull and then on the other to ensure symmetry.

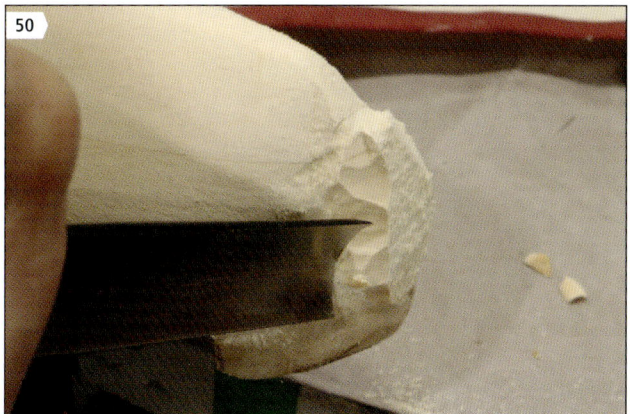

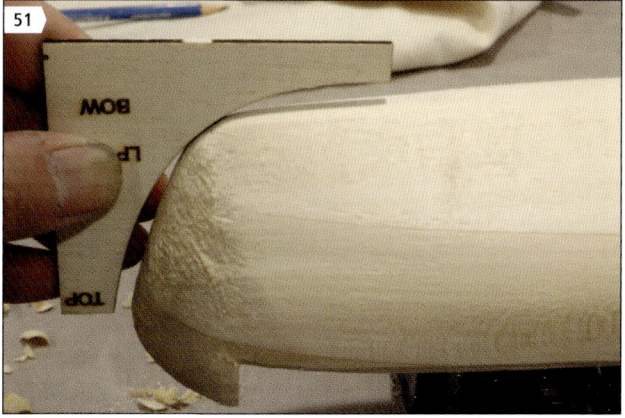

50
Carving of the bow starts with paring away the wooden plug. A sharp gouge and light cuts gets the job done.

51
The templates are offered up to the bow to see where wood needs to be removed. The same procedure applies to all areas of the hull. Take a little of the wood off, using a gouge or a rasp – whatever works best – and offer up the template again to see where else wood has to be removed.

52
The profile is getting closer. A pencil mark shows where wood is to be removed next. Note that the cheeks of the bow remain to be shaped.

must be constantly renewed. It's not uncommon to sometimes take off more wood by mistake but these gouges can be repaired with a two-part automotive filler. When the full profile of the templates touch the hull all the way around, and their inside top and bottom edges touch the centrelines, you have arrived at the proper shape.

The carving tools I use most often are Henry Taylor #1 and #5 gouges. Coarse sandpaper and a half-round wood rasp also have their uses. Be aware of the wood's grain when carving. When cutting with

53

The bow's profile and cheeks are carved to shape. The marks from the rasp are clearly seen so attention with some sandpaper will smooth this and all of the contours together.

54

The carved hull. Some sanding will be required to smooth out the tool marks. When sanding, continue to check the contours of the hull with the templates. Any gouges or dips can be filled with two-part automotive filler and sanded smooth.

55

A front quarter view of the sanded carved hull. Carving is a very rewarding activity and is a great stress reducer.

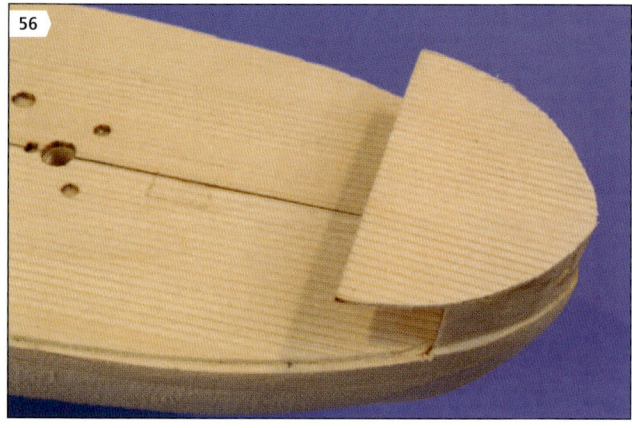

56

A rebate is cut along the hull edges to seat the bulwarks. The scribed decking is glued in place.

the grain, the wood pares away nicely, but when you cut against it the wood will tear off in ugly chunks. Stop and turn the hull around to carve with the grain. A flat area to accommodate the stem, keel and rudder post must also be worked into the hull. On *Perry* this is ⅛in wide, and an easy way to do this is to cut a piece of ⅛in wide masking tape and fix to the hull bottom as a reference to shape the hull in this area (see Figure 49).

Decks and Bulwarks

With the hull carved to shape, a rebate must be carved into the hull to seat the bulwarks (Figure 56). Cutting the rebate is straightforward with a sharp chisel, but once again beware of the direction of the grain to avoid tearing the wood. At the extreme bow and stern, you have no choice but to cut across grain, and this is tackled by cutting the rebate's outline with a sharp knife as a stop cut, and then use a file cut in the actual rebate. The wood will fall away from the stop cut leaving a clean rebate.

The kit provides scribed wood sheet for the deck that will need to be trimmed to fit inside the rebate. In some kits only a generic sheet of scribed wood is included, but in the *Perry* kit the sheet is laser-cut to provide the deck in two halves with the openings for the masts and other fittings. On the downside, the joint between the laser-cut halves is difficult to disguise, and it is also difficult to show any *nibbing* of deck planks – the angled edge cut into the end of the plank to accommodate the curve of the hull at the bow and stern. However, details such as the shift of the butts, caulking between planks, and trennels are easily drawn in with pencil (see Figure 57).

The laser-cut edges between the two halves can be gently bevelled with sandpaper to remove the char and provide neat mating faces to minimize any gaps. Deck caulking was drawn in with the tip of a sharp pencil down the grooves of the deck (Figure 58). Some modellers glue thin black or brown thread into the grooves but I find this effect a little too dramatic for my eye and I can never get the thread to lie down straight. If the colour of the wood looks a little bright to you it can be toned down with a thin wash of grey paint, made from a mix of a little burnt umber, ivory black and titanium

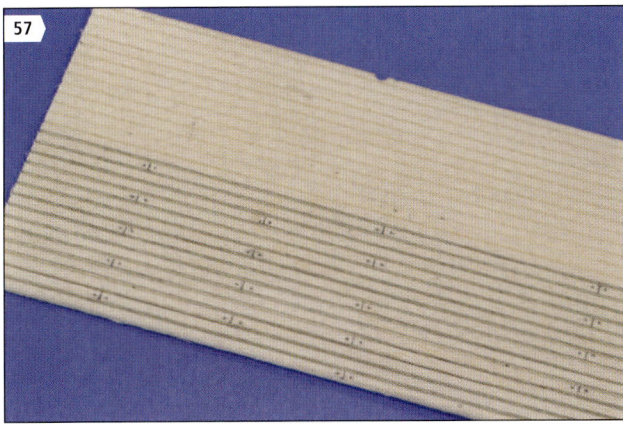

57

Scribed wooden deck sheet can be made to look more realistic by running a sharp pencil down the grooves to represent the caulking between planks. Trennals and butts can also be drawn in if desired.

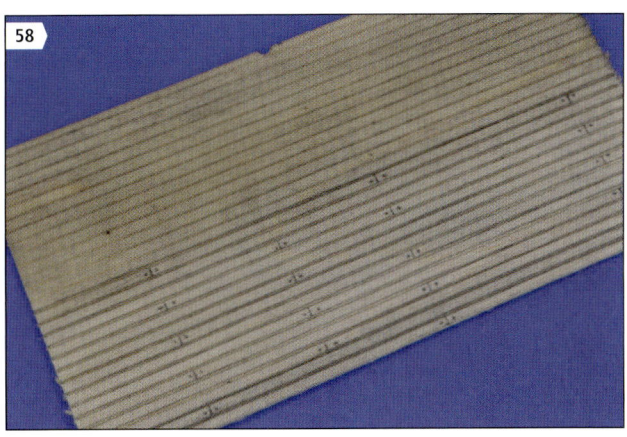

58

The brightness of the deck can be toned down with a wash of artist's oil paints. A wash looks quite effective on the plain scribed wood or on the sections that have been detailed with pencil.

white artist's oil colour dissolved in white spirits. Do not use a wash made with acrylics because scribed deck sheeting will curl up if exposed to any water. When the wash is dry, it can be buffed with some fine steel wool and held in place with low tack masking tape until the acetate glue dries.

The bulwark is a clever design of two pieces that are laminated together. One piece represents the inner bulwark with all the holes cut through for the gun tackle, cleats and other fittings; and a second piece represents the outer bulwark with no holes (Figure 59). The inner bulwark is not as deep as the outer bulwark so when they are glued together a lip is formed that fits into the rebate cut into the hull. The bulwark is glued together and allowed to dry before being curved over a planking iron to fit the hull contours. The bulwarks are overlong and when offered up to the hull will have to be trimmed to length. Test fitting the bulwark will take some time, and at each test you will induce a little more curve with the planking iron. Once you achieve a reasonable fit to the hull – note that it will never be a perfect fit – it is taped to the hull (Figure 60). Start gluing the

bulwark in place at the stern by lifting the tape and wiping in some glue. Hold it in place with a clamp, tape, and perhaps a little brass nail. Carry on along the length of the bulwark and when you arrive at the bow and the most severe curve, stop there and let the glue cure before proceeding any further.

To shape the bulwarks around the bow, a hot planking iron is pressed up against the outside of the bulwark pushing it into the hull to induce a curve that better fits the contours. Apply glue and hold into place. Ensure that the bulwarks meet at the centreline and that they are of equal height. Contrary to the instructions, I found it much easier to fix the bulwarks in place without the scribed forecastle decking in place (Figure 61). The decking was torn out and I let the bulwark fall where it wanted. In my model the bulwark wanted to flare outwards which left a sizeable gap between the forecastle deck and the bulwark. Forcing the bulwark in place to accommodate the scribed decking would have resulted in an unnatural contour to the hull sides in this area. This is part of the *art* of ship modelling when you know when to let the wood lie naturally. The gap between the

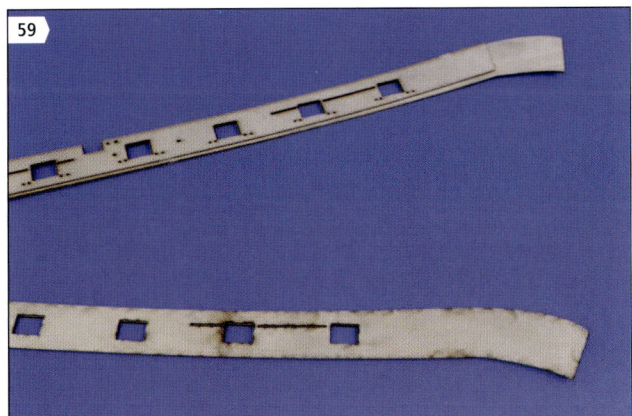

59

The assembled laser-cut bulwark components. A little pre-bending of the front has been carried out over the head of a hot planking iron.

60

The bulwarks sides are glued in place first and held to the hull with tape and clamps. The bulwarks around the bow will be shaped and glued into place later.

59

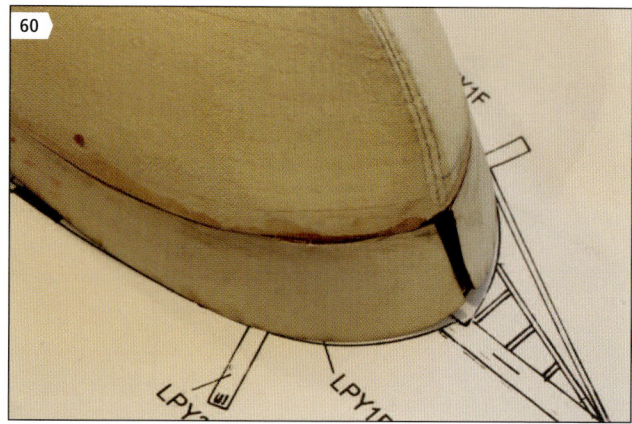

60

61

When the bulwarks were pushed in around the bow they did not want to close in neatly around the forecastle deck but tended to flare out at the top. The forecastle deck was removed and another one cut to fit the new space between the bulwark sides.

62

Double checking the shape of the bulwarks against the plans showed that the natural flare the parts took on is correct and that the laser-cut forecastle deck part is too small. Wood has natural tendencies that has to be worked with, not against.

inner bulwark and hull was made good with two-part automotive filler and a new forecastle deck was cut from spare planking sheet to fit the space. This left a nice neat joint between the bulwark and deck and, lo and behold, the flare of the bulwarks matched the plans almost perfectly (Figure 62).

The outside join between the bulwark and hull was contoured with two-part automotive filler and sanded smooth. The important thing at this point is to use enough filler to blend them together into a seamless piece (Figure 63). Shape the filler to continue the sweet lines of the hull and most of the filler I required was to build up the shape of the bow. This is the beauty of solid hull modelling. It is very

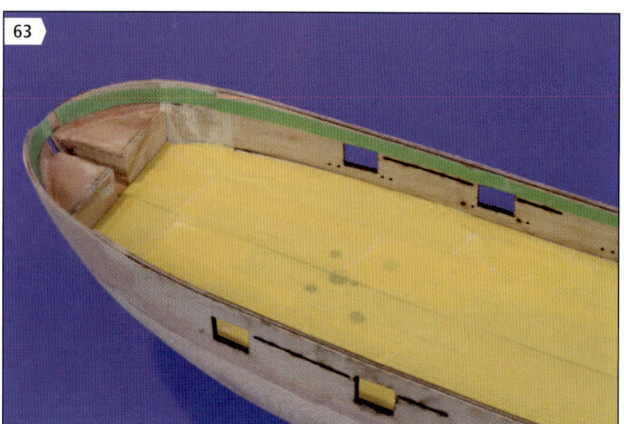

63

63

The join between the bulwark and outer hull is filled with two-part automotive filler (in light pink) and sanded to shape. A few applications of filler were required to build up the contour and preserve the sweet lines of the hull. The deck has been masked off to prevent it from damage. The band of green tape on the inside of the bulwarks marks the final height of the bulwarks. The tape was allowed to follow the sheer of the hull and any wood extending beyond the top of the tape line is sanded away.

forgiving of mistakes because the solid hull provides a very secure backing for filler and shaping. The stern transom facia piece was soaked and curved over the planking iron to fit the curve of the transom.

A ship's *keel* is the backbone of a ship to which the *stem post*, the curved upright timber at the ship's bow is attached, and a *rudder post* at the stern. On actual ships, the stem post is just one upright timber that comprises the head of the ship. The head is made up of several pieces of timber that are attached to the stem post like the *apron*, *gripe*, *rising wood*, and the *gammon knee*, for example. The stern post is also a single timber but is has several timbers attached to it such as the *inner post* and many supporting knees. The keel too is not a single timber but several scarfed together such as the *false keel*, *keelson* and the like. The complexity of these areas is shown in Chapter 8 when we have a look at building a model in frame like a real ship. Ship nomenclature is a specialist language and the terms will differ across languages. With kits coming from countries around the world, often the names and specifics of these timbers get lost in translation. To simplify matters many kits refer to the stem post and all of its related timbers as just the 'stem post' or 'stem'. The stern post and its collective parts are just called the 'stern' or the 'rudder post'. For the purposes of this book, I use common kit nomenclature to be consistent with kit convention and reduce any confusion. As such, the stem, rudder post, and keel are glued to *Perry*'s hull and small holes drilled right through them into the hull. They are pegged in place with a sliver of split bamboo skewer dipped in glue (Figure 64).

Painting and Coppering the Hull

A coat of sanding sealer filler was applied by brush, smoothed off and followed by a coat of primer. The primer highlights any flaws that must be corrected and the process continued until a blemish-free hull was achieved (Figure 65). Painting the *Perry* is quite straightforward. The white stripe along the line of the gunports was painted first (Figure 66). Pure white looks rather garish, so use a warm white or ivory colour that not only looks better, but is in keeping with the colours of paint from the era. The off-white was

SOLID HULL MODELLING

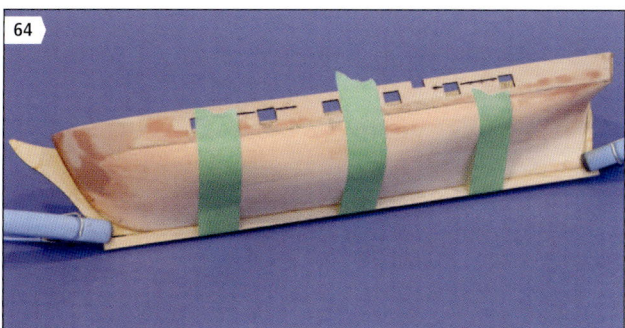

64

The stem, keel, and rudder post are fixed to the hull and she is starting to look like a ship. A trick to prevent the sharp edges of stem, keel, and sternpost parts from getting damaged is to soak the edges with thin CA. The glue soaks into the wood and solidifies it. Filler was used to fair these parts into the hull bottom and automotive glaze and spot putty corrected any minor imperfections and gaps. The extent of the putty work to fair in the bulwarks and hull, especially at the bow, can be seen

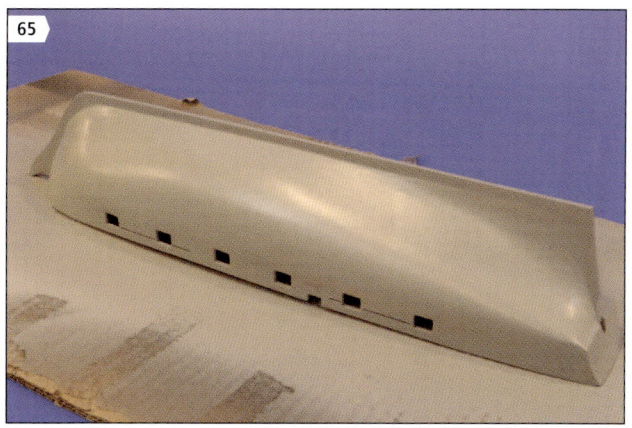

65

A coat of primer was sprayed on the hull and putty used to correct any imperfections. The process was repeated until a flawless surface was obtained. Wood is a porous material and some species have a marked grain that takes a great deal of preparation to fill before being ready to accept the final paintwork.

darkened slightly with a little brown to shade around the gunports (also called *sally ports* in American parlance). The paint is allowed to cure overnight before being masked off and the hull painted off-black. Pure black was used as a shade and sprayed around the top of the bulwarks and along the waterline to impart a more three-dimensional finish to the paintwork (Figure 67).

The waterline was marked next by first setting the hull on a flat surface. The plans show that *Perry* draws more water under the stern and the hull was set to the proper angle in its cradle. A pencil is taped to a block of wood at this height and moved around the hull marking the waterline (Figure 68). Double check the height of waterline because sometimes the pencil slips or the model shifts in its cradle. The underwater hull is clad in copper but the kit does not provide any materials for this. Instead it instructs you to mask off the waterline and paint the area a dull copper colour (Figure 69). I did this to see how it looked and just hated the result. It looked like paint so I decided to apply the cladding with real copper. A roll of self-adhesive copper foil

tape was purchased from a shop that sells supplies for making stained glass windows (Figure 70). For the *Perry*, I used 3mm wide tape cut into 12mm lengths which is about the scale size required (Figure 71).

A tip of a knife blade removes the tape's backing paper and the copper plate is positioned with a pair of tweezers and rubbed down. The copper plates are laid in rows from the keel upwards, starting at the stern working towards the bow. The plates are laid end to end with each plate overlapping the previously laid plate by about 1mm. The plates for the next row are shifted about half the length of a plate below (around 6mm) in brickwork fashion. Each row also overlaps the one below it by around 1mm as well. After two or three rows are laid, the curvature of the hull at the bow and stern will force the rows to diverge away from the previously laid row leaving a triangular-shaped gap (Figure 72). Let the copper diverge and it quickly heads up towards the waterline. Once you reach the waterline the plates are cut across to fit. The triangular gaps are filled with tape cut to shape and the ends of the keel, stem and rudder

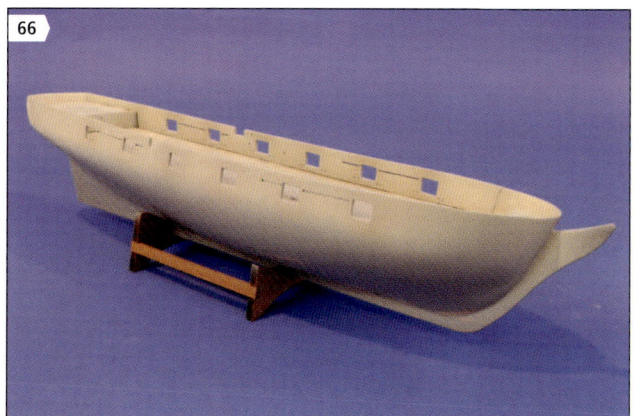

66

The hull all along the gunports were painted off-white from stem to stern.

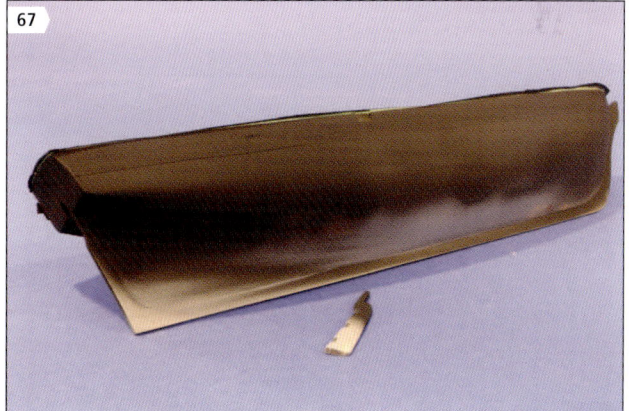

67

The white stripe is masked off and the hull and rudder are painted black to just below the waterline.

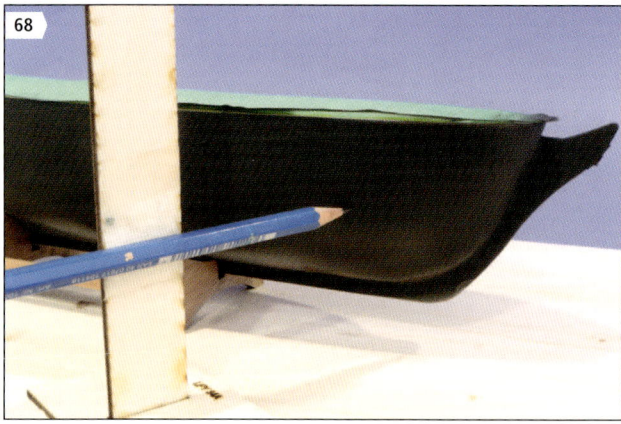

68

The waterline being marked with a pencil. The pencil is being held onto the marking tool by magic – that is, the magic of industrial strength double sided tape.

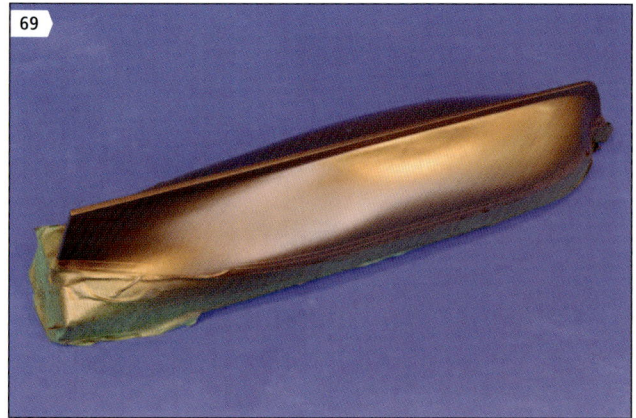

69

The hull bottom was sprayed copper to represent the copper cladding to ward against worm. To my eye, the painted bottom looked like paint and the decision was made to lay copper plates over it.

70

Adhesive backed rolls of copper tape found at shops that sell stained glass making supplies.

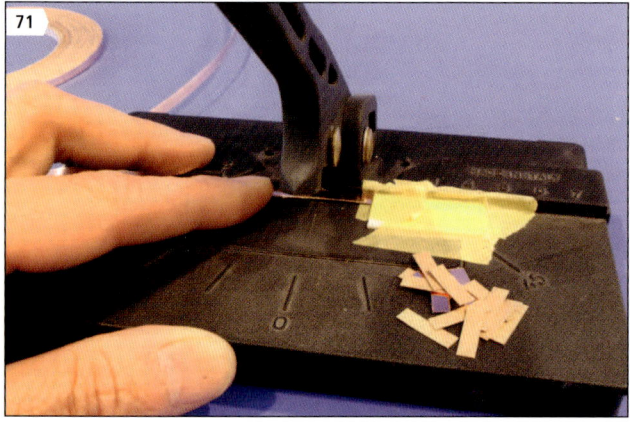

71

The copper tape is cut into individual plates with a guillotine cutter. The cutter made by Amati was ideal because its base is hard, allowing the tape to be cut cleanly. A depth stop was fashioned from a piece of scrap plastic and taped down.

72

The curvature of the hull will cause rows of copper to diverge and create triangular gaps. These gaps are filled with rows of copper in the same way as before, except the plates that fall into the apex of the triangular space are cut to fit the space – and don't forget to allow for the correct overlap with the previously laid plates.

post are covered with tape whose sides are bent over the edges for a neat finish.

The top edge of copper at the waterline is covered with thin wooden batten. On actual ships the batten prevented the edge of the copper from getting snagged and pulled off. The batten was given a wash of black and burnt umber artist's oil colour to dull down the brightness of the wood. The colour of the copper tape is also quite bright and dulled down with a matt clear coat (Figure 73). It is important to note that I coppered right along the marked waterline but if you look carefully at the stern, owing to the curvature of the hull, the line of copper appears to sag downwards. This is an optical illusion that we model makers must overcome by allowing the line of copper at the stern (and sometimes the bow) to rise up *over* the marked waterline. This line is determined by cutting a narrow piece of tape and placing one end at the point on the waterline where it looks like the downward slope begins. Move the other end of the

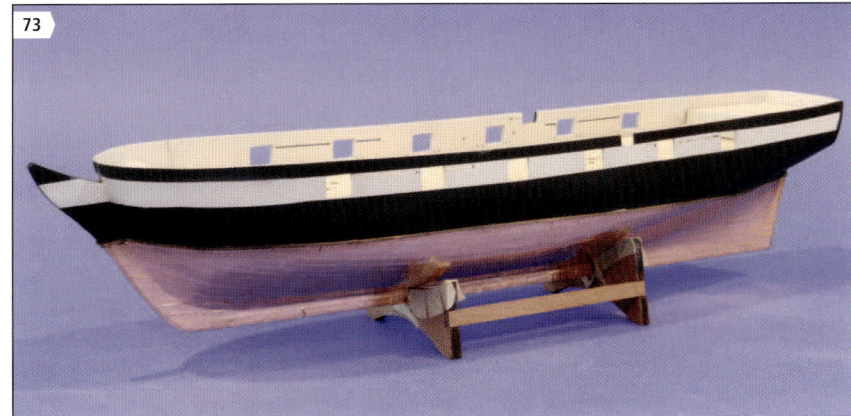

73
The coppering is completed and a wooden batten is fixed all along the top of the copper. Despite being straight, the waterline appears to sag at the stern as discussed in the text. Coppering the *Perry*'s hull is quite straightforward given its small size and gentle hull curves. The inner bulwarks are painted white, and all of the masking tape removed from the hull revealing the ship's black and white colour scheme.

tape upwards until it looks like the waterline is straight along its whole length. This will take a few trials but eventually it will look correct. Mark the new waterline positions at the bow and stern and that will be the actual line you copper to.

BULWARK RAILS

The laser-cut rails that fit on top of the bulwarks did not easily fit my hull (Figure 74). The shape of my hull differed enough from the kit parts that it was easier to make a new rail than try to modify the kit parts to fit. This is not a criticism of the kit which provides the theoretically correct shape, but rather is caused by variations in how each modeller builds his hull. The shape of bulwarks is traced onto a piece of card with a help of a plush towel (Figure 75). The card is laid on the towel and the hull is placed upside down on the card and gently pressed down. The towel provides enough 'give' so that the card is held flat against the hull's *sheer* (the upturn of the elevation of the hull at the bow and stern of the hull) enabling the hull shape to be traced. The width of the rail (and a little bit extra) is marked out with a pair of dividers and marks joined up with a French curve (Figure 76). The tracing is cut out to make a pattern that is traced onto a piece of thin ply, one for each side of the hull. The rails are cut out – and here's a tip: cut them overlong – and sanded to shape.

They are pre-painted black and glued to the top of the bulwarks (Figure 77).

SALLY PORT LIDS

A characteristic of nineteenth-century American ships is that their gunport lids are split horizontally and stow the long guns with the barrels protruding through a hole pierced through them. This arrangement is seen on many of their sailing warships like the USS *Constitution* which can be visited in Boston. On *Perry* the lids are solid because she is largely armed with carronades and the barrels are not long enough to protrude through the sally ports in the same way. The kit provides solid lids whereas the plans show pierced lids. There are times when the plans and parts do not agree, and in this case the parts are correct because the kit has been upgraded as a result of new research that showed she was largely armed with carronades as opposed to long guns. These are the little details and anomalies that one must keep in mind when building ships from the age of sail because research is always an ongoing process. To Bluejacket Shipcrafters' credit, a revised set of plans and instruction booklet arrived without warning in the post one day with a note explaining the upgrade to those who purchased the kit directly from them.

The companionways and other deck fittings were assembled as

74
The laser-cut rails didn't fit the shape of the hull so new ones will have to be made from scrap material. The waterways have been pre-painted white and glued to the deck right up against the bulwark side for a neat join.

75
The line of the bulwarks is traced onto a piece of card. The card and the hull sit on top of a soft towel, allowing the hull to be pushed down against the card so an accurate tracing can be taken.

76

A pair of dividers set to the width of the rail (and a little extra) and the inside edge of the rail is ticked off. The patterns are cut out and traced onto 1/16in plywood sheet. The length of the tracing on the wood is extended about 1/8in to provide room for adjustment.

77

The new rails are offered up to the hull and trimmed to length and shaped by rounding over the edges slightly. The rails are pre-painted black and glued to the top of the bulwarks.

per plans and instruction booklet (Figure 78) and these need little comment, just a straightforward assembly job. A tip for laser-cut companionway ladders: it is very difficult to remove all of the laser char from the edges of such delicate parts and the dark edges found on every step and stile is obtrusive and unattractive. The prominence of the laser char can be minimized by staining the assembled ladder a rich mahogany colour, or painted over with a mix of burnt umber and burnt sienna artist's oil colour mixed with a little oil paint medium. The oil paint will darken the wooden parts to better hide the laser char, and the paint can be brushed out to give an authentic woodgrain finish. A little practice with oil paints soon shows you the versatility of these paints.

Armament

The guns and their carriages are cast metal parts whose seam lines need to be cleaned up. The parts are washed, primed and painted in the base colours of a red brown for the carriages and black for the barrels. The nicely cast details are brought out with a wash of ivory black and burnt umber oil colour that is sealed under a coat of satin varnish when dry (Figure 79). When it comes to rigging the guns, many kits only provide materials for the *breeching rope*. This is the thick rope that is attached to the inside of the bulwark on both sides of the gun and the gun's cascabel. This rope limits the gun's recoil when it is fired. What is often omitted is the tackle that is used to pull the gun back into position after reloading, and the training tackle that is used to swing the gun over a little to the right or left when aiming. The training tackle is only rigged when the gun is in action, otherwise the breeching rope and gun tackle is present. Figure 80 shows a fully rigged model cannon with a breeching rope and tackle for a stowed gun. The lines of the gun tackle are *triced up* (tied up) up out of the way, a lead sheet apron (*cover*) was fitted over the touch hole, and a *tompion* is fitted inside the mouth of the barrel to keep the damp out. Many people omit these details because they want to show the guns run out ready for battle.

78

Several of the deck fittings built, painted and fixed to the hull. The pewter fittings required a little cleaning up before primer and paint. Several fittings, such as ladders, companionway doors, and hatches are laser-cut wood. The laser charring was covered up by over painting the parts with artist's oil colour. The sally port lids on the hull side are simple rectangles of plastic card painted off-white. The ship's bulwark rail has been cut to make way for the entry port. There may be small gaps between the rail and bulwark top that is filled by brushing on some *Kristal Kleer* into the join and wiping away the excess. The glue can be touched up with a bit of paint and when the model is complete an overspray of matt or satin varnish will blend in any glue marks.

SOLID HULL MODELLING

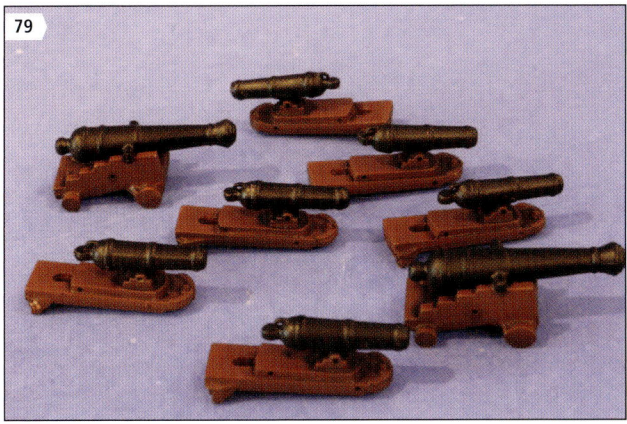

79
The guns painted and given a wash of burnt umber and ivory black artist's oils. A coat of satin clear varnish sealed the paint and deepened the colours. The wheels (*trucks*) on the gun carriages have yet to be painted.

80
A fully rigged model gun in a large 1/24 scale radio control sailing model of *Surprize*. The gun is outfitted with a breeching rope and hauling tackles that has been wrapped around the barrel when the gun is stowed. A lead sheet cover used to protect the touch hole when not in action has been fitted. If the gun lock was fitted, a square lead cover could be made to fit over it. The method of stowing the gun is copied from that used on *Victory* in Portsmouth. On a large-scale model such details are easy to replicate, but on smaller scale models the gun tackle is often simplified to give the impression of rigging.

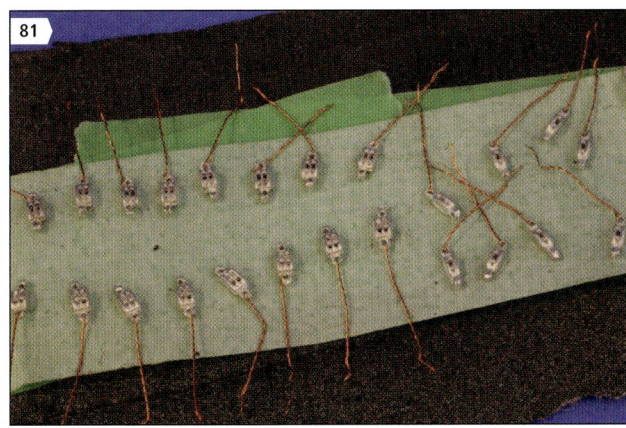

81
The pewter blocks are cleaned up, holes drilled and stuck to a piece of masking tape ready for painting. These blocks are fixed to the inner bulwark with a length of twisted wire hole to represent the eyebolt and stropping. The small 1/96 scale size necessitated some simplification of the gun rigging.

The *Perry* kit provides enough blocks to fully rig the gun similar to that shown in Figure 80. The holes cast into gun tackle blocks require clearing by drilling through with a new #77 drill bit held in a pin vice. Most of the cast holes were clear, but drilling them through makes them a bit larger allowing the rigging thread to be *rove* (threaded) through much more easily (Figure 81). You will probably break a drill bit or two so have a few extra on hand! The blocks in this kit are provided ready stropped so the loop and becket need to be drilled through to attach the line to them. On a real ship, the blocks for the gun tackle were attached with rope tied to an eyebolt fixed to the inner bulwark. In the small scale of this model, the eyebolts are very small and it would be very fiddly to feed a length of thread through their tiny holes. Instead, the rope and the attached eyebolt was simplified by a single piece of twisted wire. Wire was threaded through the block's loop and twisted tight. The twisted wire resembles a rope, but being made of wire is very stiff whose end can be glued into a hole in the bulwark. The fact there is no visible eyebolt is not really noticeable; and if you were to feed a length of thread through a tiny eyebolt and tied a knot to hold it fast it would obscure the eyebolt from view anyways. For the breeching rope, a loop is formed from wire and the breeching rope is fed through the loop. The length of the breeching rope is adjusted by pulling the rope through the loop one way or the other and knotted to hold it fast to the eyebolt.

The rigging blocks are attached to scrap cardboard and primed and then painted a dark brown. Owing to the very small size of the blocks, the guns were rigged off the model and attached to the bulwark later (Figure 82). The kit supplies white threads for the breeching rope and gun tackle. This can be dyed to a light tan if so desired. On ceremonial occasions rope was often whitened for show so I left it white. The gun was fixed to the deck with a pin. The breeching rope should be given a realistic sag by wetting the thread with a mixture of water and white PVA glue. The end of a paintbrush is used to push and prod the breeching rope into shape and the glue in the mix will hold the shape when dry. Thread doesn't have the weight of real rope so we must help it not defy the laws of gravity.

DEADEYES, CHAIN PLATES, AND CHANNELS

A *deadeye* is a pierced wooden disc encircled by a rope or an iron band that is used to set up a *shroud*, the thick rope that holds the mast up from side to side. A *chain plate* is a metal plate that is used to fasten the shrouds to the hull. The deadeyes and chain plates are attached to the hull through a wooden *channel*, a platform that protrudes from the ship's hull (Figure 83). The kit-supplied deadeyes

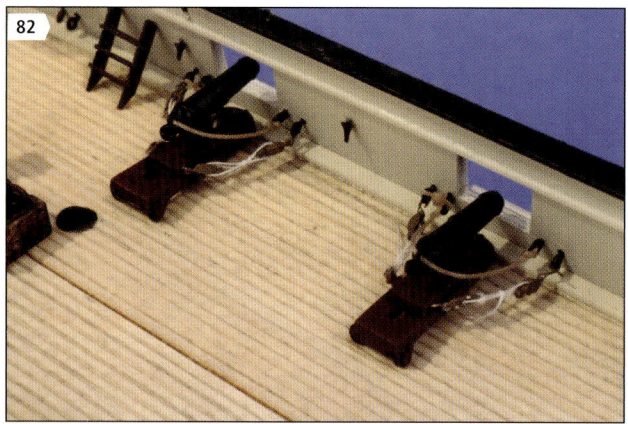

82

The rigged guns. When threading line through the blocks dip the end of the thread into some CA glue. This stiffens the thread end into a needle making much easier to thread the blocks.

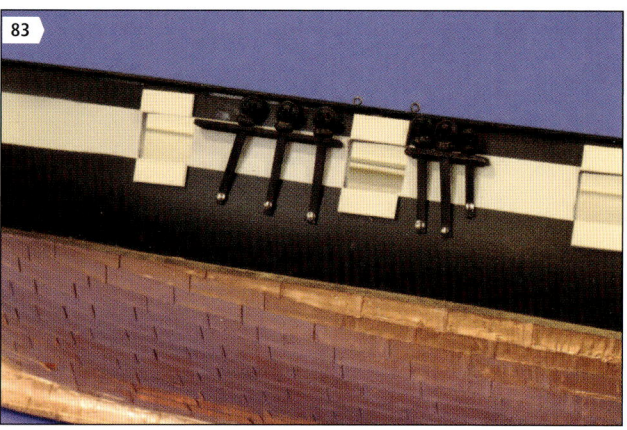

83

The deadeyes have been slipped into their respective slots and a hole drilled in the chain plate to take a pin that tacks the deadeye assembly into place against the hull.

are ready moulded with chain plates and just need to be painted black. The channel is a laser-cut part with notches cut for the deadeyes but also cleverly includes the *pin rails*, the strip of wood that runs along the inside of the bulwarks to hold the belaying pins used in the rigging. The channel/pin rail slides through a slot in the bulwark and ensures that the chain plates and pin rails are firmly fixed to the hull and will be able to take up a lot of stress during the rigging process with little fear (seen in Figure 78).

With the channel in place and painted black, the deadeye and chain plates are slipped into their respective slots as shown on the plans. The critical consideration is the angle of the chain plates. Although the plans indicate the angle, it is much easier to set the angle with a piece of string. Put a dowel into the mainmast hole and tie a piece of string to it at the correct height from the deck. The string is then pulled down towards a deadeye and the angle of the string is the angle the chain plate should be fixed. Tack the chain plate in place with a little glue and drill a hole through the chain plate into the hull. Glue in a pin to keep it there. The head of the pin is touched with black paint to make everything blend together neatly.

Headrails

The head of the ship with the headrails, carvings, and the figurehead is where much of a ship's beauty lies. The fashion and extent of the headwork has varied over periods of history from being ornate to austere, depending on the nationality of the ship and the size of it. The headwork on American ships is generally plain and, on small brigs like the *Perry*, is quite simple in design, but they do set off the lines of the hull beautifully. Simplicity of design does not mean the headwork is simple to construct. On the *Perry*, the headwork is limited to a set of headrails and it is one of the most difficult areas to build because the rails have to sit at the correct angle to complement the hull lines and hold any decorations at the correct angle.

The *Perry*'s headrails and decoration are provided as a single-piece metal casting. Painting them neatly is the first challenge because any unevenness in the paint line will stand out. The easiest way to paint the moulded detail is to first paint the headrail parts black and then dry brush the raised detail with white paint. The dry brushing defines the edges and to all you have to do is paint within the edges. Touch up any black and when dry give the part a coat of gloss varnish to seal it all in. A thin wash of ivory black artist's oil paint seeps into all the recesses to highlight the details and edges even more so. The gloss varnish prevents the black wash from staining the white painted work, keeping it bright and allowing any excess wash to be easily removed from raised areas with a cotton bud dampened with white spirit (Figure 84).

The next challenge is to bend the painted headrails to fit around the bow (Figure 85). It is a little anxiety provoking but careful planning makes the job straightforward. Offer the part to the top of the stem and mark where the bend starts. The part is gently bent a little at a time using a pair of needle-nose pliers whose jaws have been lined with masking tape so they do not mark the paintwork. The part is slowly bent and shaped until it fits. The metal is soft and good quality so it was easily shaped and did not crack. My bending was a little off and it left a small gap between the hull and the base of the headrail. Instead of trying to induce a sharper bend I left it well enough alone and filled the gap with Krystal Kleer and painted over in black when cured.

Another small detail that needs to be scratch-built is the *cathead*

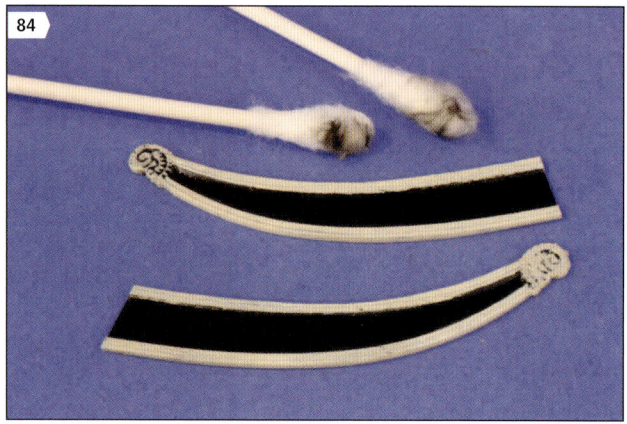

84

The painted headrails. A cotton bud is used to remove any excess wash from the white painted areas.

SOLID HULL MODELLING

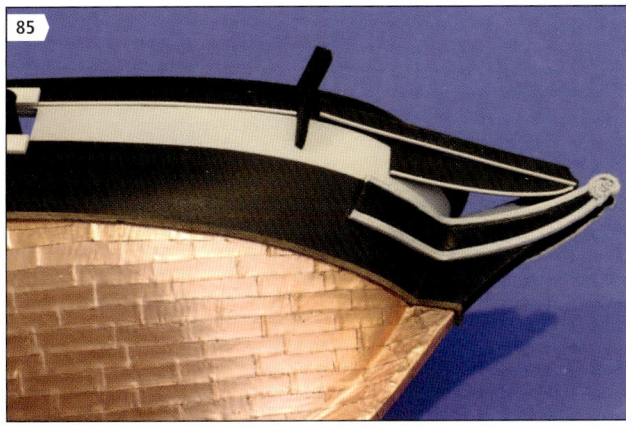

85
The headrails and headboards have been added to the hull. The white decorative moulding on the headboards is plastic strip styrene painted off-white. Pre-painting decorative rails and mouldings and fixing them separately ensures a sharp line between colours.

86
The cathead knees were scratch-built *in situ* by offering up pieces of wood whose inside edges have been angled to fit the hull and cathead. The shape of the support is drawn on the wood and the item is cut out and painted.

knee. A *cathead* is a large wooden beam attached to the bow that aided in lowering, raising, and supporting the ship's anchor. The knee is its support. When making these parts it is much easier to make them *in situ* than to rely entirely on plans (Figure 86). Like the main bulwark rail, any kit-supplied part may not fit given the unique shape of your hull. To make the knee, the cathead is first attached to the deck at the proper angle. An oversize piece of wood is offered up to the hull and cathead and the angle between the two cut. This may take some trial and error to find. Once the angle is cut the shape of the knee is drawn and itself cut out. The part is painted black and glued into place (Figure 87). The remaining hull details and deck fittings were built following the kit instructions and need little comment except to say that many of the deck fittings are painted white. Painting white is best accomplished with an airbrush or aerosol spray. Brush painting white invariably leaves brush marks and requires several coats to cover that clogs holes and leads to a thick finish. The hull is looked over and any paintwork touched up, followed by a coat of satin varnish that yields a consistent finish and blends all the touch ups and paintwork together nicely.

The *Perry*'s handsome hull is now complete and ready for rigging, and that topic will be covered in Chapter 9. With the basic elements of solid hull modelling in mind, let's digress from the *Perry* and introduce other ways a solid hull can be carved. The carving of *Perry*'s hull shows that solid hull models are quite straightforward to make, and can serve as the basis for any ship you choose to make. The *Perry*'s hull was carved from a single roughly shaped block of wood. It takes little stretch of the imagination to see it could have been carved from a solid square piece. In some ways, starting with the flat surfaces of a square piece makes the marking of the station and centrelines easier. To simplify matters further, a hull can be carved from two halves joined together along the centreline during final assembly. Figure 89 shows my carving of a waterline hull for *Victory*. The port and starboard hull halves were each carved from a separate piece of wood joined together with pegs of wood. After the rough carving

87
The completed cathead knees. The pin rails and windlass are painted pewter castings and the *bitts* (cylindrical metal or wooden posts that extend up from a base plate that's fastened to a deck to secure a ship's lines) made out of wooden dowel. The coamings for the gratings are laser-cut from a piece of thick wood, and the gratings themselves from thin ply. The coamings were painted brown and the gratings black to cover up the laser char found on the parts. Sanding the char off these delicate parts would have meant broken pieces.

88

A limitation of solid hulls is that if you wanted to show windows with any real depth you would have to drill out the hull at the window location. Window frames and panes would have to be built up and placed over the openings. A modeller's expedient that is effective on small-scale models is to make a solid window and frame. Paint the frames the required colour (white for *Perry*) and the panes dark grey. Add a little false reflection with blue and white paint.

89

Carving *Victory*'s waterline hull from two halves of wood. The hull has been carved and the first coats of red paint applied to the inside of the bulwarks and rubbed down to seal the grain. The edges of the top and bottom of the wales have also been painted black before planking so there is a crisp painted edge between the hull planks and wale. The hull features extended forecastle bulwarks which some historians have postulated were fitted to *Victory* at the Battle Trafalgar in 1805.

90

Captain Cook's *Endeavour*'s carved hull ready for planking above the waterline with wooden strips and the bottom ready for light brown paint to represent the 'brown stuff' antifouling. The wood grain on the hull bottom has been sealed with a few coats of shellac. Shellac is a traditional sanding sealer for wood. The keel, stem and sternpost have been fixed to the hull. These are made of pear; the same material will be used for the hull planking.

was completed the hull halves were joined and the final shaping done together as a single unit to ensure the halves were symmetrical.

On this model the hull halves are hollowed out to form the bulwarks because this ship had a pronounced tumblehome that would be difficult to capture from ply sheet. To guide the thinning, the location of the three decks were marked by drilling holes through the block of wood before carving so show where they lie. The thickness of the bulwarks was checked by callipers and holding the hull up against a bright light. The more light that shines through, the thinner the wood, and this was a very handy way of ensuring the bulwarks were thinned to a consistent thickness.

Another variation is one shown on the carved hull of Captain Cook's *Endeavour* (Figure 90). This time the hull was carved in four parts: split along the centreline and the waterline. The hull was split at the waterline in order to make it easier to reproduce her appearance of being bright finished above the waterline, while the bottom was covered with *brown stuff* – an antifouling mixture of tar, pitch, and brimstone to protect the wooden planking from rot and ship's worm. The bottom half of the model would be painted the colour of brown stuff so it made no sense to plank it just to have it disappear under a coat of paint. Accordingly, the hull below the waterline was carved to the correct outside dimensions. The hull above the waterline would be planked over in 1mm thick strakes so the top quarters were carved 1mm smaller to accommodate the wood, bringing the hull to proper dimensions. The upper hull would be planked before permanently joining it to the painted lower hull. One of the finest carving woods if you can find it is jelutong. It cuts cleanly and is soft enough to carve easily without losing the crispness of the cuts and can be had from fine wood retailers.

Carving a hull is not very difficult to achieve. The key is to have a good idea of how you envision the completed model, and set the parameters of how much of the hull can be carved from solid and what will have to be built up from sheet later. If you intend to show all of the internal decks fully fitted out with gunports open, then the hull up to the level of the main gundeck, or to the waterline can be carved from solid. The hull above can be represented by bulkheads that are sheathed over with wooden strips to form the remainder of the hull. Plank-on-bulkhead modelling is the subject of our next chapter.

5: Single Plank-on-Bulkhead Modelling
Cutty Sark

The *Cutty Sark* is perhaps the most modelled tea clipper in the world and now repaired after the devastating fire in 2007, the ship is back to her full glory with her sweeping lines and towering masts. Her enduring popularity has spawned many books and kits in plastic, wood and card, and some kind of model of her is perpetually available in many different scales. One such kit is the 1/84 scale model by the Spanish firm Artesania Latina. This particular kit is available in many model shops at a reasonable price in very attractive packaging (Figure 91).

The type of hull we will tackle in this chapter is the 'single plank-on-bulkhead' model. This type of model builds a framework comprising a central profile and cross sections that is planked over with a single layer of wood. On this particular kit there are a few other considerations to be aware of:

- The keel, stem, and rudder post are separate parts that are attached to the hull *after* the planking has been completed.
- The model is designed to be 'decorative'. Although the general features of the model are accurate to the original, the finish of the model is not entirely authentic and features many semi-scale parts.
- To represent the *Cutty Sark*'s copper bottom, the hull below the waterline is left in its natural wood finish whilst the area above is painted black like the actual ship.
- The *Cutty Sark* is a flush deck ship with just a small raised forecastle and poop so the model maker will not have to contend with enclosed decks.

91

Artesania Latina's 1/84 scale *Cutty Sark* kit. The kit is designed to be assembled like a conventional plastic model kit with a pictorial construction booklet. Unlike a plastic kit, there are no part locators on many of the items, and because no scale drawings are included it makes it impossible to check the location of parts. In a bid to make the model easier to build the designers have made it more difficult.

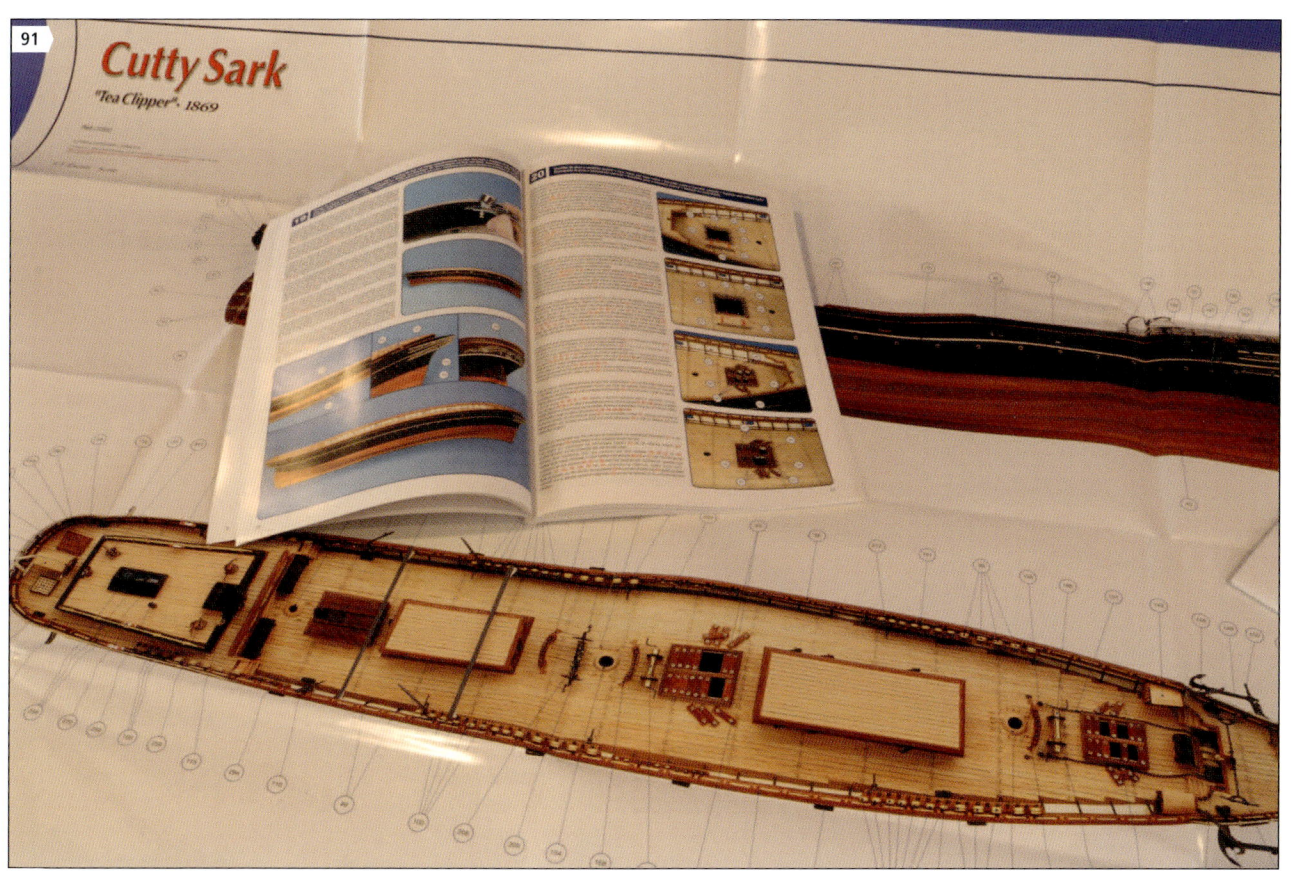

92
Drawings by George F Campbell and C Nepean Longridge's book on building a solid hull model were key references for the project. Another fascinating book is Basil Lubbock's *Log of the Cutty Sark* which details the life of the ship and, most importantly for the model maker, when and what changes were made to her appearance taken from the ship's logs and repair orders.

With these features in mind, you will have to make some decisions as to how to tackle the kit and what to change to meet your expectations. Personally, having visited the *Cutty Sark*, I was determined to reduce the decorative features as much as possible and build a more authentically finished model. This means the model would be painted like the original and proper copper plating and scale deck planking laid. Moreover, the *Cutty Sark* was a *composite built* ship, meaning that her frames and bulwarks were of iron and the hull below the bulwarks were planked with wood. I wanted to represent this and my thinking was that the hull below the bulwarks would allow some of the planking lines to show through the paintwork and finishing the bulwarks smooth to represent the iron sheets.

To help in building a more authentic model, a set of drawings by George F Campbell was obtained from the *Cutty Sark* gift shop by mail order (Figure 92). These 1/128 scale or 3/32in = 1ft plans are highly detailed and would have to be enlarged 152% [Enlargement Ratio = (plan scale ÷ kit scale) × 100 = (128/84 = 1.52) × 100 = 152%] to match the kit. The other vital reference used was C Nepean Longridge's book that described in detail the building of a 1/48 scale model from scratch. The book goes far beyond the model making techniques he used, but describes the ship's appearance and fittings at different times in her career. Measurements in his book are to ¼in = 1ft (1/48 scale) so his dimensions are divided by 1.75 to match the kit.

Constructing the Framework

Like many modern kits the parts are laser-cut (Figure 93). Marking the part numbers in pencil on all of them will save a lot of frustration later and it's recommended that the numbers are put on both sides of each part. Assembly begins with the hull's framework. The profile piece (false keel) and bulkheads are cut out of the carrier sheets with a sharp utility knife to score the tab on one side and then flipping the sheet over to finish cutting through. This will avoid any splintering of the part that would occur if you tried to cut all the way through on one side. It also means less pressure on the knife blade, reducing the risk of broken blades and shards of flying metal penetrating your flesh. The kit parts are cut from 6mm plywood

sheet which means that the false keel at the stem and rudder post will have to be thinned down to accommodate the thickness of the planking added later.

The laser-cut slots are not exactly square, caused by the deflection of the laser beam cutting through the thick material. A little truing up with a coarse sanding stick will remedy that and help obtain easy, but not loose fit of the bulkheads to the false keel. Test fit all the bulkheads and pay attention to where the top of each of the bulkheads fall. In this case they should be flush with the top of the false keel. If not, the slot on the false keel should be filed deeper until the bulkhead sits perfectly flush. If the bulkhead sits too low then the slot must be packed with a sliver of wood to raise the bulkhead to the correct position. Test fitting is critical because the shape of the hull depends on an accurate framework.

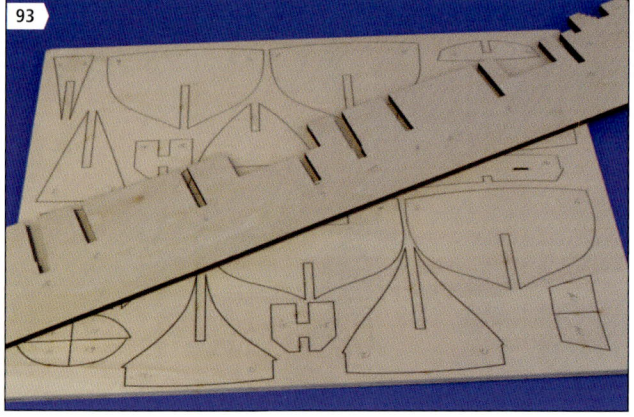

93
The major structural elements of the *Cutty Sark*. Shown are the laser-cut bulkheads and the false keel or the 'backbone' of this style of model. Part numbers have been pencilled on the parts before they are removed from their carrier sheets. The kit also provides (not shown) strip wood for planking, dowels for masts, and a very large selection of neatly cast white metal and brass detail parts, and a set of fully sewn fabric sails.

SINGLE PLANK–ON–BULKHEAD MODELLING

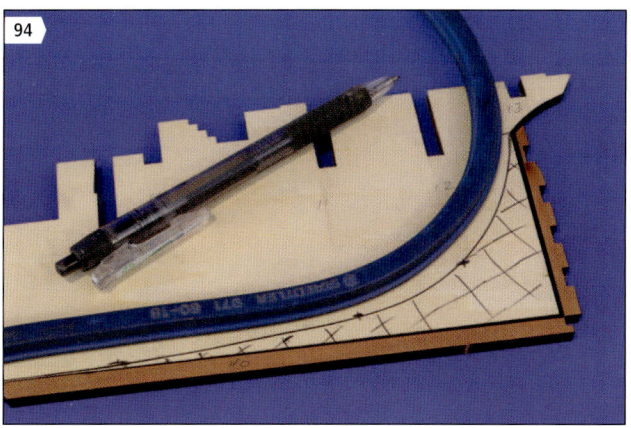

94

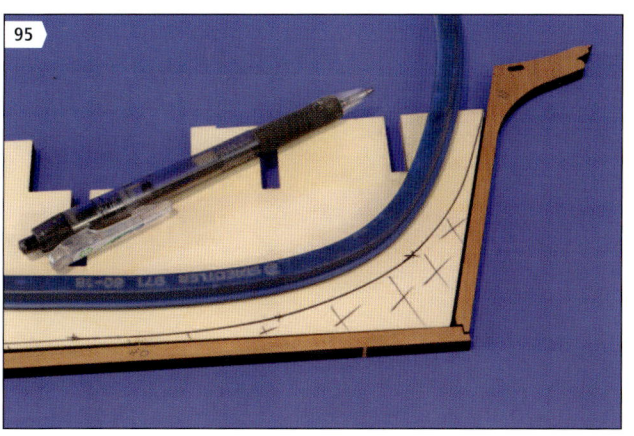

95

94
Marking out of the bearding line at the stern. The crosshatched area under the bearding line is where the false keel is thinned by the thickness of the planking on both sides.

95
Clipper ships are narrow at the bow requiring a bearding line to be marked and the false keel thinned like the stern. The laser-cut stem post and keel are shown to illustrate why thinning the false keel is so important for the planks to fit.

When satisfied with the fit, mark where the bottom of each bulkhead falls on the false keel in pencil. Join up the tick marks and you have marked the *bearding line* (Figure 94) and the area below the line defines where the false keel is thinned to accommodate the hull planking. On the *Cutty Sark* the stern and stem areas have to be so thinned. Usually the stem area is not thinned because the bows on sailing ships are often round (bluff), but on *Cutty Sark* her bows come to a narrow knife edge cut through the water for speed (Figure 95). The hull planking is 2mm thick so this amount must be removed from each side under the bearding line. To ensure that the same amount it taken off both sides a 2mm wide piece of tape is cut and laid down the centre of the false keel (Figure 96) to provide a line to which you can pare and sand down to (Figure 97).

Slip the bulkheads without glue into their slots and spend some more time examining the hull. Familiarize yourself with the hull curves and take a strip of wood planking and lay it across the bulkheads down the hull's length. You will see that in the bow and stern area the plank does not lie flat across the bulkhead, but rather sits on an edge indicating where the bulkhead must be bevelled so the plank comes into contact across the entire edge. You will also notice where the plank will have a tendency to curve upwards – again notably at the bow and stern as it follows the sheer of the hull and the planks will have to be bent to accommodate it. Test fitting a plank across the bulkheads also gives an idea where the planks might be unsupported and may tend to sink in between bulkheads.

Departing from the instructions I put some of the bevel on the frames before gluing them to the false keel. The bevel itself is easily cut with a sanding drum mounted in a rotary tool or with a fine rasp (Figure 98). Ensure that you mark the side of the bulkhead where the bevel is to be cut with an 'X' so you don't bevel the wrong side; and on laser-cut parts the charred edges on the opposite side of the bevel serve as a handy guide to avoid taking off too much wood by keeping the far back edge black (Figure 99). The pre-bevelled bulkheads are permanently glued to the false keel and an easy way

96

97

96
A tape strip is laid down the centre of the false keel to guide an even removal of wood below the bearding line.

97
A carving gouge is used to remove the wood followed by a rasp and sandpaper to smooth out the cut marks to bring the wood right down to the tape line.

98

Each bulkhead that required bevelling was gripped in a bench vice and bevelled with a fine rasp. A rotary tool fitted with a drum sander could also be used to quickly remove wood. Either way, be careful not to bevel too far. You are just getting the bevels started and they will be completed by sanding once all of the bulkheads are permanently attached to the false keel.

to keep them square to the false keel is to use children's building bricks held by a clamp (Figure 100). Coat all mating surfaces with glue and remember to wipe away any excess that squeezes out of the joint. Let the glue well cure before moving on to the next phase of construction.

Filler Blocks

Most kits provide some form of solid wood block to be cut, glued, and shaped into the stem and and stern areas to provide a solid landing place for the hull planks. A good practice is to expand the number of filler blocks and fill as many spaces between bulkheads where you feel the planks might sag. On this model the planks are supported over a large 70mm area by nothing but air. It not necessary to fill all of the spaces but to focus on the most difficult areas to

101

Filler blocks made from balsa wood. Any wood will do, I just happened to have off-cuts of balsa in the scrap pile and it is a very easy wood to shape.

99

The importance of bevelling the bulkheads can be appreciated in this photograph of the three stern bulkheads. The plank when laid across them will lie neatly all along their edges.

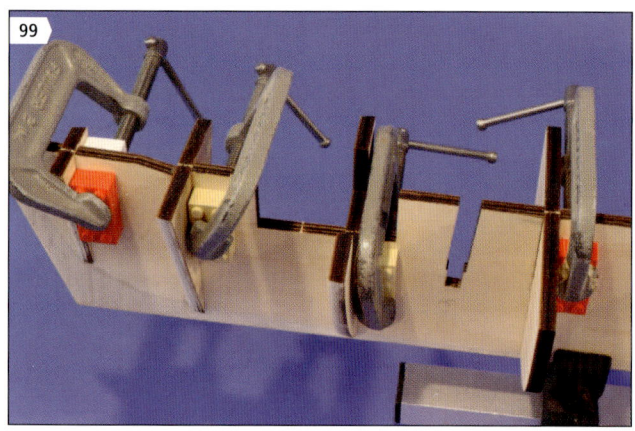

100

Keeping the bulkheads square to the false keel is vitally important to avoid a lopsided hull. Children's building blocks are clamped to the false keel on both sides against the bulkhead. The false keel is being held in a keel clamper.

102

Filler blocks at the stern. These have been roughly shaped.

SINGLE PLANK–ON–BULKHEAD MODELLING

103

The roughly shaped filler blocks at the bow. Any remaining spaces will be filled with two-part automotive filler.

104

Masking tape is used to define the area along the bearding line to limit where the two-part automotive filler will be applied.

plank, defined as any place where the planks must be acutely bent to round up a stern or around a very bluff bow. On *Cutty Sark*, the bow area requires some attention because the planks are bent albeit fairly gently over a long area over widely spaced bulkheads (Figure 101). The stern area (Figure 102) requires additional filler blocks because the planks must curve up at a fairly sharp angle under the transom. The kit provides a few filler blocks just for the extreme areas of the bow and stern and these were duly fitted. Additional filler blocks were made from chunks of balsa wood. Often hobby shops will carry bags of economically priced balsa wood offcuts that come in a wide variety of random shapes and from them it is easy to find blocks and strips that will fill the adjoining areas. It's not critical that these blocks fit exactly because any gaps can be filled with two-part automotive filler. All that is important is that the hull contours are maintained throughout the area so the planking to come has a solid surface to land. Once glue has set, mark on the filler blocks the edge of the deck, bulkheads, and the bearding line to define where the blocks must be shaped with chisels, rasps, and sandpaper (Figures 103 and 104).

Any gaps are filled with two-part automotive or wood filler (Figure 105). An important place to focus on is on any gaps between the blocks and the top of the bearding line. Lay some masking tape along the bearding line to protect the areas where you do not want filler and trowel the material into the area. It is easier to build the putty up in thin layers as opposed to a single thick application. Remove the tape just before the filler dries and you will be left with a clean line between the filler and the bearding line.

Sanding back the filler is a messy job that was done outdoors while wearing a dust mask. Hand tools can be used but, in my case, I used a small hand-held oscillating power sander fitted with a fine (#220) sandpaper. At this time a sanding block long enough to span at least three bulkheads was prepared with a rougher #120 grit to finish off the bulkhead bevels (Figure 106). When sanding by hand, a coarser grit is necessary to efficiently take off wood and filler because your arm cannot match the speed and torque of a power tool. Allow the sanding blocks to come into contact with at least two

105

Two-part automotive filler is applied over the filler blocks. The tape is removed just as the filler cures leaving a sharp line. If you allow the filler to cure hard it will be very difficult to remove the tape.

106

The bulkheads are given a final sanding with a long sanding block to finish all the bevels and fair them.

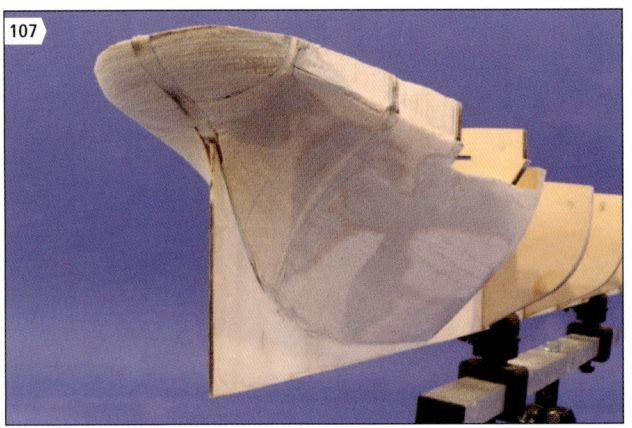

107
The filler is sanded back and the final bevelling of the bulkheads completed.

108
The false deck is wider than the bulkheads. The bulkheads must be widened with shims to match the width of the false deck.

bulkheads at a time. As you sand, continually look down the length of the hull ensuring the bulkhead edges all line up and you can imagine a plank lying flat against all of them at once (Figure 107). Sand a little at a time and with a plank continually checking that it lies flat against the bulkheads. Sometimes a supplied bulkhead is cut too small and its proper width can be restored with a shim of wood glued along its edges to match the flow of the hull (Figure 108) as opposed to sanding down all the other bulkheads to match the undersized one!

Any filler blocks that protrude above the bulkheads will also need to be sanded back flush. This is best done by hand and take care not to change the deck's *camber*. Camber is the deck curvature measured as the height of deck at centreline above the height of deck at sides. This transverse curvature directs water off the deck into the waterways to drain off through openings in the hull called *scuppers*. On our build of *Perry*, there was no noticeable deck camber owing to the small scale of the model and the deck was carved flat. On larger scale solid hulls it is important to shape camber into the deck because it is quite prominent. Plank-on-bulkhead models allow the camber to be cut into the bulkhead tops directly so it appears in models of all scales. The top of the bulkheads and filler blocks are sanded until a test fit of the false deck shows that it lays flat with no bumps or voids felt when running your fingers along its length.

Permanently glue the false deck to the framework and hold the edges down with pins tapped into the bulkheads. A little problem made itself evident at this time – the width of the false deck was found to be greater than the bulkheads. This was corrected by shimming up bulkhead (Figure 109). It is not really clear if the bulkheads were too narrow or the deck too wide, but the simplest solution was to shim up the affected bulkheads as opposed to sanding down the false deck. This is the problem with kits that do not provide scale plans. There is no way of checking if the bulkhead or the false deck is correct. Keeping the false deck whole was deemed safest because the other deck parts are matched to its shape.

110

The plank on bulkhead hull framework now complete and ready for sheathing with deck and hull planking. In retrospect, the large space between the midship bulkheads should have had filler blocks added to fully prevent any of the hull planks from sagging as they most certainly did later.

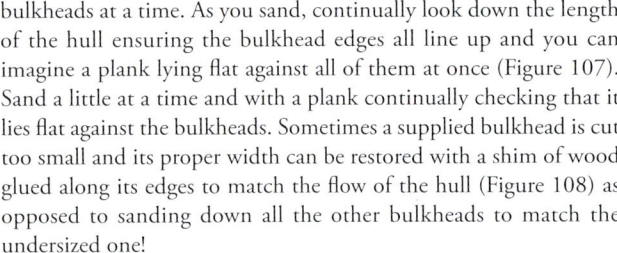

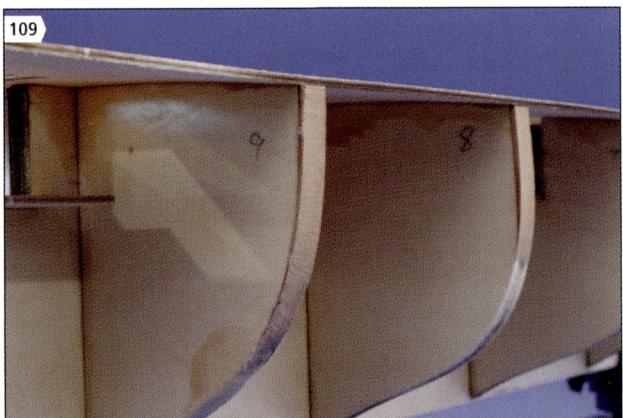

109
Scrap wood was glued to the edges of the bulkheads and sanded.

Planking the Hull and Deck

Modeller's new to wooden ship models often report that the hull planking is difficult and a huge source of frustration that often leads them to give up on the model. Even experienced modellers find hull planking difficult at times, especially on extremely bluff hulls of a collier (coal carrying cargo ship like Captain Cook's *Endeavour*) or a ponderous line-of-battle ship. The planks must be bent to such an extreme that they just do not want to sit properly. And this brings us to one of the reasons why planking can be difficult – we often try to force a plank into a shape it does not want to go. If it does not go where we think it should go, we assume it is the fault of the plank or the design of the kit, but never ourselves. As model shipwrights we must overcome the urge to force a plank into position instead of allowing it to lay more or less where it pleases. Another source of frustration is that despite our best efforts using proportional dividers and slide-rules to work out the area to plank and the shape of the plank to fit it, the piece still doesn't lay neatly against the hull or the neighbouring plank below it. This all may sound a bit discouraging but shaping a plank (a process called *spiling*) is readily conducted with simple tools and an understanding of how to take advantage of the natural tendencies of wood. After some practice spiling and planking, the process will become second nature and you will be able to do it all by eye.

Measurement and Measurement Error

The shape of a hull side is not flat. You will be planking over a curved surface and the areas to be planked will be different at the bow and stern from the middle of the ship (called *midships*). Coming to an understanding of the fluid shape of your hull will take some familiarization before starting to plank by measuring the area to be planked at each bulkhead. The primary measurement tool is called a 'tick strip' which is no more than a strip of thin card approximately 1cm wide (Figure 111). Cut one strip per bulkhead and number them. Place one end of a tick strip at the deck level and allow the strip to lie along the edge of the bulkhead until it reaches the bulkhead's bottom against the false keel. Mark the tick strip where it reaches the bottom of the bulkhead. This defines the area to be planked on each bulkhead and automatically takes into account the curve of the hull. Measure between the marks on the tick strip with a ruler and keep a record. On each tick strip mark the halfway point in red ink.

On my model the distances were:

Bulkhead #	Length (in mm)
Bow	100
2	100
3	97
4	97
5	107
6	111
7	114
8	117
9	100
10	100
11	100
12	100
13	110

The greatest area is on Bulkhead 8 at 117mm. The hull planks provided in the kit are 5mm wide so 117mm ÷ 5mm = 23.4 or just about twenty-four 5mm wide planks will be required to cover the widest part of the ship's side. This figure also tells us that the 5mm planks are a little too wide and need to be narrowed. As we move along the hull towards the bow (around Bulkhead 4), the space begins to narrow and tells us where the planks need to be tapered to fit. At end of the bow the space opens up a little indicating where a gap will form between adjacent planks that will require an additional plank to be inserted to fill the space. Similarly, the planks running aft will have be tapered, but at the extreme stern (around bulkhead #9) the area widens up again indicating where additional planks will be required to fill up the gaps that will form. Having a good understanding of these points in your head will help with the planking process. In general, the amount of tapering required for each plank on *Cutty Sark* is generally small given the long and straight nature of the hull shape. The most difficult area to plank will be at the stern where planks must be curved in a sharp sweep to accommodate the shape of the stern and transom.

Use each tick strip to mark the halfway point on each bulkhead. You have now split the area to be planked in half. Subdividing the area helps keep the run of the planks consistent and allows you to spot errors quickly because they will show up that much earlier than if you were planking the entire space at once. A *planking batten* is made from a single thin and flexible piece of wood, say 2mm square or 1mm by 2mm; it is cut longer than the hull. The hull will be planked starting at the level of the main false deck downwards towards the keel. As such, the top edge of the batten is laid along the tick marks starting at Bulkhead 8 and tacked into place with little brass nails. It helps if you drill a hole in the batten to accommodate the nail and prevent the wood from splitting. Moving on to Bulkhead 7, the batten is tacked into place and the process continues with each bulkhead (Figure 112). Once the batten is tacked into place, it should form a sweet run along the hull. If you find a bump or waviness in the batten, remove the pins for the offending areas and let the natural springiness of the wood determine the run of the line. That is the first lesson in the art of shipbuilding: let Nature help guide the process. When it comes to ships, if ever in doubt, remember the old adage: 'If it looks right, it is right'. Additional battens can be fixed in place if desired to help you visualize the areas to be planked.

111

Tick strips measure the area on each bulkhead to be planked.

111

112 Planking batten tacked into place at the half way point between the keel and the deck edge as measured by the tick strips. There are a few marks that do not lie along the batten, probably caused by measurement error. What is important is letting the natural properties of the wood and your eye determine the run of planking.

The space between the top of the false deck and the batten on Bulkhead 7 is 58mm. This would mean that if 5mm planks were used, 11.6 would be required. If the plank width was reduced to 4mm, 14.5 planks would be required. However, I decided to use scale planking and in this model's 1/84 scale, *Cutty Sark*'s actual plank width would be 3.2mm or about ⅛in wide requiring 18 planks to fill the space (18.125 planks to be exact. The .125 planks equals .375mm that will be taken up by measurement and cutting error). The kit-supplied planks could be cut down or ⅛in strips purchased but I decided to cut my own planks from well-seasoned pear wood I had in my shop. I bought this wood many years ago to build a fully framed model, but as with all natural products, some of the laths had a heavily figured grain and could not be used. The wood was saved because it is perfectly suitable to plank models that are to be painted, and a tight grained hardwood like pear takes paint very well with a minimum of surface preparation. This wood also bends easily with the application of heat and a dip in hot water to make severe curves. These fine properties made pear a favourite of model makers for centuries.

The stock I had was 76in long, 3in wide, and 5mm thick. These were cut into 25in lengths and thickness sanded down to ⅛in (Figure 113). Planks 1mm thick were ripped on a table saw fitted with a carbide blade (Figure 114). Let me apologize here and now for mixing Imperial and metric measurements. Being of the generation of Canadian school children who had to convert from the Imperial to the metric system in 1971, we were taught to use both systems interchangeably. As a result, today we continue to order beer by the pint as opposed to a 568 ml glass, but the 1mm mark on a ruler is much easier to find than the 3/64in mark. A typical Canadian compromise!

Laying the First Plank

The first plank is a full-length single strip that runs from bow to stern. It is fixed to follow the main deck because the kit's designer uses the deck sheer to determine the sheer of the hull planking. Be aware that on other models the deck and hull sheer can be different. The planking can also start at the level of the main wale (which on warships does not follow the same sheer as the gundeck). Planking can also begin at the keel and work upward or at some other starting point. It will vary by model kit. If ever in doubt, you can always start planking at the keel and work your way upwards which is how actual ships are planked. The curves of the hull and turn of the bilge will naturally determine the sheer of each plank and you cannot go far wrong.

On this model of *Cutty Sark* there is little or no tapering to do on the first plank (Figure 115). All you have to do is to induce a slight

113

114

113 A sander reducing the wood stock to a thickness of ⅛in. Out of view is the set of clamps used to hold the thickness sander securely to the portable work bench.

114 1mm thick strips being ripped off ⅛in thick stock. Safety is very important and although you cannot see it, the table saw is clamped to the portable work bench. The blade guard has been removed for clarity (do not operate a saw without one) and a shop vacuum was used to take up most of the sawdust.

SINGLE PLANK–ON–BULKHEAD MODELLING

115

The first plank is laid starting at the level of the deck. The plank will require just a little bending to lie along the deck's curve.

116

At the stern the plank will have to be twisted to lie flat along the hull. The plank was soaked in hot water and held against the heated head from a planking iron while twisting and bending the plank to the required shape.

curve to fit around the bow and stern by running the plank between the fingers. With pear, inducing the curve was quite easy. In contrast, the kit-supplied mazonia is relatively stiff and if using this you will need to soak the wood in hot tap water for about 5 minutes and make the curve over the head of a heated planking iron. The wood is drawn back and forth along the planking iron head, gently pulling down on both ends until the curve is set. You will hear a hissing sound as the water in the plank is turned to steam that softens it up while bending. Keep the plank moving over the head to avoid scorching the wood.

The gentle curve of the hull at this point meant there was no need for clamps or pins and a dot of thick CA at each bulkhead is sufficient to hold the plank firmly in place. Start by dotting thick CA on the first two bulkheads and fix the plank; then dot the next two or three bulkheads and continue laying the plank making sure the plank follows the deck's sheer. Once in place, repeat on other side of the ship. It is important to alternate planking on one side then the other to avoid building in any stresses and twists into the hull framework. At the stern the plank will need to have a little twist put into it as well (Figure 116). A twist is induced by heating the area up on the planking iron and giving the wood a little twist with your fingers. Hold the twist for a few seconds and let the wood cool and lock the twist in place. The nice thing about adding the keel, stem and rudder post after all the planking is in place is that we do not have to fit and trim the plank ends into these parts. The planks can simply run past the false keel and the planks are trimmed flush with the false keel so that the stem, keel, and rudder post can be fixed into place with a simple butt joint.

The second plank is test fitted by pushing it up against the first plank in the midship area first and working towards the bow. The front end will probably ride up over the first plank a little at the bow area. The point where the overlap begins is marked and it indicates where the start of the plank taper begins and the degree of overlap is the amount that must be taken off. If you are feeling unsure about the amount, this can be checked using the tick strips. Holding the plank against the hull, mark the location of each bulkhead on the plank and set aside. A new tick strip is used to measure the space under the first plank to the top of the planking batten on each bulkhead. Divide that space by the number of planks to be fitted, in this case 17 planks. The result is the width of the plank at each bulkhead. If you plot this on the plank and join up the points will show how much wood must come off the top of the plank and where. The overlap and tick strip methods should produce similar results. If not, then error has crept in somewhere so repeat the procedures until the results tally up.

To cut the taper, lay the plank on your workbench and align a steel straightedge along the marks and cut off the sliver of wood with a sharp knife. Once the taper has been cut, you should test fit it again to ensure it will lay right up against the first plank without excessive force. The hull at this stage is fairly flat so it should fit quite well. As you plank downwards the planks will develop a noticeable gap between their front faces, especially where the hull rounds at the turn of the *bilge* (the area on the outer surface of a ship's hull where the bottom curves to meet the vertical sides). These small gaps are caused by back edges of the planks butting up against each other causing the front face to gape. This is easily corrected by scraping a little wood off the inside upper back edge to allow the edges on the front face to come together. The plank is now bent using your fingers or soaking and bending with a planking iron and fixed to the hull with thick CA. After every three or four planks laid, PVA wood glue must be wiped onto the inside back of the planks to seep into the joint between the planks and bulkheads. Wipe off any excess PVA that gets on the outside of the hull before it cures with a damp cloth. Once your planking reaches the batten the batten is removed because the run of the planks has been well established. The area below the batten is planked using the same techniques and methods.

The planks at the stern not only curve around the hull but sweep upwards as well (Figure 120). In this area, the planks will not want to lie up against each other but curve upwards like an open palm of your hand with the planks splaying out like fingers. This was shown by the tick strip measurements indicating that additional planks need to be added to cover the area. Continue laying the planks but allow

117

A view of the bow planking. Nine planks per side have been fixed to the hull and note that the planks are starting to require tapering to accommodate the area. Two planks were used for each row because it is easier to fit shorter lengths of planks.

118

A view of the planking at the stern. The starboard and port side planks come to meet under the transom to form a triangular area (marked B).

the planks to splay out and lay where they wish. What is important is that they splay out roughly symmetrically on each side and the run of the planks in that row is fair. The additional filler blocks really help in this area because the double curvatures being put into the planks will make them want to spring out. Having a solid gluing surface allows you to press the plank down across the stern area and glue to keep them in place.

The triangular gaps between the splayed-out planks are where a *stealer* or *drop plank* is cut to fit the space. These planks are essentially triangular-shaped pieces of wood but it is not a simple matter to just cut out a piece of wood and glue it into the space. The ends of the stealer planks on actual ships do not end in a point, but are rather cut off square to provide sufficient area for a trennel to hold the plank in place, and the space between planks is cut to the squared-off shape. For *Cutty Sark* there was no need to cut a properly shaped stealer and a simple triangular piece was cut to fit because they would be covered by the copper plating or painted and would not show (Figure 121). In areas where a stealer would show the area and the plank would have to be prepared properly as I will show in the next chapter.

The basic hull is now fully planked and it can look a little rough (Figure 122). My model looks particularly rough because I ran out of pear and finished the hull planking below the waterline with the kit-supplied wood. I did not even bother to cut the strips down to scale width because all of these planks would get covered over with the copper plating. It can be discouraging to compare your work to the instructions and wonder 'where did I go wrong?' or think 'is this just too much for me?' and give up. Don't fall into that trap! The planking will look a lot better once the plank ends are trimmed and the hull sanded smoothed. The plank ends that overlap the false keel at the bow are sawn flush. The planks at the transom require a little more care. These need so be sawn off to match the curve of the

119

The area under the transom is planked. Most of the triangular area will be covered with planks that meet on the centreline. However, small planks will have to be cut to fit the left-over space right behind the stern post.

120

As planking continues towards the keel, the strakes will want to splay out to accommodate the shape of the hull. This phenomenon also happens at the bow.

SINGLE PLANK–ON–BULKHEAD MODELLING

121
The gaps between the splayed-out planks are filled with small triangular planks called 'stealers'.

122
The planking nearing completion. It can often look a little rough at this stage of the build.

transom and tape is used to guide the saw blade (Figure 123). The transom itself is planked over after the trimming is complete (Figure 124) and the hull is ready for final shaping (Figure 125).

SANDING THE HULL

Sanding the hull (or *fairing*) takes time and elbow grease. By hand, use a sanding block faced with 60 grit garnet paper. The power and speed of an electric palm sander can make quick work of this task. A random orbit sander is best because it leaves fewer sanding marks and you can use a much finer grit of sandpaper (start with #120 grit or finer). Have a care when using this tool because it is very easy to sand through the planking. I do this work outside as its very dusty work, and once again, safety gear is essential. Begin by taking off the edges of the planks and move the sander to shape the curves. Do not be tempted to apply pressure to the tool, rather let the tool do the work.

Sand the hull until most, if not all, of the planks are flush with each other and the curves look smooth. Pay particular attention to the stem and rudder post areas. On kits that are designed to add the

123
The transom is marked off with a piece of tape and a razor saw used to cut back the planks.

124
The transom is planked over.

125
The hull planks have been trimmed back flush with the false deck and false keel. The hull is starting to look like a majestic tea clipper.

126

A mistake! I have sanded through the planking right down to the edge of a bulkhead. The error was caused by some unsupported planks that sagged. My hunch that filler blocks should have been fitted in all the spaces between bulkheads was correct and I should have not second-guessed myself.

127

The wood was soaked with thin CA to solidify the area.

128

Two-part automotive filler is trowelled into the area and sanded smooth. It was good fortune that the repair fell under the waterline and would be covered by the copper plate.

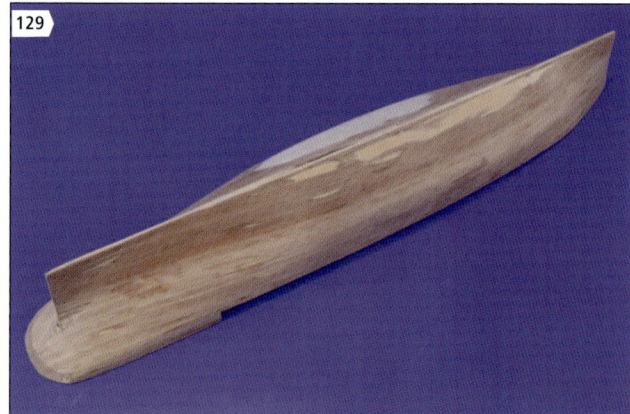

129

The *Cutty Sark*'s planking sanded smooth and trimmed. Any dips were corrected with filler. The keel, stem and stern posts are ready to be fitted.

stem and rudder post after the hull is planked, the planking must be sanded down to the thickness of the posts. The bottom of the keel area must also be sanded flat to seat the keel. There may be some planks that cannot be sanded flush because they have sunk slightly below the others. Trying to sand the surrounding areas to match will surely lead to sanding through the planking (Figure 126) or sanding the planks so thin that they are springy. This state of affairs can be made right by:

1. Stabilize the wood by impregnating the area with thin CA (Figure 127). Wood turners and carvers use this trick to repair broken parts all the time.
2. Fill the area with two-part automotive filler. Spread it on just beyond the area to be repaired.
3. When the filler is set, smooth the filler and feather the edges into the rest of the hull by hand sanding with a fine grit paper, such #220 garnet or a light touch with the power sander (Figure 128).

KEEL, STEM AND RUDDER POSTS

Most kits provide stem, rudder and keel parts to a common thickness. However, on real ships the stem and rudder posts are tapered to be narrower at their *heel* (bottom) than the top. The keel itself is also tapered along its length at both ends to accommodate the narrowed bottom ends of the stem and rudder posts. The drawings of *Cutty Sark* show this tapering very clearly and for a realistic model these kit parts must be altered to suit. Starting with the keel, the kit provides it in two parts that are glued and pinned together on a flat surface. Use a metal straightedge along the bottom of the parts to ensure it runs true. Following the Campbell plans, the keel must be reduced to 4.8mm at a point approximately 50mm from each end to 2mm where it attached to the stem and rudder posts (Figure 130). With the keel laying on its side, a sanding block equally removes the wood on both sides until the desired taper is achieved. The keel is fixed to the bottom of the hull with glue and pinned in place with a sliver of bamboo. Sand a taper into the stem

SINGLE PLANK–ON–BULKHEAD MODELLING

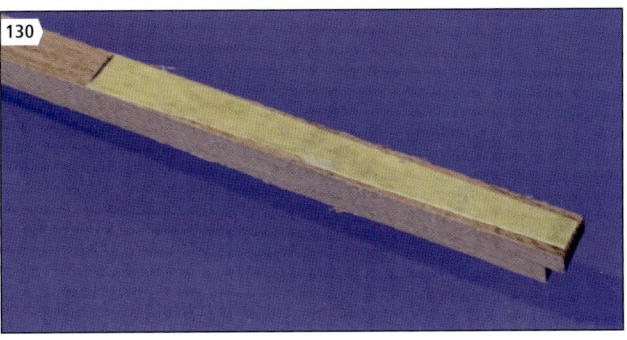

130
A piece of tape marks the taper on one end of the keel.

131
The new rudder post was properly grooved like the original to accept the curved forward edge of the rudder. A round riffler file cut the groove.

and rudder posts from top to bottom until the heel matches the keel thickness. These parts are attached to the keel and hull and remember to check that the stem and rudder post assemblies are perfectly vertical. For my model, I decided to build a new rudder post from scratch because the kit part was the wrong shape and had huge notches cut into it to accommodate the non-prototypical kit-supplied *gudgeons* and *pintles*. The rudder is attached to rudder post with gudgeons – socket-like fittings attached to the rudder to enable a pivoting or hinged connection when slipped over a pintle, a type of pin that is attached to the hull. Together the gudgeon and pintle enables a pivoting connection that can be easily separated. The new rudder post was built according to the Campbell plans and is grooved at the backside to accommodate the rounded front edge of the rudder (Figure 131) and glued to the hull and faired into the planking with wood filler (Figure 132), as is the stem post (Figure 133).

Main Deck

Cutty Sark's deck is long and visible so it really benefits from a neat and proper job of planking. The kit provides 3mm wide strips of maple to be cut into lengths laid in brickwork fashion as befits a decorative model. However, an authentic model requires scale deck planks to be cut and laid. In this scale, the deck planks need to be 1.75mm or about 1/16in wide. A few sheets of 1/16in basswood was purchased, deliberately picking sheets that were slightly different colours to bring a little variety to the deck. One face on each sheet was painted in a dark grey enamel to represent the caulking between the planks. Basswood is an inexpensive, readily available bland-coloured timber making it an ideal wood for a deck. Planks 1mm thick were cut from the sheet (Figure 134) with a miniature table saw. These planks are a little oversize but they are already thinner than matchsticks and any finer would render them difficult to work with.

With a bundle of deck planking at hand the next set of considerations is how to lay them:

- Three- or four-shift of the plank butts?
- Will planks known as *margin planks* be fitted around each of the hatches and deck houses?
- Will waterways be represented around the decks?
- How to handle the join or *break* between the main and poop decks?

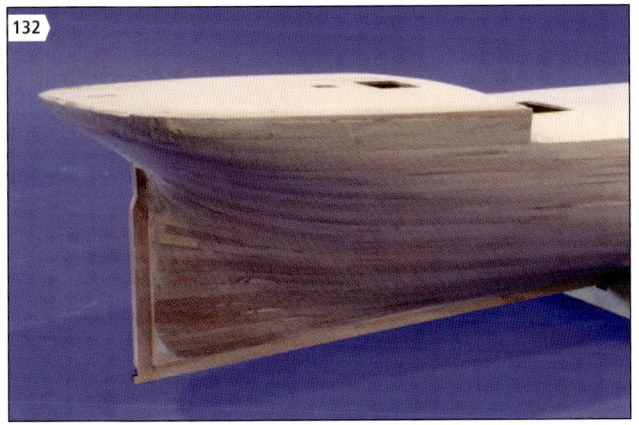

132
The new stern (rudder) post and the keel have been fixed and faired into the hull.

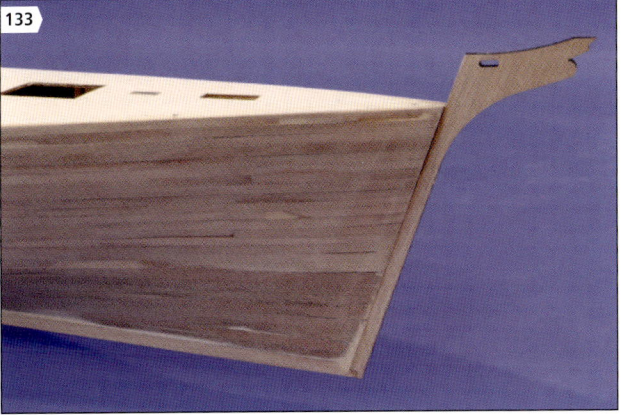

133
The stem post fitted and faired into the hull planking.

134

Cutting deck planks on a miniature table saw. If you do not have a miniature saw you can purchase strips of pre-cut wood and rub one edge of the plank with the side of an HB pencil to represent the caulking.

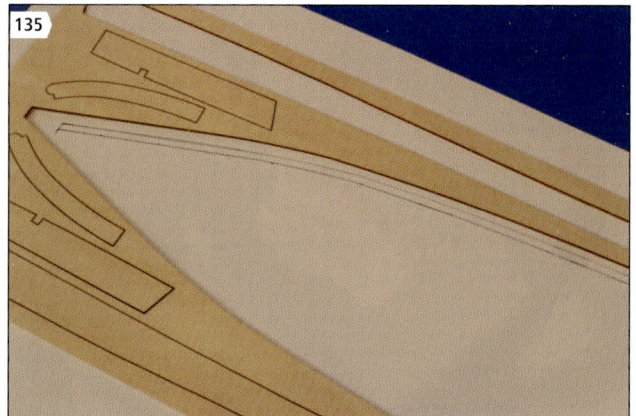

135

Never throw anything away! The laser cut-out for the false deck pieces makes a fine stencil to trace out the shape of the deck to make the waterway.

First, I would include the waterways. The shape of the waterway is the same as the deck so the false deck cut-out left over from the kit can be used as a pattern to get the precise shape. Lay the cut-out on a sheet of .5mm plastic card and trace along the edge (Figure 135). Offset the pattern by 4mm (taken from the Campbell plan) and trace again. The waterway can be cut out a little over length at stem and stern and glued down to the false deck (Figure 136) and painted grey (Figure 137).

The next task is to use Campbell's plans to mock up the location of the hatches and deckhouses. A simple square of card is used to represent the maximum length and width of each item. These pieces of card are laid on the false deck in the correct positions and traced around with a pencil to become the datum points. The margin planks that surround each deckhouse and hatch are made from 3mm wide strips of basswood cut from 1mm thick basswood sheet. The edges are jointed at 45° angles and rubbed with a pencil to simulate deck caulking. The margin planks fitted alongside the waterways were laid with a single length of basswood for each side.

The remaining deck spaces are filled with the deck planking cut to scale lengths and laid with the proper shift of butts. In 1/84 scale a plank is 73mm long. Following Longridge, the planks were laid with a four-step shift of butts so in our kit scale the length of first plank in each series of five planks is:

Row	Plank Length
1	73mm
2	29mm
3	58mm
4	14mm
5	44mm

Planking begins at the centreline aft at the break of the main and poop deck and works towards the bow (Figure 138). These small planks are difficult to lay straight so use a straight edge or fit a planking batten to true up each row as you go along. As you plank

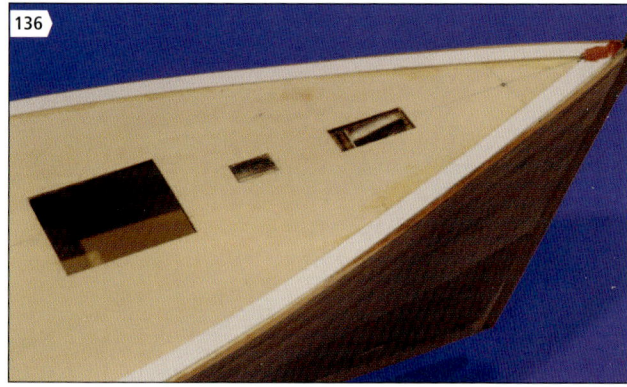

136

The waterway is cut from styrene sheet and glued to the false deck. A bit of putty is used at the bows make them look seamless under paint. A gap was left between the waterway and deck edge to accommodate the bulwarks that will be fixed in place later.

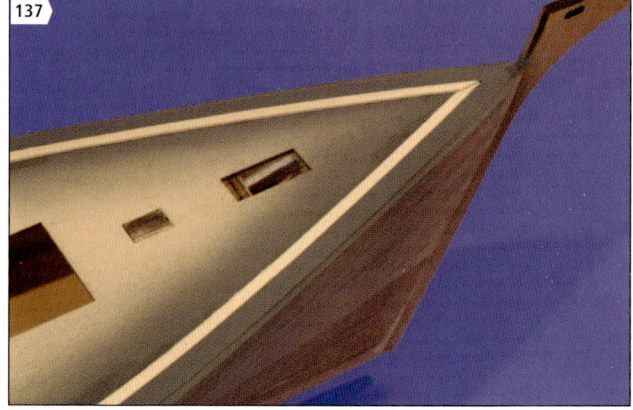

137

The waterway was painted grey and the margin plank that surrounds the entire deck was glued up against it.

SINGLE PLANK–ON–BULKHEAD MODELLING

138
The deckhouse and hatch margin planks have been laid and the planking will be fitted in between and around them. Deck planking starts from the deck's centreline and a planking batten was tacked along the deck centreline to ensure the planks run true. The waterways and margin planks surrounding the deck are masked off with tape to protect them from any damage.

139
Deck planking underway. Any gaps between the planks were filled with a mix of wood glue and earth colour to represent the tar and oakum used in caulking. Note the shift of plank butts.

the deck, there will be times when you get the shift pattern mixed up. Don't worry. The shift is a rule of thumb and no self-respecting shipwright would discard a perfectly good piece of wood if it was a little short. If you look at ships like *Victory* in Portsmouth, the shift pattern is clear but there are a number of places where the pattern falls off. Perhaps a plank was repaired or replaced that threw the perfect pattern out of alignment, but that is of little significance because maintaining structural integrity was paramount. For us model makers, we are trying to give an impression of how a deck was laid (Figure 139), and despite all of our hard work a number of the butts will be covered by deckhouses or other fittings so the pattern won't appear perfect anyway. As planking progresses towards the bow the deck curves inwards and the planks will have to cut to a point to fit. Like hull stealer planks, they are not cut to a point but are squared off and set into the margin plank. This is called *joggling*

the plank. With a very sharp knife, cut away the margin plank then lay the final plank in the row to fit the space as shown in Figure 140.

The fully planked main deck (Figure 141) was gently rubbed down and wiped over with a damp cloth to raise the wood grain. Once dry it was sanded back again using very fine sandpaper and given a light coat of tung oil to impart a warm colour (Figure 142). I did not attempt to portray trennels simply because they would be very hard to do and look out of scale on these narrow planks. They can be simulated with dots made with a tip of an artist's brown coloured pencil if desired.

The poop deck is a little different from the main deck in that there is only a waterway but no margin plank. The deck planks around the curved section are not joggled into anything but are instead curved or cut at an angle to fit the curved waterway edge. Start work by finishing and painting the break between the main deck and the

140
At the bow the planks are joggled into the margin plank.

141
The broad expanse of the main deck is planked ready for rubbing down.

142
Tung oil was applied to the deck to bring out the colour of the wood and caulking. Don't forget to wipe off the excess. If you do not like the warm yellow colour that tung oil imparts, use a clear acrylic matt varnish that will keep the wood a whitish colour. Enamel or oil-based varnishes all have an amber tint that will colour the wood.

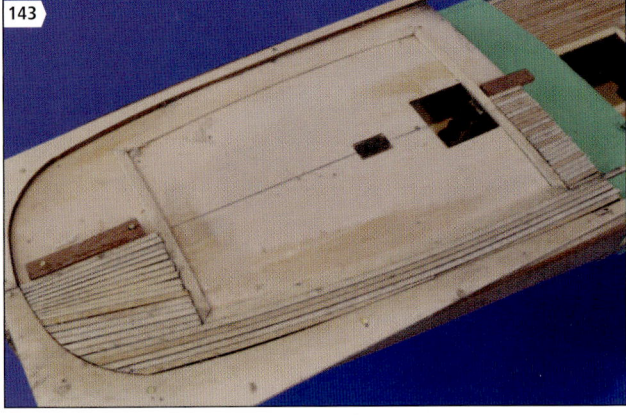

143
The false poop deck cut was very useful to ensure the planking matched the shape of this deck.

poop itself. Add the deck house margin planks as before. The laser-cut carrier sheet that held the poop sub deck is an ideal pattern to plank to. Having a pattern in place ensures the deck planks are laid to the correct shape so that a waterway can be easily fitted (Figure 143). A styrene waterway is traced and cut using the laser-cut carrier sheet as before and painted grey before fitting (Figure 144).

BULWARKS

The main bulwark is a laser-cut from 2mm thick ply. The inside of the bulwarks received several coats of a creamy off-white paint, gently sanded down between coats to fill the wood grain. The goal is to make the surfaces quite smooth so as to differentiate the grain-free 'iron' bulwark from the planked wooden hull, to highlight *Cutty Sark*'s composite construction. At the bow, the bulwarks are attached to the *knightheads*. The kit's knighthead is very one-dimensional and only detailed on the front and back faces. Scores were cut on the sides to complete this detailing and the tops were bevelled as shown in the Campbell and Longridge references. This work took just a few minutes to complete and it certainly makes the part look a lot more realistic (Figure 145). The knighthead is pinned to the deck and the bulwark is glued to its sides with the ends trimmed flush (Figure 146). When fixing the bulwarks to the hull, make sure they follow the hull's sheer and that both sides flare out from the hull symmetrically.

144
The planked poop deck with the pre-painted styrene waterway ready for installation. The importance of pushing the deck planks up against each other is highlighted here by the unsightly gaps made worse with the black glue. These planks should be cut out with a knife and fine chisel and re-laid.

SINGLE PLANK–ON–BULKHEAD MODELLING

145
The knightshead is detailed by cutting groves all around the part and bevelling the top to match the shapes shown in the G W Campbell plans. It is painted black before attaching to the deck.

146
A view of the bulwarks at the bow. The pre-painted forecastle deck supports have been installed between the inner bulwarks. Lengths of quarter round styrene strip has been glued to the waterway right up against the bulwark to give a neat joint and additional reinforcement to the bulwark to hull joint. The outsides of the bulwarks are faired into the hull using two-part automotive filler.

The joint between the main bulwark and the waterway revealed some gaps. Although not prototypical, the gap was covered with a 1mm quarter-round plastic rod painted grey that makes a very neat joint. Using wedge-shaped wood or plastic rod to cover up the joint on a model is often considered a model maker's bodge, but on warships at least it is quite accurate because the waterways were not shaped channels, but a wedge of wood serving as a spurn water and to stop the wheels of the gun carriage. This style of spurn water can be seen back in Figure 79. The gutter-type waterway on *Cutty Sark* is an example of how naval and mercantile practice differ. With the bulwarks in place, the forecastle subdeck can be fitted and the deck planked as before (Figures 146 and 147).

DETAILING THE INNER BULWARKS

A feature that makes the *Cutty Sark* so beautiful is that her inner bulwarks were of varnished teak decorated with painted wooden appliques. This detailing begins with the fitting of the *strengthening* rail clearly shown in the Campbell plans and Longridge's book. The best way to visualize how the bulwark is constructed is to think of it as divided into a lower and upper sections. The lower bulwark (which is the main bulwark we just fixed to the hull) is capped with a wide rail, called the strengthening rail. The second section is fixed on top of the strengthening rail to form the upper bulwark.

The strengthening rail itself is composed of two parts. The first part is a thin 1 x 1mm wooden batten that is fixed to the inside top edge of the lower bulwark (Figure 148). This rail is not prototypical, but is a model making expedient to provide more of a surface area to fix the actual strengthening rail to the bulwark. Once the batten is in place, the lower bulwark is detailed with the fitting of metal bulwark stanchions. The bulwark stanchions were made of short lengths of dark grey painted brass rod. From the plan, the stanchion locations are marked on the waterway and a hole drilled. The brass rod is bent as per the drawings and one end of the stanchion goes into the hole and the other end tucks just under the 1 x 1mm batten. It should be noted that Campbell's plans indicate they were white, but pictures of the stanchions in Longridge's book show them a dark colour. Which is correct? Probably both are, as the ship had subtle

147
The fully planked forecastle deck. The main deck has an amber hue from the tung oil compared to freshly sanded forecastle deck whose light colour looks like a new deck. A weathered deck has a grey tone that can be reproduced with washes of grey artist's oil colour if desired. The Campbell plans show that forecastle deck planking ends butt up against the waterway and there is no margin plank for the deck planks to be joggled into. The margin plank laid was painted grey to represent the waterway.

colour scheme changes throughout her life. The key is to pick a time period and stick to it as best you can. Longridge's book also shows that the stanchions were fitted with rings and cleats for lashing down

148

The first part of the strengthening rail (1x1mm square batten) has been glued to the inside top edge of the bulwarks. The stanchions were shaped out of brass rod and were inserted into holes in the waterway with the top ends fitting under the rail. The break of the main deck and poop has also been finished with a coat of black paint (it could have been off-white) and a length of styrene strip fixed in the junction between the deck and the break for a neat joint.

149

The strengthening rail proper is glued to the top of the bulwarks and the batten. The strengthening rail rides up over the waterways on the forecastle. The knighthead has sustained some damage and is chipped. This chip was repaired with two-part epoxy putty (*eg*, Milliput or Apoxie Sculpt) that is easily shaped and sculpted.

cargo and rigging, but I did not add them because they would be very small in this scale. If you enjoy super-detailing, Campbell's plans and Longridge's book feature these little fittings exquisitely. The actual strengthening rail itself was added next (Figure 149). The rail is 5mm wide and after being cut out, the inside edge was rounded over to give it a finished look and glued on top of the 1x1mm batten and bulwark edge.

The upper bulwark is a .5mm thick x 5mm wide strip of pear that was edge-glued on top of the strengthening rail using medium viscosity CA (Figure 150). The upper bulwark is quite fragile at this time so be careful where you put your fingers. The join between the upper bulwarks and strengthening rail is reinforced considerably once the upper bulwark rail stanchions were added (Figure 151). These stanchions are 1mm x 1mm square strips of pear cut into short lengths (a little longer than the height of the upper bulwark) and glued in place. When the glue had set they were trimmed flush with the height of the bulwark. The upper bulwark was finished with a coat of tung oil to bring out the colour of the wood and hide any glue stains (Figure 152).

The final item is to fit the oblong-shaped panels between each upper bulwark stanchion. A strip of styrene 3mm wide by .25mm thick was painted off-white. A guillotine cutter cut the strip into 10mm lengths and all four corners of each piece were trimmed off to form the oblong shape shown on the Campbell drawings. A panel

150

A thin strip of pear was glued to the top of the strengthening rail to form the upper bulwark. In the foreground the extent of the two-part automotive putty required to fair the bulwark into the hull can be seen.

151

The upper bulwark stanchions are glued in place using a small block of wood to space them evenly.

SINGLE PLANK–ON–BULKHEAD MODELLING

152

The upper bulwarks and stanchions given a coat of tung oil to represent the varnished teak bulwark of the ship.

153

Plastic card panels are cut from .25mm sheet (thin cardstock is an alternative). Note that the two-part automotive putty used to fair the main bulwark to the outside hull has been sanded smooth. It may take a few applications of filler to obtain a smooth transition between these parts.

was glued in between each upper bulwark stanchion and being made of thin flexible plasticard they were able to follow any curves easily (Figure 153).

PAINTING AND COPPERING THE HULL

The basic hull structure is largely complete and it is time to prepare it for paint and coppering. It is good practice to give the hull a coat of the base colour before moving on to coppering. In preparation for paint, I prefer a 'blank hull', that is one that is devoid of all details such as decoration and mouldings. These can be added later and painted over to match. If the details are a different colour, such as natural wood finished decorative side rails, then they can be pre-finished and fixed to the painted hull leaving a crisp colour separation line that is very pleasing to the eye. Painting started by giving the hull a coat of non-filling sanding sealer because we wanted some of the lines between planks to be visible under the paint. Sanding sealer was also applied to the unpainted bottom because it gives a smooth hard surface. The adhesive backing on the copper plates stick better to a smooth surface. On *Perry*, if I had not already painted the hull with copper paint, I would have sealed the carved surface with sanding sealer or primer to aid adhesion. The area above the waterline was given a coat of off-black paint by airbrush. This coat was rubbed down with #1000 grit sanding sponge and recoated until a smooth finish was achieved. A little subtle shading was done with black paint because the airbrush was out (Figure 154).

The waterline is marked off and the top edge masked with tape. The hull's bottom is covered with 4mm wide copper tape cut into

154

The hull has been painted black and any other flaws corrected with automotive glaze and spot putty. The paint has been shaded and highlighted to break up the monotony of an all-black painted hull.

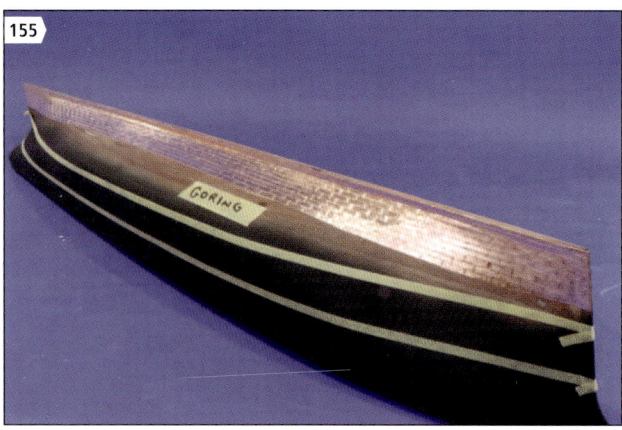

155

The first (bottom) strake of coppering has been laid and the *top strake* has been marked off with tape. The elliptically shaped centre area is *the goring strake*.

156

Coppering the goring strake. The first few plates of each row are cut at an angle to accommodate the curve.

14mm lengths which is about the scale size required. Unlike a warship in which the coppering starts at the keel and works its way up to the waterline, on a merchant ship the copper is divided into three distinct belts known as *strakes* (Figure 155). The first strake starts at the keel and consists of 8 or 9 rows of plates. The second or *top strake* starts at the waterline (around 8 or 9 as well) and runs parallel to it. These space between the top and bottom strakes is an elliptically-shaped space called the *goring strake* (Figure 156). To fill this space lay plates as before (I worked upwards) but now trimming the copper plates to fit. Once all three strakes are completed, examine the waterline and use a piece of tape to correct for the optical illusion that makes the waterline droop down at the bow and stern (Figure 157) as discussed in the previous chapter. You have to do this by eye and play around with the position of the tape until the waterline looks straight. This additional area is filled with shaped pieces of copper tape and any slight gaps between plates can be touched in with copper paint. The *Cutty Sark*'s hull is quite large and the area to be coppered will take some time over several days. It is best to do the work in short bursts.

When I last visited the *Cutty Sark*, her copper had oxidized to a warm rich copper brown colour. To replicate this, the shiny copper tape was weathered by first dulling it down with a coat of a matt acrylic clear varnish. The matt varnish seals the copper and provides a microscopically rough surface for the subsequent washes of paint to adhere. A dark wash of raw umber and burnt umber oil paint thinned with white spirits was applied to the copper and allowed to dry (Figure 158). Additional coats of the wash can be applied to suit your taste and when finished, a coat of acrylic satin polyurethane was sprayed over that deepens the colours and provides a consistent sheen. A wooden batten was added to the top of the copper to finish the job. The batten was given a wash of ivory black and burnt umber artist's oils to kill the whiteness of the wood.

157

The top strake was completed to the waterline, but the optical illusion makes it appear to sag downwards. Tape was used to correct the line and the additional space is coppered yielding a visually straight line of copper.

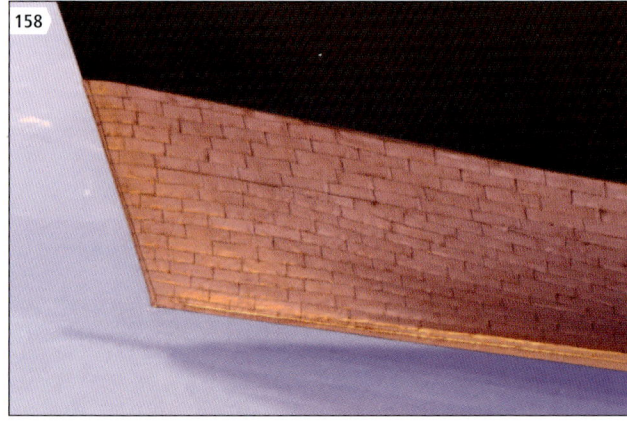

158

The copper is weathered to give an authentically dull and warm finish. By following the rows of copper you can make out the top, goring and bottom strakes. The keel, stem and stern posts have been wrapped with copper plates as well.

SINGLE PLANK-ON-BULKHEAD MODELLING

OUTSIDE HULL DETAILS

A prominent decoration on *Cutty Sark* are two parallel varnished wooden rails that run the length of the hull. Ensuring that the rails are evenly spaced is important because they draw the eye to the ship. A piece of masking tape was cut as wide as the space between the two rails (Figure 159). Mark the location of one of the rails and apply the tape. Keep adjusting the tape until it follows the sheer of the hull and is symmetrical on both sides. Another very important point is that the distance between the two rails is wide enough to accommodate any of the cast and etched brass parts that need to fit between them. The space shown on the kit instructions or width of kits parts might be different from that shown on Campbell's plan because it is not clear what sources were used to design the kit. I relied on Campbell's plan and the etched decoration at the transom only just fits and looks a little cramped. In retrospect I should have made the gap a few millimetres wider.

The rails themselves are 2mm x 2mm Swiss pear strips. Later in her career the rails were replaced with white painted ribbands. If you choose this scheme the ribband is best applied to the hull using white vinyl pin striping tape as opposed to painting it. The wooden strips were soaked in hot water and tacked to the hull with a little dot of thick CA every inch or so along their length using the edges of the tape as a guide. Lightly tacking them into place allows you to easily – and with the least amount of damage to the paintwork – pull them off the hull to correct their position if something goes awry. Once they are tacked into place, remove the tape and run thin CA down their length and press the entire length against the hull firmly securing them. Don't worry about shiny glue spots, they will disappear under a coat of varnish at the end.

The headwork on *Cutty Sark* is quite simple (Figure 160). Like the *Perry* in the previous chapter, there is only a single cheek knee and a head board for each side. The challenge to fitting these parts is getting the bevels correct so all the parts sit correctly against each other. There is no other advice than to take your time and bevel and shape each part until they fit against the hull and each other. The decorative rails added to the headwork are pre-painted plastic strips to give a crisp finish. The scuppers are holes drilled through the hull by marking their position on a strip of masking tape (Figure 161). The tape also prevents excess slivering of the wood that would leave an unattractive jagged hole. The kit instructions locate the scuppers in a different position from the Campbell plans, but I relied on the plans.

Bulwark Rails. The rail that sits on top of the upper bulwark (also called *gunwale covers*) are fitted next. Like the *Perry*, the kit-supplied parts didn't really fit my hull because my construction varied a little from the kit designer's calculations. As demonstrated with *Perry*, a pattern for a new rail was made and the item cut from a 4mm wide and 1mm thick strip of pear. Normally I try to find a piece of wood wide enough to cut the rail in one piece to avoid joins. My wood stock would not allow this so I would have to put the rails together from a few pieces and do my best to hide the joints. This is not easy

159

The natural wood side rails added. The rails or painted ribbands draw the eye to the sheer of the hull so it is important to carefully lay out their location with masking tape, if necessary repositioning the tape so they run sweet and true. Note that a wooden batten has been added to the top of the copper.

160

The headwork consists four parts, the head boards (top) and the cheek knees (bottom). The cheek knees provide lateral support to the stem and knee of the head. The assembly has been given a preliminary coat of black paint.

161

The scuppers are drilled through the hull. A piece of tape is used to ensure the scupper holes are straight and properly spaced. Decorative rails added from plastic strip, and the anchor billboard is shown in place.

162

The rail around the stern was built up from several parts to accommodate the hull curves. The rail has been oiled and given a coat of satin varnish that has highlighted the joins between pieces of wood. If these joins are too prominent to your eye, they can be hidden by retouching them with artist's oil colour and gently brushing it out to blend the colours.

to do on *Cutty Sark* because the rail is clear varnished wood. Moreover, the stern is round and to make a rail to fit it would mean having to use more pieces than I would have preferred. The problem with having to use several different pieces is that the grain of the wood shows and the pieced-together rail looks disjointed when the grain on one piece is laid to the next.

The rail was made *in situ* using as few strips of wood as possible. Each piece of rail is glued to the top of the upper bulwarks and is supported by the upper rail stanchions. The rail parts were glued down, a little at a time, ensuring it followed the curve of the hull as much as possible. Once they did not fit, another piece was fitted with the ends cut off at an angle to accommodate the curve. Care was taken to ensure that the edge of each piece was allowed to overhang the stanchions and the outer bulwark by at least 1mm on each side. As the rail nears the end of the hull the curve becomes quite round and several short curved pieces of pear were cut and fitted together (Figure 162). Once all of the railing pieces are attached, the outside and inside edges are sanded smooth to a consistent 1mm overhang.

Despite the rail being made of a fine-grained hardwood, under a coat of oil and varnish the grain and the joints between the parts would be highlighted, too much so for my sense of aesthetics. There are two ways to reduce this effect. The first is the joinery itself. I used straight joints that looked like the rail was just cobbled together (well, it was!). What could have been done is to cut proper scarfs between the pieces of wood. When proper joins are used the viewer's eye will be drawn there and will be impressed by the fineness of your work, diverting attention from the graining. Second, and this was my approach, the entire rail is carefully over-painted with artist's oil paints. Oil paints can be mixed to match almost any colour of wood and when applied to the surface and brushed out and blended will do an effective job of covering up a multitude of sins. It will not hide all of the graining and joins entirely, but certainly reduces their overall prominence.

Rudder. The rudder is laser-cut out of 6mm wood stock and was thinned down to scale thickness of 4mm. As you can see in Figure 163 the kit rudder also has big square chunks laser-cut out of its front face into which the grossly over-scale brass gudgeons were to be fitted. The Campbell drawings can be used to cut and shape a new rudder out of wood stock, or guide the modification of the kit part as I did. The kit part is first cut away from the carrier sheet leaving the bit of the carrier sheet that is attached to the front of the rudder intact (Figure 164). A little wood glue was wiped into the laser-cut line that reattaches the carrier sheet to the rudder. The rudder now has a solid front edge and new, properly located and shaped gudgeon notches can be cut. The rudder is tapered from top to bottom, and then to an aerofoil shape using a square of sandpaper taped to a flat surface. The front of edge the rudder is rounded over and the rudder stock itself filed round to complete the job. The rudder is next painted black and copper plated (Figure 165). Given the scale of the model, fitting working gudgeons and pintles would be difficult to make out of brass strip and tube, so instead their presence was faked. The rudder was pinned into place on the rudder post with pins and the straps that hold the gudgeons and pintles were added to the rudder and hull sides using strips of black cartridge paper.

Etched Decoration. Photo-etched brass has been a real boon to period ship modelling because it brings delicacy and finesse to so many fittings that in the past were chunky and oversized metal castings. It is frequently used in many kits as a way to add carved *bas relief* decoration, and here the medium is less successful because the details are flat and very one-dimensional. To give these flat etched parts more depth, white PVA glue is painted onto the part to build up the details (Figure 166). It may take a couple of applications to get the effect you want because PVA glue shrinks and flattens out when it dries. Relief carved details like leaves and scrolls really benefit from this attention. With the glue modelling complete, the decoration was painted gold and fixed to the model (Figure 167). The hull paint work was touched up and additional shading and highlighting added with different mixes of black and white paint. The tonal variations in paint were blended with a few overall thin washes of well diluted ivory black and burnt umber artists oil colour. A clear coat of matt or satin polyurethane as you desire will seal the paintwork and help blend the shades together even more so.

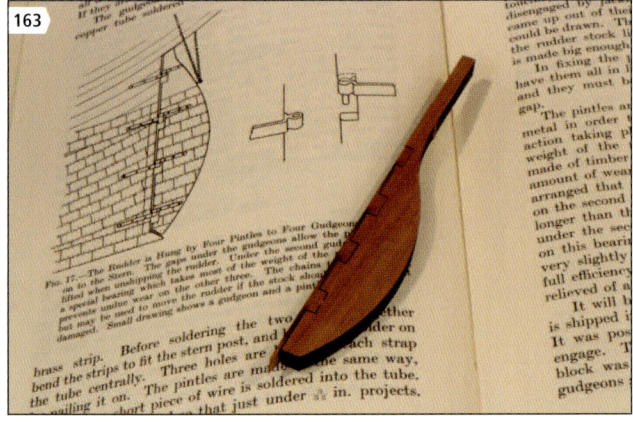

163

The kit supplied rudder is over-scale and has shape issues compared to the Longridge book.

SINGLE PLANK–ON–BULKHEAD MODELLING

164
The rudder was completely reshaped. The gudgeon cut-outs were reduced in size, its thickness reduced to scale, and the blade sanded to a proper aerofoil shape and tapered down its length. The rudder shaft and front of the blade was rounded over.

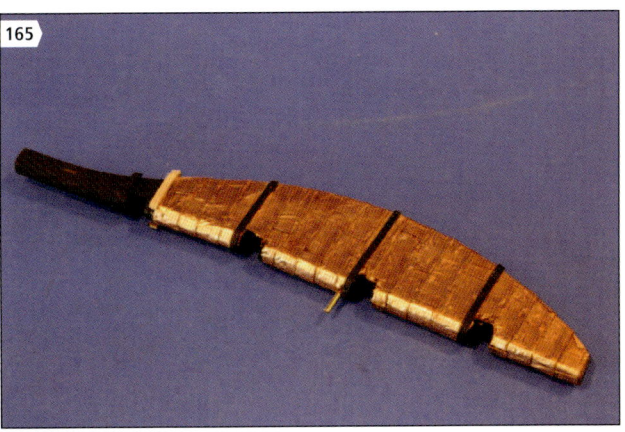

165
The painted and coppered rudder. No attempt was made to have a working system of hinges and instead the rudder was fixed to the hull with a pin. The rudder's gudgeon and hull's pintle straps are made of heavy black cartridge paper.

DEADEYES

The next major task is stropping the deadeyes. The kit provides soft wire for you to make the strops by bending it into two loops – a figure-of-eight shape with a large loop at the top to fit the deadeye itself, and a small one to fit a pin so the strop can be tacked to the inner bulwark. The kit method is less than satisfactory for two reasons. First, to pin the strop to the inner bulwark means a hole must be drilled right through the bulwark creating holes on the exterior that must be repaired and repainted. Second, it does not really replicate or remotely resemble how the deadeye strops were actually fitted to *Cutty Sark*. Indeed, it would be easier to replicate actual practice than to use the kit method!

On merchant ships like the *Cutty Sark* the deadeyes are stropped differently from warships like the *Perry*. *Cutty Sark*'s strop is actually a single eye with a straight long shank. A plate, called a *palm* is attached to the end of the shank and the palm is riveted to the inner bulwark. Adding a palm to the end of the shank is fiddly and can only be securely attached by soldering. Moreover, the palm would be glued to the inside bulwark and a small dot of glue does not provide enough sheer strength to take up the strain of the rigging later. A model making solution is to do away with the palm and have the shank inserted into a hole drilled into the waterway close to the inner bulwark. This better replicates the look of the actual construction and also provides a very secure fixing point for the deadeye to take up the strain of the rigging.

167
The PVA glue treated etched decorations appear much more like ronde-bosse (encrusted enamel) decorations than the flat etched decoration as supplied. The hull's paintwork has been touched up and given a few washes of ivory black and burnt umber oil colour to blend in all the shaded paintwork together. A coat of clear satin polyurethane varnish evens out the sheen and provides protection to the paintwork.

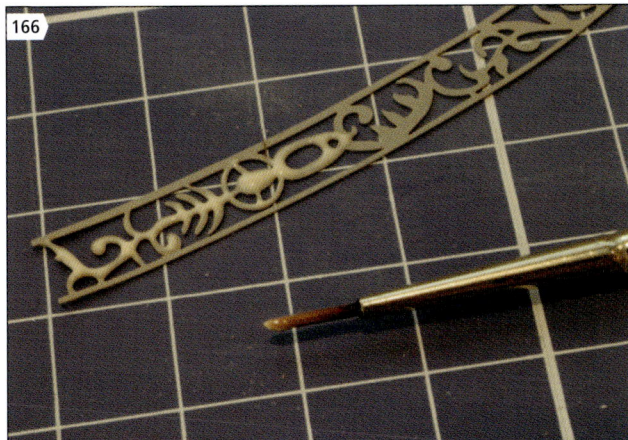

166
The etched part is cleaned up and given a coat of primer. One or more applications of PVA glue is used to build up the details. When cured, the part was primed and painted gold.

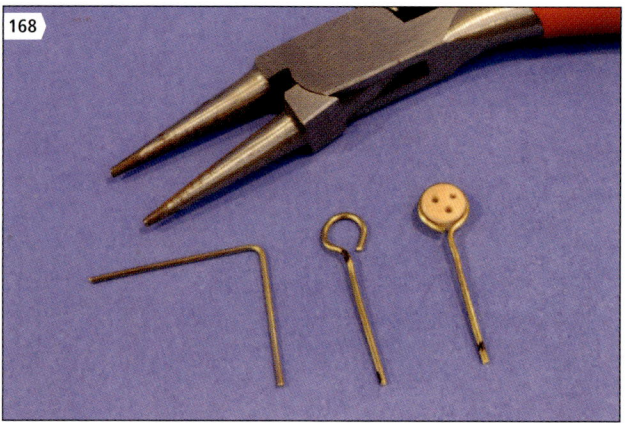

168
The steps to bending wire to form a deadeye strop. It takes practice but once you get there they are quick to make.

169
Deadeyes stropped and ready for priming and painting black.

The strops were made by taking a length of 1mm diameter wire, annealing it in a flame from a gas torch (heat the wire to a cherry red and allow to cool. The tip of the blue flame is hottest) held in a pair of pliers. The wire is pulled straight by placing one end in a vice and the other end in a pair of pliers. Figure 168 illustrates how the one end of the straightened wire is shaped into a loop into which the deadeyes is fixed. The deadeye loop is formed by measuring down from one end of the wire approximately 17mm for a large deadeye (and approximately 15mm for a small deadeye) and bending the wire 90°. A pair of round needle-nosed pliers is used to curl the wire over to form a loop. The excess is cut away and the loop can be adjusted with more inward bending and trimming until the exact size is obtained. This takes a bit of practice but after doing a few you get the feel for it and making them becomes quite easy. The deadeye is inserted by pulling them open slightly and closing them tight around the deadeye (Figure 169).

The kit and Campbell drawings also differ in the number and sizes of deadeyes required, as well as their position. For example, the kit provides 20 large deadeyes for each side of the mainmast, but the Campbell plans indicate 9 large and 4 small deadeyes per side; the kit provides 12 large and 6 small, in contrast to 9 large and 3 small per side around the foremast. In terms of sheer numbers, the kit provides 47 deadeyes per side whereas the actual ship has 32 in total. Given the different sizes required (indeed, three sizes are indicated on the Campbell plan whereas the kit provides two generic sizes), I had to make up any differences. Most of the extra deadeyes were scrounged from my spares box. However, some were made of boxwood, white metal, and some of walnut, so to make them all look the same I painted all of the deadeye and strop assemblies black, as if they were all covered with a protective coat of paint.

With these changes, the kit's pre-cut kit-supplied deadeye channels must also be discarded and new channels made to accommodate the corrected number of deadeyes. These channels were also pierced to hold belaying pins, and the number and location

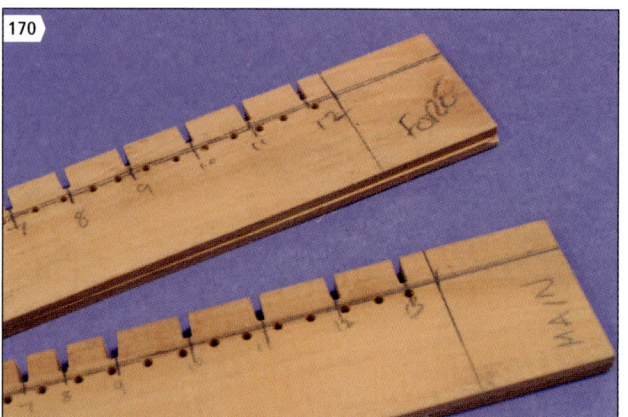

170
The channels also serve as a rail for belaying pins. The picture shows the layout for drilling belaying pin holes and slots for the deadeyes on oversized pieces of wood. They were made in handed pairs by holding the pieces of wood together with double sided tape.

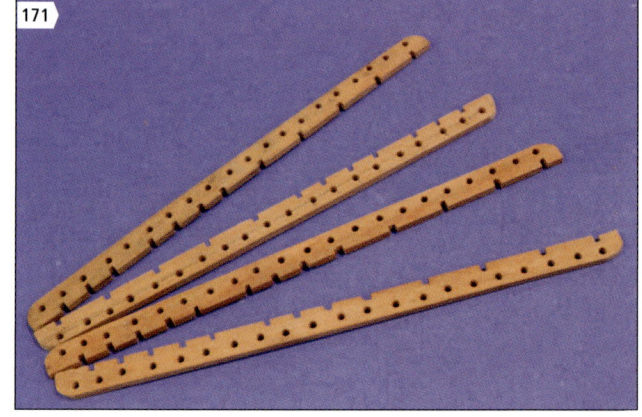

171
The fore and main channel/pin rails were trimmed to their proper shape.

SINGLE PLANK–ON–BULKHEAD MODELLING

172
The channels are attached to the bulwark under the strengthening rail to give a greater gluing surface because they will come under a lot of strain during rigging. In reality, the pin rail was cut as an integral part of the strengthening rail.

173
The shanks of the deadeye strops are fed through the slots in the channel and into a hole drilled at the edge of the waterway close to the bulwark. A few of the deadeyes shown will need to be rotated to the correct orientation. It's important to check this otherwise you may rig the deadeyes upside down.

of these elements taken from the Campbell drawings. Channel construction started with an overly long and wide strip of pear (20mm wide) of the correct thickness (1.5mm) marked out with the locations of notches for the deadeye stops and holes for belaying pins (Figure 170). Double-sided tape is used to temporarily attach a second strip of wood of the same length to the underside of the marked piece. In this way you can make identical channels for both sides of the ship at once. The notches are filed out (I used my miniature table saw) and the holes drilled. The strips are then ripped to the correct width and cut to length. Separate the two channels and round off the outer corners (Figure 171). The new channels are fixed in their location on the inner bulwark as per the Campbell plans (Figure 172). For strength, I glued the channels *under* the strengthening rails so it is simultaneously supported along its top and side edges. Once in place, the notches are used as a guide to mark the location on the waterway near the side of the bulwarks where the shank of the deadeye strop will be fixed. A hole is drilled and the deadeye assemblies are tested for fit, the shanks trimmed to length and solidly glued into place (Figure 173).

DECKHOUSES AND HATCHES

The deck of a clipper is festooned with cargo hatches and deckhouses. The deckhouses are usually beautifully panelled in teak and handsome. The kit supplies the shell of each deckhouse from pre-cut ply parts, and the decorative panelling is provided by overlays laser-cut from a sheet of walnut. Unfortunately, the walnut overlays are extremely thick and must be replaced. I thought about thinning the overlays by temporarily fixing them to a flat board with double sided tape and running them through a thickness sander. However, being reduced to such a thin veneer makes them very fragile and difficult to remove from the tape without breaking. It is much easier to build up the panelling on each of the deckhouses from thin strips of pear wood ripped using my miniature table saw.

Deckhouse construction began by assembling the kit shells and painting them off-white. Following the Campbell plans the panelling was made up of thin strips of wood shown in the Figure 174. Along with the panelling, the deckhouses have simple mouldings around the roof and base made up of square pieces of pear. These mouldings can be rounded off to provide a more finished look. The roofs were planked with scribed basswood sheet – left over from the *Perry* model. The wooden parts were given a coat of tung oil to bring out their colour and the deckhouses were finished off with doorknobs made with a head of a pin, and the kit-supplied brass eyelets for the portholes (Figure 175).

The deck hatches are very simple to make. Each hatch frame (known as the *coaming*) was made up of wooden strips following the Campbell plans and the hatch covers were made of styrene strips cut to fit inside the frames (Figure 176). I deliberately used styrene for the hatch covers because they are painted grey and the surface of

174
The assembled deckhouse shells are painted an off-white colour. The roof planking was scribed wood sheet and pear strips were cut for the panelling.

174

175

Completed deckhouses and hatchways. If you look carefully I made a major error. The deckhouse is a little too large for the margin plank surrounding it. This is a lesson to check and check your measurements before cutting or gluing anything. The problem will be corrected by gluing the deckhouse to the deck and using very thin strips to lay a new set of margin planks. The new margin planks will be slightly proud of the deck, but that is far less noticeable than the fact the deckhouse just doesn't fit.

176

The cargo hatch was made up of wood strips for the coamings and covers from plastic card. Holes have been drilled for eyebolts and lifting eyes to be added later. The hatches were painted grey and highlights added with an airbrush to break up the monotony of a single colour and further deepened with a wash of black artist's oil paint.

176

styrene does not need any special preparation to paint, unlike wood (Figure 177). The painted hatches were fitted with brass ring bolts (eyelets) and lifting rings. For an authentic model the ring bolts and lifting rings were blackened. Many modellers leave these parts in a shiny brass because they look pretty, but actual ships blacken all their ironwork. Brass fittings such as these can be blackened in two ways. The first it to paint them and the second way is to use a chemical blackener that oxidizes the surface of the brass black (Figure 178). Painting is straightforward by sticking the eyebolts to a piece of folded over masking tape or by pushing the shank into a blob of putty and spray painting. An acrylic lacquer paint, such as those contained in the excellent aerosols by Tamiya must be used because the layer of paint is thin, shrinks when it dries, and sticks well to metal.

Far better than painting is to use a chemical blackener. These are called 'patina solutions' and are available from jewellery and some model railway supply shops. There are specific solutions for brass, copper, or steel and they can turn the metal different colours such as black, brown, or green, for example. For our models, turning brass black is the most common task. The metal parts are first cleaned (*eg*, water and detergent to remove any grease) or by 'pickling'. Pickling is when the part is soaked in a warm solution of acid (there are different acids for different metals – consult the jewellery supply house) that ensures an even finish from the patina solution. A little patina solution is poured in a glass jar and the parts dropped in. They change colour quite quickly so remove and rinse in clean water to stop the process. If you leave the parts in the solution, they will eventually dissolve away or the patina will flake off. I often dilute the patina solution with water to slow down the process and allow a more gradual oxidation and provide more control as to when to stop the process. You will have to gently swirl or stir the parts in the solution to ensure all faces come into contact with it. Do not stir with a metal object, but rather a wooden coffee stir stick. The solution can be reused a number of times, but the effect gets weaker

SINGLE PLANK–ON–BULKHEAD MODELLING

177
A completed deckhouse and painted cargo hatch (eyebolts and lifting rings yet to be added) fixed to the deck.

178
Patina solutions to colour metal easily and quickly. These are caustic chemicals so treat them with respect and follow the manufacturer's instructions.

179
The copper plates were first given a patina of green before gluing to the hull. Copper turns green when exposed to the elements over time.

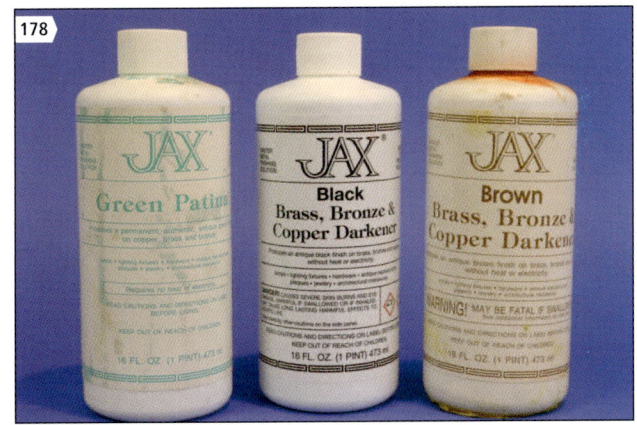

179

180

The *Cutty Sark*'s completed hull. Deck fittings, masting and rigging are left to be done.

with each use until it has to be discarded. Even in this state it should not be poured down the drain but disposed of at a recycling/disposal depot that take chemicals and old paint. The use of patina solutions takes a bit of practice and experimentation, and results will vary depending on the hardness of the metal and strength of the solution.

The resulting finishes are very durable and extremely authentic. Brown patina solution is useful for parts such as cleats that are brown in colour to resemble wood but the item is provided in brass. Green can be used to colour copper plating on a hull (Figure 179). The copper plates are cleaned and laid out on a piece of cardboard. The patina solution is brushed over the top of each and when the desired colour is reached the plate is dipped in water to stop the reaction. The green patina solution yields several different shades of green, but also white and black. The plates are glued to the hull as usual. I do not recommend that the hull is coppered and then the patina solution is brushed over the whole area. In my experiments it was difficult to get a consistent finish simply because the glue used to attach the plates may have smeared on top of the plate preventing contact with the solution. Stopping the reaction would also be a problem in that how do you wash the bottom of the hull without getting the wooden parts of the model wet or damp? Damp will surely lead to warping somewhere.

With the hatches and deckhouses fixed to the deck, and the rest of the fittings such as pumps, the ship's wheel, belfry, bitts and whatnot can be made up from the kit-supplied parts. Don't forget to add the figurehead of *Cutty Sark* herself now that the major construction work on the hull is complete and she is out of danger from getting damaged. To the kit's credit, the deck fittings can be used from the box and are generally to scale. Armed with the Campbell plans you are well equipped to improve them. In general, the remaining fittings require little in the way of any special skills and any particular considerations for larger items like the ship's boats will covered in other chapters of this book.

At this point we will leave the *Cutty Sark* (Figure 180) and the challenges of a single plank-on-bulkhead hull. Of particular concern are the difficulties in planking with the ever-present danger of sagging or springy planks inherent in this style of kit, and that a natural wood finished model is very difficult to achieve without perfect planking. With a single layer of planks, there is only one chance to get it right. Moreover, the build of this kit shows that although it was designed to be largely decorative in nature, the model can be built into something far more authentic with some straightforward techniques and a little forethought.

6: Double Plank-on-Bulkhead Modelling

HM Brig *Speedy*

Our next build focuses on tackling a double plank-on-bulkhead model. The ship is the brig *Speedy* in 1/64 scale by Vanguard Models. The designer is Chris Watton who has designed many kits for Amati in Italy and Jotika in the UK. Under his own label, he has incorporated several innovations not seen in other kits before. These are a real aid to the modeller, which, coupled with highly detailed instructions and plans, make this kit an ideal project for anyone with limited experience to have a go.

The 14-gun *Speedy* should need no introduction to the naval historian. This little brig, under the command of Lord Cochrane, forced the surrender of the much larger 32-gun Spanish xebec *El Gamo* on 6 May 1801. *Speedy* was so small she sailed under the guns of *El Gamo* and Cochrane and his men boarded, overcoming a Spanish crew six times greater in number. This daring action has inspired characters in several naval novels and movies. The kit featured here is a limited-edition version that includes pear blocks and boxwood planking (Figure 181). The standard version of the kit provides pear for the second planking, and several optional extras can be purchased such as ladders in pear or sets of highly detailed rigging blocks.

The considerations to keep in mind if contemplating this kit are:
- Double planked hull.
- Separate keel, stem post, and rudder post assembly.
- The model is historically accurate but can be finished semi-decoratively in natural wood or be painted authentically.
- Pre-cut stem post rabbet to assist with planking.
- Laser-etched deck – all of the deck planks are etched onto a clear sheet of wood that shows all of the planks with proper shifts of butt, nibbing and trennels, all beautifully rendered. No deck planking is required.
- Full scale plans and illustrated instruction booklet to guide construction and rigging.
- Large scale allows for more detail to be incorporated, but the rigging of the guns is simplified and additional blocks will need to be purchased to rig them properly.

181

Vanguard Models' 1/64 *Speedy* kit incorporates all the latest developments in double plank-on-bulkhead model ship design.

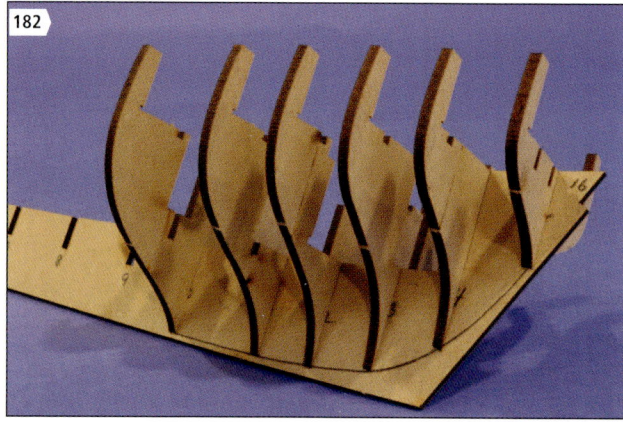

182

As with *Cutty Sark* the first task is to mark the bearding line. Of particular note is the design of the framework – the framing is composed of many closely spaced bulkheads that obviate the need to add filler blocks. The area under the bearding line is easily thinned with coarse sandpaper because HDF is easily sanded.

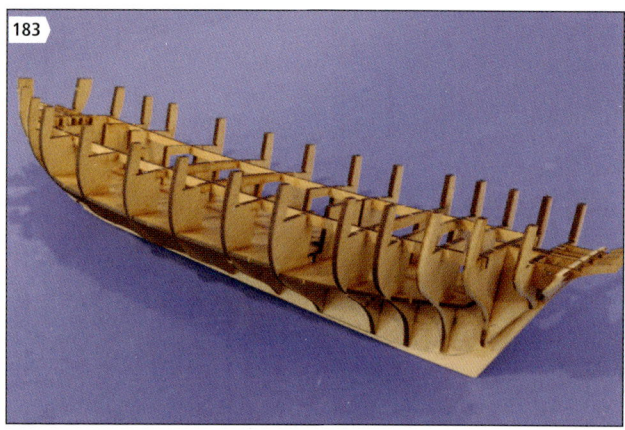

Frame Assembly

One of the first innovations of this kit is that the bulkheads and false keel parts are laser-cut in high density fibreboard (HDF) and not plywood as was case in the *Cutty Sark* kit. HDF is a very dense and heavy material that is exceptionally strong and, most importantly, does not warp, ensuring a straight framework. There is a lot of bias amongst modellers who are used to plywood parts, but in my experience of working with HDF, this bias is unfounded. Test fitting the bulkheads to the false keel without glue shows they fit well and as before the heels of bulkheads are marked on the false keel to define the bearding line (Figure 182). It is important to keep in mind that the area below the bearding line is thinned to accommodate the thickness of the first planking *and* the second planking as well. Figure 183 shows the bulkheads glued in place and, in contrast to the *Cutty Sark* model, the *Speedy* has been designed with a lot of closely spaced bulkheads that prevent the planks from sagging in between them. Moreover, being double planked, any problems with the hull shape can be rectified with sanding and filler on the first planking before being planked again with the finish wood to produce a nicely shaped hull with no bumps or dips. This is the key advantage of the double planked design.

After the bulkheads have been bevelled, the main sub deck is glued to the framework and here we find another modern design feature (Figure 184). The top of each bulkhead has a laser-cut slot in them to hold the sub deck edges in place obviating the need to tack down the edges with pins while the glue dries. Another neat design feature is that the stem post has laser-cut slots in it to form a *rabbet* – a groove into which the ends of the first planking fits. The stem rabbet holds the plank in place while it is bent around the curves of the hull and keeps it in place while you tack the wood to

183

The assembled framework and bevelled bulkheads. The framework incorporates a number of supports and strengthening pieces to ensure the bulkheads are square and true.

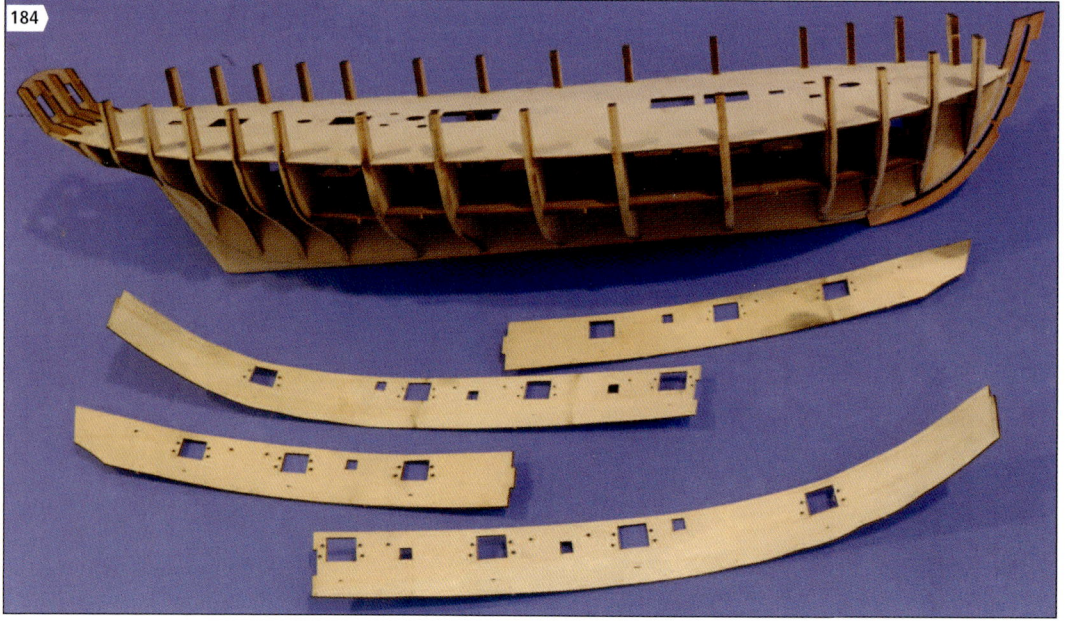

184

The false deck has been glued to the top of the bulkheads. The gunport patterns were soaked in hot water, temporarily clipped to the hull and left to dry to lock in the shape. Of note is that a slot has been cut into the stem to form a rabbet. The rabbet will hold the ends of the planks in place while fitting them, making the job much easier and neater.

185
The gunport patterns are glued to the bulkheads with pins to hold them in place until dry. The hull is ready for first planking in record time.

the bulkheads. In models without this feature, the job is much more fiddly because the end of the plank must be held tight in place against the stem post while at the same time getting the pin in place and hammering it home, all the while keeping the plank from slipping out of place from the plank above it. The job often needed three hands to complete while we humans are born with just two.

The bulwarks or 'gunport patterns' are added next and it is a laser-cut piece of ply like the previous models but the design is a little different as it is only one layer thick but is cut into a front and back end to fit on the wood carrier sheet. The two halves should be taped together and offered up to the hull to determine where they need to be curved to fit the hull. The parts are taken off the hull and the parts soaked in hot water for an hour, then put back on the hull, this time clamping and pinning it into place *without* glue. When fully dry, they will have taken the shape of the hull and can be glued permanently to the hull. It is really important to ensure they are glued in exactly the right place on the hull framework so the gunports are the correct height in relation to the deck or the guns will not fit. With the gunport patterns in place the basic hull framework is now complete and ready for the first planking (Figure 185). The thoughtful design of the framework means that construction went quickly, easily, and accurately. No modifications were required.

First Planking

The first planking will not be seen but this does not mean you can be sloppy just because any problems can be corrected with filler. The first planking should be carried out as you would the finished planking to give you practice in how to shape, bend and taper a plank to the point where you will intuitively know where a taper should begin and its shape. The planking starts under the gunport pattern. The first wood strip will need no tapering and is soaked and bent as is. The tip goes into the rabbet and is glued and tacked into place on each frame (Figure 186). The procedure is repeated on the other side of the hull that keeps any stresses on the framework caused by the planking to be equalized. As with *Cutty Sark*, the next plank is test fitted into position and any overlap with the previous plank is trimmed and bevelled where necessary and fixed into place. Given the small size of this hull, the planking was carried out in full wood

186
The first two planks on each side need no tapering or bevelling. The use of the bow rabbet is shown. The tip of the gunport pattern has a tab that fits into the rabbet, and the plank ends notched to fit as required. The gunport patterns have pre-drilled holes for the gun tackle around each gunport. A helpful innovation is that the designer has included a laser-etched mark below the gunports that show where the main wale is located. Pins hold the planks in place temporarily until the glue dries and are then removed.

187
Planking continues using full length strips of wood.

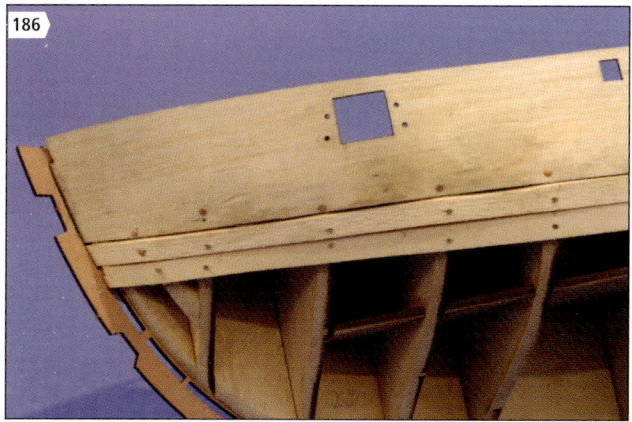

188

As the hull shape changes, the planks will want to splay out leaving triangular shaped gaps between planks.

189

The gaps are filled with triangular stealer planks. This is not prototypical practice but being the first layer of planking, the main consideration is just making sure all gaps are filled.

190

The first planking has been sanded down. There are some gaps that need to be filled and the plank ends at the stern needs to be trimmed back.

strips (Figure 187). As with any hull, triangular-shaped gaps will appear between planks as they fan out to accommodate the shape of the hull (Figure 188) and will require stealer planks. Because this is the first planking, gaps can be filled with simple triangular pieces of wood (Figure 189).

After the first planking is completed a slightly thinned down coat of PVA glue should be brushed over the plank seams. The thinned glue will seep into the joints between the planks to fully bond themselves to each other. Leave the glue to cure for 24 hours and remove the pins, and the plank ends overhanging the stern can be roughly trimmed back. I strongly suggest covering the stem and rudder posts with layers of masking tape to protect it from nicks and bumps as we move to sanding the hull (Figure 190).

The first planking was sanded using a power palm sander and finished off by hand. The sanding showed no dips attesting to the excellent design of the framework. A few gaps between planks appeared that were filled with a spackling compound (Figure 191). The one area I should have changed was the planking at the rudder post. I took the planking all the way to the rudder post and planks had to be sanded down to

191

The first planking was sanded through while trying to accommodate for the thickness of the second planking. This hole was filled with two-part automotive filler to restore the solid base required for the second planking. In retrospect, the first planking need not be taken to the stern post, but rather just to the bearding line.

DOUBLE PLANK-ON-BULKHEAD MODELLING

192

Transom and counter planked in boxwood. The coloured glue was used to simulate the caulking.

1.5mm total thickness to accommodate the second planking. In order to get to this thickness, I sanded right through the planks in the area! Two-part automotive filler was used to fair the planking into the false rudder post. In retrospect I should have just taken the hull planking to the bearding line and not beyond.

SECOND PLANKING – BELOW THE WALE

A decision will have to be made at this point. Will the model be left in natural wood or will the second planking be painted in an authentic manner? The special edition kit I purchased provided boxwood for the second planking which when finished produces a nice warm tan-yellow colour and is in keeping with the finest period ship models. If you decide on a natural wood finish, you have to decide if you wish to simulate the caulking between hull planks similar to the way we did with the deck planks on *Cutty Sark*. Instead of rubbing the edge of a hull plank with a pencil lead, caulking between the planks can be simulated using black/brown coloured glue. Coloured glue is made by mixing PVA wood glue with some earth colour. Earth colours are finely ground dry minerals (ochre, bitumen, zinc oxide) that are mixed with varnish to make different colours of stain used by woodworkers. They are available from good woodworking supply shops and come in a variety of colours running from dark browns, reds, white, and blacks. Earth colours are preferable to paint or ink to colour glue because they do not soak into and stain the wood, but rather they sit on the surface it is applied to. They also provide additional consistency to the glue so it becomes a natural gap filler. On the other hand, if you decide to paint your model authentically, boxwood is a nice tight grained hard wood that takes paint well with little surface preparation. The second planking begins with planking over the transom and counter areas. Although I decided to paint my model in authentic colours, in Figure 192 I planked the area in natural wood and used coloured

glue to show you how it looks.

The main wale is added next. This is a thick band of planking that is two layers thick. The kit is designed so that this thickness is built up in layers which makes shaping and bending the wood easier. The first layer – and this is important – is called the *key plank* that sets the location for the wale and all planking above and below it. When the second planking is completed, the second layer of the wale is glued directly on top of the key plank to bring the wale up to its proper thickness. The kit helpfully provides laser-etched marks on the gunport pattern for the location of the key plank. When fitting this plank ensure that it is symmetrical on both sides of the hull and adjust as necessary.

The second planking is carried out in the usual way but only plank the areas below the key plank for now. If you are leaving the planks in natural bright finish, they can be cut to scale length and a shift of the butts for hull planking can be incorporated. I suggest that the backs of the planks are coated with dots of thick CA and the edges with coloured PVA. The thick CA ensures the plank is firmly fixed to the first planking without the need for clamps while the coloured glue fills any slight gaps between planks just like real caulking. My model is to be painted so the planks were cut into two or three lengths that made tapering and bending easier to handle, and fixed

193

Second planking underway. At the bow, there is no rabbet for the plank ends but instead they are fitted flush against the stem post. When fixing the second layer of planks, apply dots of thick CA glue to the back of the planks and PVA wood glue to the edges.

194

Like the first planking, the planks for the second planking want to splay out from one another at the bow and stern areas to accommodate the curves of the hull.

195

In reality, stealer planks do not come to a point but have a squared-off end. The gap between planks on the hull must be shaped to accept a plank with this squared end (as shown marked in pencil).

196

The space for the stealer is cut out of the second planking.

197

Stealer planks fitted with coloured glue on a natural wood finished model.

198

The second planking is smoothed off and the effectiveness of the black glue and properly shaped planks is shown. A coat of tung oil brings out the beauty of the wood and darkens the black glue lines.

to the hull with thick CA and regular woodworking PVA glues. As a personal choice, I did not fill the gaps between planks with filler so the run of some of the planking would show under the paint. To another person, these lines are distracting and will fill them to yield a clean surface. The choice is very personal and what you do defines your style. Having a firm base of the first planking makes it much easier to properly shape stealer planks (Figures 193 to 198).

DECK AND INNER BULWARKS

The deck is a beautifully laser-etched part with all planks, butts, nibbing and location marks for the deck fittings included (Figure 199). It is literally a drop-in part. Laser-cut decks have been around for some time, but the grain of the wood sheet (usually made of basswood) has always showed through and spoiled the effect. On this deck, the wood is carefully selected to be as grain-free as possible, and the laser-etching is finely done with no evidence of scorching anywhere. After the deck was glued in place (Figure 200), the inner bulwarks were planked, sanded and painted. Note that the bulwark plank closest to the deck was pre-painted red ochre to ensure a neat separation of deck and bulwark (Figure 201). Take care not to mar the laser-etched deck with glue or paint drips. You cannot simply sand away any mistakes without sanding away any of the etched detailing. A repair of sorts to any damaged etched detail can be made by drawing the lines back in with a sharp pencil.

The remaining second planking above the wale is now added. This planking is probably the easiest because there is very little tapering or bevelling required. The hull is now fully planked and the advantage of a well-designed double planked hull is evident (Figure 202). The key to this model is the design of closely spaced bulkheads, especially in the bow and stern, that keeps the planks from sagging. Large gaps were filled with automotive glaze and spot putty and given a coat of primer (Figure 203).

COPPERING THE SHIP'S BOTTOM

In preparation for coppering, the ship's waterline was marked off in pencil. Once again, the hull is placed on a flat surface. *Speedy* did not draw more water at the stern so the keel is positioned so that the whole length of the keel is set at a uniform height above the

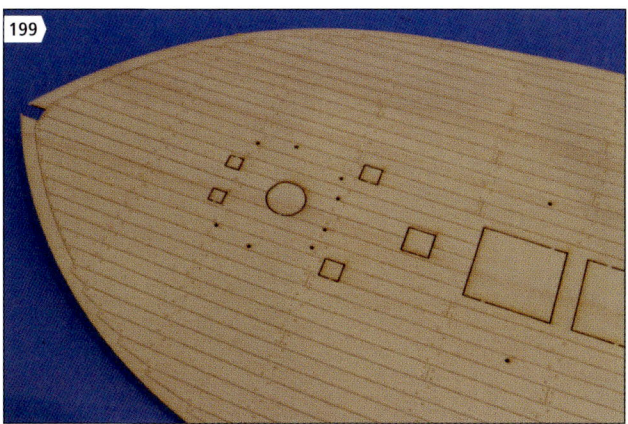

199
The entire deck is a laser-cut with etched details.

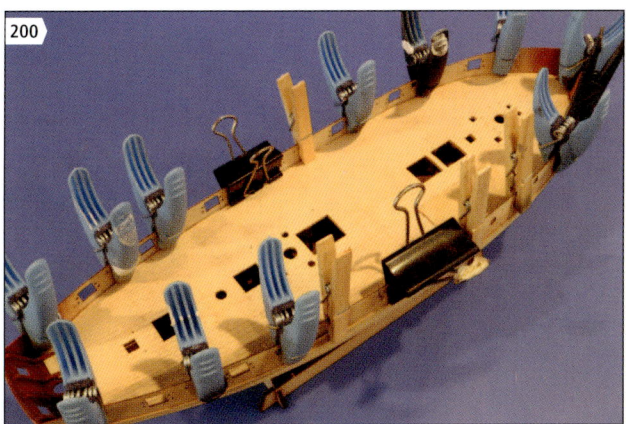

200
The deck was glued down and the edges held in place with clothes pegs and clamps. A small piece of wood can be used to spread the pressure along the edges. The deck fitted perfectly.

201
The inner bulwarks have been planked and the gunports trimmed out. The planking has been given a few coats of red ochre paint and sanded back. The clever design of the kit allows the holes for the gun tackle to be drilled from the outside inward.

202
The hull after the remaining area is planked over, the main wale, keel, stem and stern post fixed in place. The gunports are filed to their final shape and any gaps filled with spackling compound (Polyfilla type filler). The red painted bulwarks have been shaded to impart depth. *Speedy* is looking very much like a ship now.

workbench surface (Figure 204). A pencil is taped to a block of wood at the height of the waterline at the stem and then traced all around the hull. Tape a strip of masking tape with its top edge about 1mm or 2mm *below* the marked waterline. Press the tape down firmly and paint the area above the tape, say 1in or so, in black. When the paint is dry, remove the tape and you have simultaneously marked the waterline and pre-painted the area just above black.

Unlike the *Perry* and *Cutty Sark*, the copper plating in this model

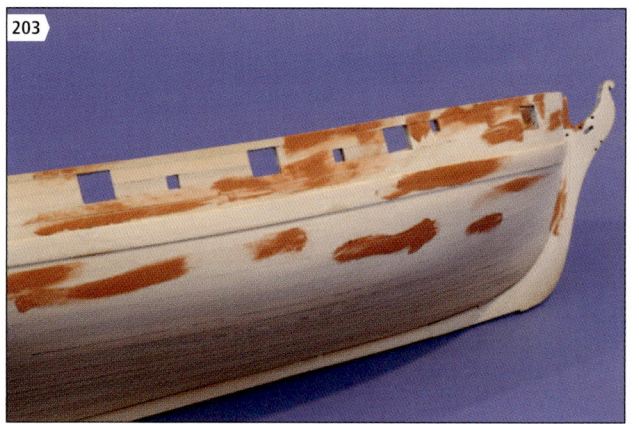

203

A coat of primer revealed a number of flaws that were corrected with automotive glaze and spot putty. Despite multiple coats of paint and filler, each coat seemed to reveal another flaw that needed attention! Such is the wonder of wood and the ham-fistedness and the poor eyesight of this modeller.

204

Once the waterline is marked, lay a thin strip of tape along it and examine it from all angles and adjust the tape at the bow and stern to overcome the optical illusion of any sagging. A lead weight was placed on the deck to hold it down into in its cradle while marking the waterline.

is composed of photo-etched copper rectangles, complete with nail head detail (Figure 205). The design has thoughtfully provided sheets for the port and starboard hull sides that change the nail pattern at the front edge of each plate to simulate the overlap of plates. In this way, the plates can be butted up together end to end. Moreover, the kit provides uniquely shaped copper pieces to cover the exposed bottom edge of the keel, stem and rudder post. In the past one had to cover these areas with bent plates of copper or paint the exposed area with copper paint. In addition, these shaped pieces carry the correct rivet detail for a very authentic looking ship's bottom.

Coppering begins at the keel and works its way up to the waterline (Figure 206). Unlike the self-adhesive copper tape used earlier, these copper plates have to be glued in place. The easiest way to attach the plates to the hull is to put a dab of thick CA in the middle of the plate. A pair of tweezers holds the plate at the aft end and the front of the plate is positioned. Press down on the plate and stroke it with your finger to spread the glue underneath to cover the entire gluing area. These plates are stiff, and some may need to be dished or curved a bit in between your thumb and forefinger before being fixed to the hull. As the copper reaches the waterline, they are cut off flush and it may look a little ragged. This is corrected by laying some masking tape along the top of the copper and dabbing

205

A view of the coppering underway at the bow. The photo-etched copper plates are very detailed but are a little more difficult to lay down and shape than thin copper tape. Any gaps between plates can be touched in with copper paint.

206

A view of the stern copper plating underway. The copper plates are cut off flush at the waterline, keel and stem. The plate is very tough and it is hard to cut with a hobby or craft knife. A sharp pair of manicure scissors worked best but this task will dull them over time. Keep a pair reserved just for this job. When the coppering was completed, a wooden batten was added to the top of the copper. The copper bottom and batten were given a wash of ivory black and burnt umber artist's oils to dull the finish, followed by a matt clear coat to protect the copper bottom's patina.

DOUBLE PLANK-ON-BULKHEAD MODELLING

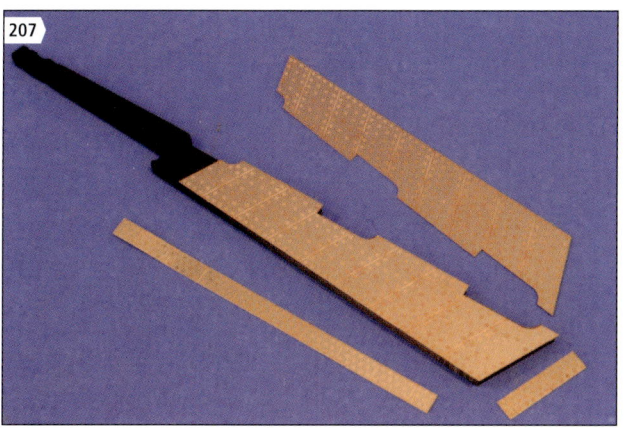

207
The copper for the rudder is provided as shaped pieces that fit the wooden part perfectly.

208
The hull received a black pre-shade before the yellow ochre goes on.

in copper paint into the area to create a neat line. The top is further finished by laying a thin wooden batten across the top of the copper to protect the edge. Keel, stem and rudder post edges are covered with the specially shaped parts, as is the rudder (Figure 207). The copper plating is over-sprayed with a matt clear varnish to subdue its brightness and then given a few overall washes of burnt umber and black artist's oil colour. A second coat of matt clear seals in the washes and deepens its colour.

Hull Painting

The copper plate and the inner bulwarks are masked off and a coat of primer applied to the hull. The black areas were painted first and shaded with pure black and shades of very dark grey (Figure 208). The black was masked off and the yellow ochre stripe was painted allowing some of the black to show through to give the colour some depth. Highlights were sprayed in with yellow ochre lightened with white and masked off when dry (Figure 209). This is my style and it is perfectly acceptable to work toward a single homogeneous colour if that suits your aesthetic. Paint your model as you see it in your mind's eye and have fun with it. To be honest, I think I choose to shade and weather my models because I am too impatient to work towards a perfectly flawless paintwork others are able to achieve!

The separation of colour between the black wale and the yellow hull side is an area requiring special attention (Figure 210). The trick when masking is to get the tape edge exactly into the apex of the joint between the hull side and wale. This is impossible for me, so I do my best and correct any unevenness with a 'pin wash' made of black artist's oil paint and white spirits. I flow the wash into the joint and capillary action takes it right into and along the junction to create a neat separation of colour. You can repeat the pin wash a few times until you get a nice clean edge. Any spillover can be removed with a cotton bud moistened with white spirits once the wash is dry. The hull's transom (Figure 211) and side fittings (Figure 212) are added next and they are pre-painted before fixing to the hull. Any marked paintwork is touched up, and don't worry too much if the touch-ups aren't a perfect match to the rest of the paint or slight

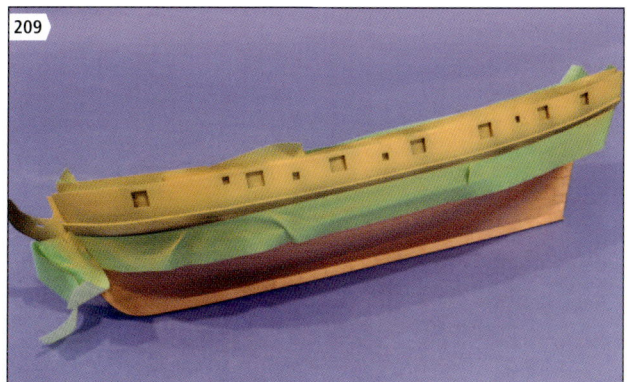

209
The yellow ochre was sprayed on allowing a little of the black pre-shade to show through, followed by highlights with lightened ochre. The ochre stripe was masked off and a coat of black applied and shaded.

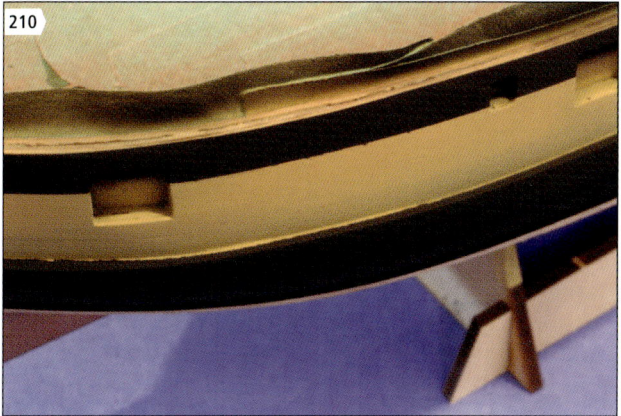

210
The junction between the black wale and ochre sides and any unevenness in the paint is corrected by flowing into the joint a wash of black artist's oil paint.

211
Hull side fittings at the stern under construction.

212
Hull side fittings in the bow area. There will be a lot of paint touch-up work to do.

213
The side fittings are complete and ready for touching up with paint. Note how the planking lines on the inner bulwark can be clearly seen through the paint, reinforcing the fact that the ship is constructed of wood to the viewer.

214
Headwork under construction. The cheek knees, rails and hairpins shown in place. The eagle-eyed among you will notice that I fixed the cathead knee (in white) upside down. I left it alone as an ever-enduring reminder to remember to check the plans before committing the glue … The gunport edges have been painted red.

215
A view of the headwork from above. The photo-etched parts and design made construction straightforward and yields an exquisite delicacy to the area.

DOUBLE PLANK-ON-BULKHEAD MODELLING

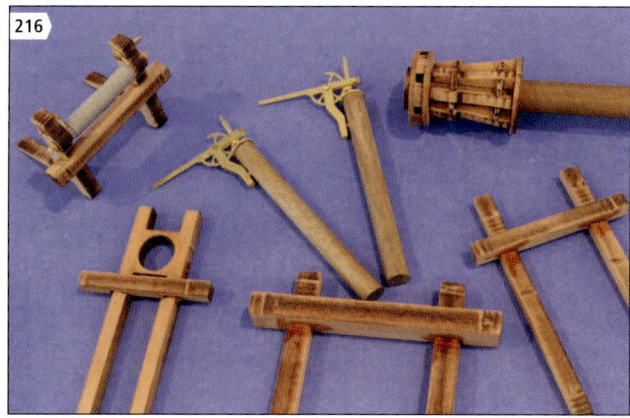

216
A selection of deck fittings: windlass, pumps, capstan, and bitts. Each is composed of laser-cut wooden parts and wooden strip or dowel. Highly detailed etched brass parts feature prominently in this kit.

217
A selection of deck fittings painted and ready for installation.

218
Deck hatch coamings, gratings, ladders, stove pipe and swivel guns assembled and painted. All went together with minimum fuss.

brush marks are visible because the final overall clear coat will help blend the different shades and textures together (Figure 213). The next chapter will cover in detail how to repair damaged paintwork.

THE SHIP'S HEADWORK

On *Speedy*, the ship's headwork is relatively simple and straightforward to assemble being composed of etched metal parts that are bent and glued into position. Figures 214 and 215 show where the cheek knees, rails and hairpin brackets are positioned. Just take your time and test fit before committing the glue and careful painting will pay dividends. Careful painting is easier said than done. The hair brackets and rails are relief etched metal parts that are yellow with a central blue stripe along its length. It is difficult to keep the blue line of a consistent width and straight within the etched recess. One method is to use blue decal sheet or blue vinyl striping applied over the yellow painted part. Another method is to flow a pin wash of Windsor blue artist's oil into the recess, similar to what as we did with *Perry*'s cast metal parts. The wash will fill the recess and neatly define its edges. A fine brush can be carefully used to paint within the edges.

DEADEYES, DEADEYE STROPS, CHAIN PLATES, AND CHANNELS

The channels on this model are laser-cut wooden parts that are first painted black and small holes drilled into their inside edge with a bit of brass rod inserted as a mounting pin. A corresponding hole is carefully drilled into the hull and the channels are glued into place. They are very fragile at this point so take care not to grab them by mistake. The deadeyes are stropped with highly detailed brass-etched parts that are pulled open and the wooden deadeye inserted and closed around them. I decided to leave the deadeyes in their natural wood colour and soaked them in tung oil and buffed them to a nice sheen. It's best to use a pair of pair of smooth round-jawed needle-nosed pliers that minimize risk of damage to the strops when you open them. The paint will probably get scuffed up in the process, so a little touch-up will be necessary.

The stropped deadeyes are put into the channels and the chain plates are fixed to the hull at the correct angle using a string. A brass pin is pushed through the chain plates into the hull to fix the assembly into place. The kit is highly realistic with several other brass fittings such as iron knees that are fixed to the channels to strengthen their attachment to the hull.

DECK HATCHES AND FITTINGS

The primary consideration for deck fittings is whether or not they are in scale and accurate in shape. Many kits provide generic fittings and are often oversize, especially items such as belaying pins. In this kit, the fittings are well detailed, in scale, and most importantly, resemble the style and shape of the period. If you are ever unhappy with a kit fitting, I urge you to try to make a better one from scratch. Figures 216 to 220 show a number of the fittings under construction and installed on the ship, and these highly detailed parts set the standard for fittings that are not only authentic, but delicate as well.

ARMAMENT

Speedy was armed with both swivel and long guns. The kit parts are well detailed and can be used right out of the box. There are two

219
Guns and fittings installed in the bow.

220
Guns and fittings fixed in the midship to stern area. All parts were pinned in place where possible to ensure they stay put.

considerations when it comes to the guns. For the swivel guns, kits often provide more than the ship actually carried or used in battle. This is because modellers often want to fit a gun to each of the gun mounting posts forgetting (or ignoring) that these guns were moved from post to post as a fight went on. This is artistic licence and the choice is yours. With the long guns, many kit designs have all of the guns sticking out of the gunport ready for battle. Most times the guns were stowed, and if the gunport has lids, the gun was kept inside the hull with the lids closed to reduce corrosion from being directly exposed to the elements. How you show your guns is up to you and I tend to show the guns on my models stowed.

The kit provides a simplified arrangement for the gun tackle and breeching ropes which I followed. The primary difference is that I *triced* (to haul up or in and lash or secure) up the breeching ropes following an example found on *Victory* in Portsmouth (Figure 221). To properly rig the guns requires purchasing extra blocks beyond those provided in the kit. The other challenge is to find blocks that match or replace them all with ones from the same range so they are consistent in style and wood species. Simplified gun rigging is common on many kits because the designer often wants to make the kit easier to build, and just having breeching ropes gives a good impression. Figure 222 shows fully rigged guns on a model of the sloop *Pegasus* to the same scale for you to compare and make a decision about how your model looks best to you.

Ship's Boat

The ship's boat(s) is a focal point of any model and is indeed a model within a model. *Speedy* carried an 18ft cutter and it is built over a frame of bulkheads like the main hull (Figures 223 to 224). The trick to getting a good-looking boat is to add detail to it. This means adding framing, thwarts and, most importantly, filling the boat with items like oars, casks, boat hooks and sails for example (Figures 225 and 226). This draws the viewer's eye to the boat and is a source of great admiration. If the boat is left empty, it looks bare and uninteresting (like my *Perry* model; I will have to go back and fill the ship's boat up with many interesting boaty items) so you may as well just cover them up and make boat covers for them. However, don't think that covered boats are uninteresting. Well-rendered cloth

221
Speedy's guns fitted with simplified rigging of just a triced-up breeching rope.

222
Fully rigged guns on *Pegasus* to the same scale as *Speedy*.

DOUBLE PLANK-ON-BULKHEAD MODELLING

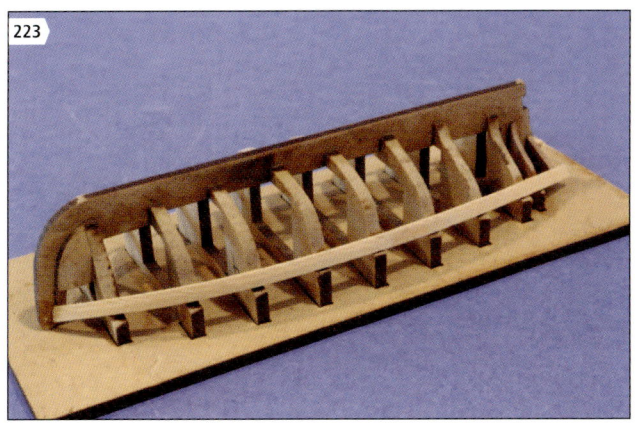

223

The ship's boat is a miniature plank-on-bulkhead model. The first plank has been glued to the framework.

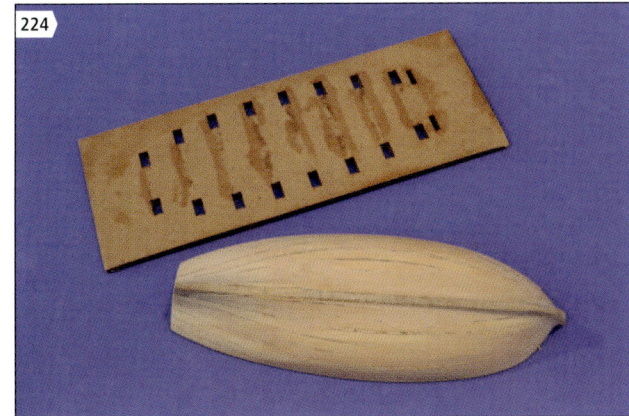

224

Once the hull has been planked and sanded down, the boat is removed from the jig.

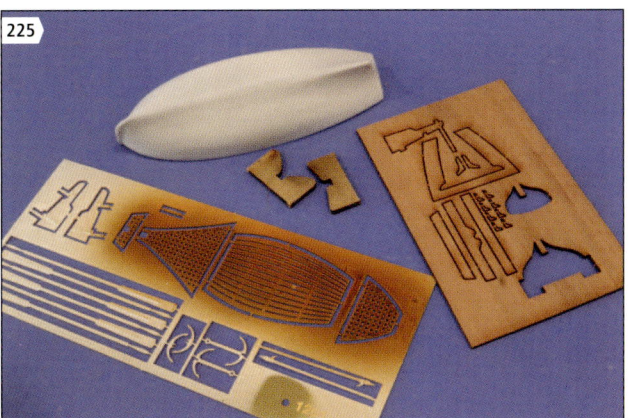

225

The kit supplies a lot of fittings and gear in chemically milled brass and laser-cut wood. The boat has been primed white.

226

The completed boat full of gear is set in her cradles and lashed to the deck.

covers are hard to make, to get it to look like more than tissue paper soaked in PVA glue that so many modellers use. Sculpting boat covers takes effort but when you get the folds right and they don't look like they defy gravity, they are a joy to behold. Modelling boat covers will be covered as part of the next chapter. One other item to consider is how to add some charm to your model. For example, to impress my daughter who loves

227

Ship's boats included in kits come in many different forms. For *Cutty Sark* the boats are metal castings that have to be planked over. All other detail for these boats, such as ribs, thwarts and gunwales for example, have to be made up from wood stock.

228
CAF Models provides a resin jig and notched frames to build a 1/48 scale clinker planked boat. The resin jig is in two parts so it can be easily removed from the hull when finished. The planking supplied has been ready shaped to fit the frame notches saving the effort of spiling the planks yourself.

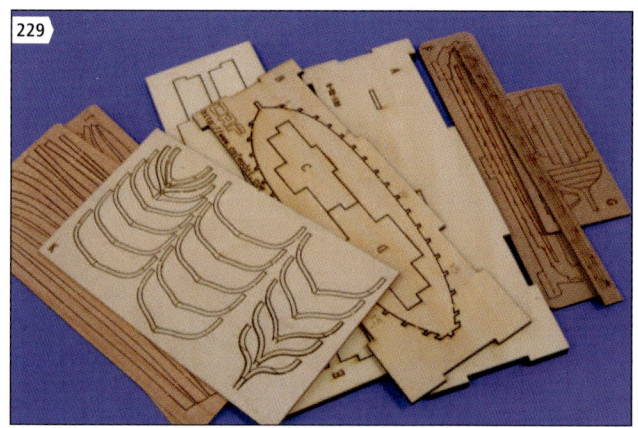

229
CAF Models also offers realistic carvel planked ship's boat to 1/48 scale. The keel, stem and sternpost are assembled from separate parts in prototypical style and the frames are built into the keel and held in the proper position by the plywood jig. The frames are then planked over with pre-shaped planks.

pets, I will place a little model dog or cat in the boat as the ship's mascot with its little head peeking up over the thwarts. I don't always add a mascot, but just once in a while to test if she's paying attention. It is charming touches like these that makes all the difference and keeps the viewer engaged.

While we are talking about ship's boats, kit manufacturers provide quite a variety of different options ranging from the most basic to the ultimate ship's boat in detail. For the *Cutty Sark* model of the last chapter, the ship's boats were provided as neatly cast metal items (Figure 227). *Cutty Sark*'s actual boats were a mix of *carvel* planked (hull planks are laid edge to edge forming a smooth surface) and *clinker* planked (the edges of the hull planks overlap each other giving the hull a stepped appearance). For the carvel planked ship's boats the modeller can simply paint the cast hulls, but for the clinker planked hull the modeller is supposed to plank over the castings with fine strips of wood. This is very difficult to do, but it is possible to purchase either cast metal or plastic clinker planked boat castings. CAF Models offers miniature kits of ship's boats that are constructed over a frame just like the real thing. The kits can produce a clinker planked hull (Figure 228) with properly notched frames to accommodate the planking that gives the stepped appearance, as well as carvel planked hulls (Figure 229).

Conclusions

At this point the hull of *Speedy* is pretty much complete and ready for rigging. The wisdom of a double plank-on-frame model is that the first planking allows you to get the shape correct and form a solid base for the second planking. The second planking is done more to scale and the proper scarfs and so on can be easily shown if so desired. The fact that you have a solid base or canvas to work from permits the inclusion of such details. The fully detailed etched deck is a new innovation that works well when done correctly. Should you wish to plank the deck yourself that is still possible but it is nice to have options.

Well-designed kits such as provided by Vanguard Models have taken all of the common issues a modeller would have to contend with into account to assure success for even those with little experience. The next phase of construction of *Speedy* is the rigging and that starts in Chapter 9. In contrast to *Speedy* that is built right out of the box to a high standard, our next project will entail a lot of scratch-building.

7: Semi-Scratch Double Plank-on-Bulkhead
The 74-Gun Ship *Vanguard*

When a modeller thinks of a sailing ship it is usually focused on a majestic rated man-of-war like the 100-gun *Victory*, the *Royal Sovereign*, *L'Orient*, *Santissima Trinidad*, or a 74-gun two-decker that comprised the majority of the battle line. These ships of the line were huge, and building one from a kit or from scratch is a major undertaking. As we have seen with the *Perry*, *Cutty Sark*, and *Speedy* hulls, there are a number of repeated operations that are common to all. Planking, planking decks, coppering, rigging guns, stropping deadeyes all have to be done, over and over again. A large three-decker has all these and there is a great deal more of it! Beyond the volume of repetitive work, there are new elements to contend with. The head work is very complex, composed of a multitude of knees, timbers, head boards and hairpins, not to mention that these parts carry a lot more decoration. Moreover, the previous builds we've covered so far had simple sterns, just a transom board that did not require much in the way of comment. A ship of the line has a towering stern replete with sumptuous decorations, windows, balconies, and balustrades. The fact that there are multiple decks, each having to be fully completed before the next one goes on, requires a lot of forethought and forward planning. At this point we have not yet discussed rigging, and one of these magnificent ships will require three masts and a lot of rigging to control the wind as they push through the water. A three-decker is the ultimate sailing ship. With our previous three builds, the models were pretty much built out-of-the-box. I had introduced a few scratch-built items or modification of kit parts but on this next build I will be providing a lot more examples of scratch-building. In this way, you will never be limited by what is provided by a kit, and if you decide to build your ship from scratch, you will have the basic fundamental skills to do so. For this step, we are building a semi-scratch model of Lord

230

The 74-gun ship *Vanguard*.

229

Nelson's flagship *Vanguard* to 1/72 scale (Figure 230). *Vanguard* was a 74-gun third rate ship of the line launched at Deptford in 1787; technically a two-decker as she had two complete battery decks, she also carried guns on the forecastle, quarterdeck and poop. She was the sixth vessel to bear the name and best known for flying Rear Admiral Sir Horatio Nelson's flag at the Battle of the Nile. At this famous action Nelson attacked the French fleet under the command of Vice-Admiral Françoise-Paul Brueys d'Aigalliers which was moored in a line of battle in Aboukir Bay. Nelson's strategy was to trap the French fleet between two lines of his ships. On the shoreward side, *Goliath* and four other ships broke through the French line to anchor and fight. *Vanguard* remained on the seaward side and soon the French van and centre was overwhelmed by six ships on either side of their line losing 11 ships of the line and two frigates.

Model Considerations

The impetus for this build was a gifted rag-tag box of parts from a fellow modeller who gave up on a kit of *Vanguard* that he did not have the skills to build to the standard he wished. The original kit was designed by Chris Watton for Amati of Italy several years ago and it remains a deluxe package today. My friend had a licenced version manufactured by Model Shipways in the United States to similar specifications as the Amati kit. My friend told me he had managed to build the hull framework but commented that Model Shipways' version cut the bulkheads and false keel in basswood and that this wood was not stout enough for a framework and that the parts, especially the bulkhead extensions that held the upper decks snapped off easily. He also found planking too difficult for his skill level. The plans were marred by a printing error so that none of the dimensions matched across sheets and after a time struggling he gave up the project in frustration. Over the years, the remnants of the kit moved house and moved again, and more and more items were lost over time. When it came to me most, but not all, of the brass etchings, some of the metal castings, and a few of the laser-cut wood sheets were present but even these were missing parts. None of the main structural parts such as bulkheads or false keel parts were included and these would have to be made myself.

The original Amati kit is presently available and it is an excellent double plank-on-bulkhead model. The kit can also build two equally famous sister ships of the class: *Bellerophon* or the *Elephant*, each of which has its own unique decoration and paint scheme. *Vanguard* itself can be painted in the Nelson chequer, *Elephant* in black and yellow ochre with a broad blue stripe, and *Bellerophon* is bright finished. Although designed by the designer of *Speedy*, the kit does not supply laser-etched decks or stem post rabbet to aid the first planking as it was one of his earlier designs.

On With The Build

The first order of business was to purchase from Amati a complete set of kit plans. This is a hefty set of 20 sheets, an illustrated construction manual and a written set of step-by-step instructions. The Amati plans contained full size drawings of all the laser-cut parts and etched brass sheets. As I pondered how to create all the missing parts I also thought about how I would depict the model. The model was designed to be authentic so I thought about how to make it even more so. The ship had spent many months at sea on blockade duty before going into action and would have become heavily weathered;

repairs at sea and tasks such as painting and maintenance would be done where the crew could reach that would result in a patchwork appearance. To keep the weather out the gunports would be closed and just a few opened to let in light and air. Modelling the closed gunports would allow the 'Nelson Chequer' to be shown with the black gunport lids against the yellow ochre base. Weathering a sailing ship model would pose a fun challenge in that, unlike a modern steel warship where there is a lot of rust, being made of wood, weathering on *Vanguard* would have to be largely fading the paintwork, grime and some general wear and tear.

The first task was to make the missing false keel and bulkhead parts using the plans as a pattern. The time-honoured way would be to lay a piece of tracing paper over the desired drawing and with draughting tools trace out a copy of the part that can be glued down to a piece of good quality plywood. The part is cut out using a hand-held fretsaw or power scroll saw. Instead of tracing, the plans could be taken to a copy shop and copied full size and cut up and pasted to your wood stock with rubber cement. Copying plans is permissible if they are for your own use only and copies of it (or parts made from it) are not provided or sold to anyone else. These two methods are laborious and we are living in the 21st Century and I found it much easier to learn laser cutting myself to cut out the parts.

Laser cutting services come in two types. In the first, you let a commercial service do all the work. You send in the plans, they scan them and cut the parts out for you on whatever stock they offer. All the time the service spent scanning your plans, talking to you, time taken on the laser cutter (not to mention test cuts) and material becomes part of your bill. This service can be expensive. The other method, if it is available in your locality, is to join a *makerspace* (ours is known as *MakerLab*). A makerspace is a workshop open to the public that has all the tools you could ever desire to use – laser cutters, 3D printers, table saws, thickness sanders, planers, routers, computers and scanners, and the expertise you would need to use them. A membership is taken out to the makerspace, and you take training courses on how to use the tools of interest. Training courses have tuition fees, or in many of these facilities, you can offset these costs by volunteering your time to help run the place (*eg*, serving at reception or operating tools for someone else). Each makerspace has its own rules and programs.

For your own project, you can do all the work yourself or ask someone to assist you, usually for a small fee. Often times members will do it for free because they are nice and you are now a member of a merry band of craftspeople. In a way there is an informal bartering system – you help me, and I help you. The other benefit of a makerspace is that you can supply the material you want cut, or they can obtain it for you at discounted prices. Joining a makerspace provides you new skills and control over the scratch-building process. These spaces invariably have a hipster coffee bar on the premises so you can sip a skinny soy café latte mochaccino with your new-found craftsperson friends as you discuss the finer points of laser cutting. I found in my experience that model ships were not something done at these labs - most of my skinny soy café latte mochaccino friends were into building furniture or were graphic artists designing lamps so they were truly intrigued by my model boat projects. You indeed become part of a community of artists who are keen to offer advice, support, and a good laugh.

Vanguard's plans were scanned (by a young person who knew all about 'vectors' and other requirements for laser cutting) and fed to

SEMI-SCRATCH DOUBLE PLANK-ON-BULKHEAD

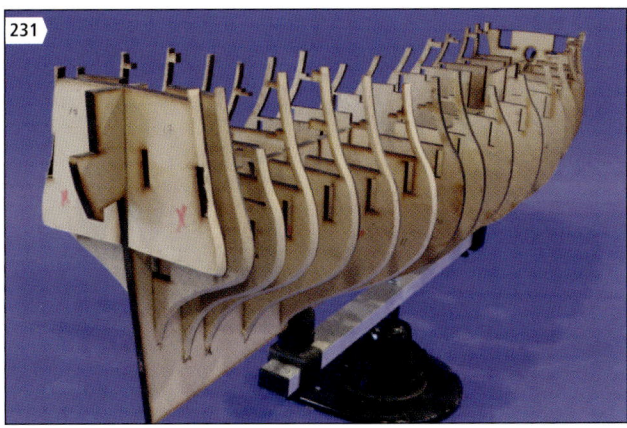

231

The bulkheads are test fitted to the false keel. The bulkheads at the stern and bow are pre-bevelled.

me to cut with laser assisted by another young person. I could not locate stocks of HDF as provided in the original Amati kit and instead used medium density fibreboard (MDF) that was planed to be 5mm thick (I knew how to use a planer from my secondary school woodworking days so I did this by myself). HDF is much more preferable because of its density and I prefer it over plywood because of its structural homogeneity. MDF is quite a bit softer and does not sand as well as HDF or ply, and it has a tendency to tear like thick cardboard when worked. However, it is very inexpensive and I think just about useable for this project.

ASSEMBLING THE FRAMEWORK

The false keel is in two pieces and when dry fitted the joint is slack. Lay some cling film on a dead flat surface and assemble the parts on top of it with plenty of wood glue. The cling film prevents the false keel from being glued to the workbench. The parts are trued by using a straight edge to line up the bottom of the false keel parts. Lay some cling film on top and weight the whole assembly down so that it dries flat and straight. If the false keel dries (or any wooden part) with a warp to it, this can be easily corrected by loosely wrapping the warped assembly along with a damp, nearly wet tissue together in some cling film. Weight the assembly down and let dry over a few days in a warm place. The dampness from the tissue penetrates the wood and when dry locks the shape in place. If you are not using the part right away, keep it under weight to prevent the warp from coming back. Any warp will be permanently prevented from returning once the ship's frame is assembled thanks to the interlocking parts that hold each other in place.

With the false keel assembled, the bulkheads were test fitted (Figure 231). Being made by ourselves, it's important that these parts are tested for fit. The laser used was not the same as the one used by the original kit manufacturer and the beam could deflect more or less. Any scanning errors could creep in so really check and double check that they fit into their slots and into the correct position as shown on the plans. Note which bulkheads will need bevelling and examine the shape of the hull and think about where a filler block might be helpful in the upcoming planking operation. It is also time to determine how the model will be displayed. Will you use a cradle to hold the hull, or a set of pedestals? If the latter, then the location of the pedestals must be decided and marked on the false keel. A slot can be cut and nut fitted that will accommodate a bolt fed up from the bottom of the display plinth; alternatively use scrap pieces of wood glued into the area to accommodate a wood screw passing through the display plinth and pedestal into the false keel.

The kit's false keel is designed with the keel and stem as an integrated unit. Only the rudder post is added after the planking is complete. As shown with the *Speedy* kit, having a rabbet into which the ends of the planks can fit really helps planking so it was decided to cut a *full* rabbet which means a slot cut into the stem and all along the keel as well. A rabbet is not critical for the second planking because this wood is thin (usually 1mm or less) and the planks themselves are cut narrower (closer to scale widths) and can easily butt up against the stem and keel with little effort. The top of the rabbet is determined by the bottom of all the bulkheads and kit-supplied filler blocks. Not only are we marking the bearding line as before, but the line is now extended along the entire length of the keel and around the stem post. By joining these marks in pencil you have marked the top of the rabbet. The rabbet itself is the thickness of the wood strip used for the first planking which in this model is 1.5mm. This distance is measured down from the top of the rabbet and the lines joined up to mark the bottom of the rabbet.

On *Vanguard*, the bottom of the rabbet lands right on the edge of the false keel below the bulkheads and is cut first. The saw is set to 1.5mm to 2mm height and a 1.5mm width (or whatever the thickness of the first planking is) groove is cut on both sides of the bottom of the false keel. This is called the *keel rabbet*. If you do not have a table saw, the groove is marked out with a pencil and a utility knife and straight edge are used to score the rabbet line keel and chiselled out (Figure 232). The stem rabbet is next marked out and cut by scoring the rabbet and chiselling out the groove (Figure 233). The area below the bearding line is sanded down to the depth of the rabbet to accommodate the thickness of the planking. Now, when the proper keel and stem parts are glued to the false keel a neat continuous rabbet is formed to accommodate the planking (Figure 234).

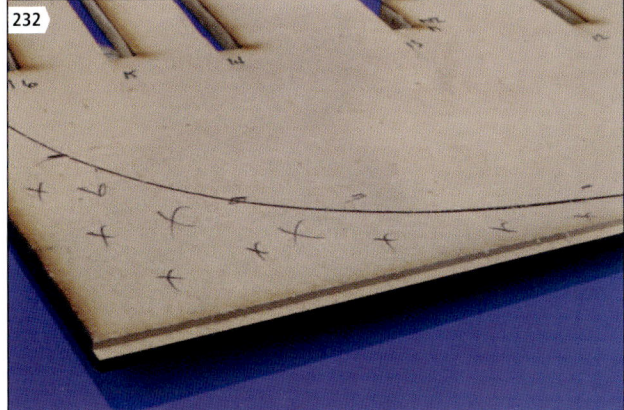

232

The bearding line was marked out as usual, and the rabbet is a continuation of this line along the entire length of the keel defined by the bulkhead bottoms and filler block profiles at the bow. The slot was cut on a table saw and the cross hatched area will be thinned to the thickness of the rabbet.

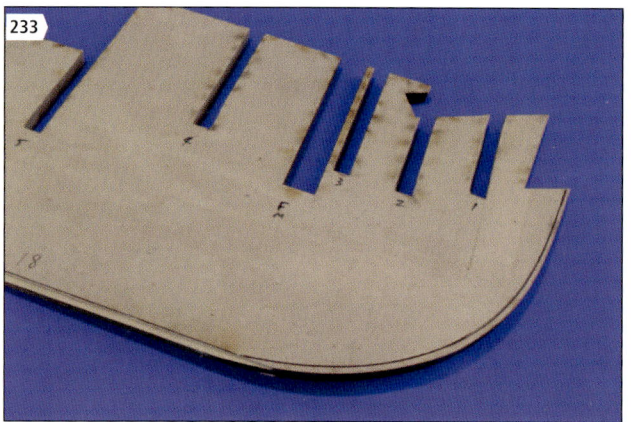
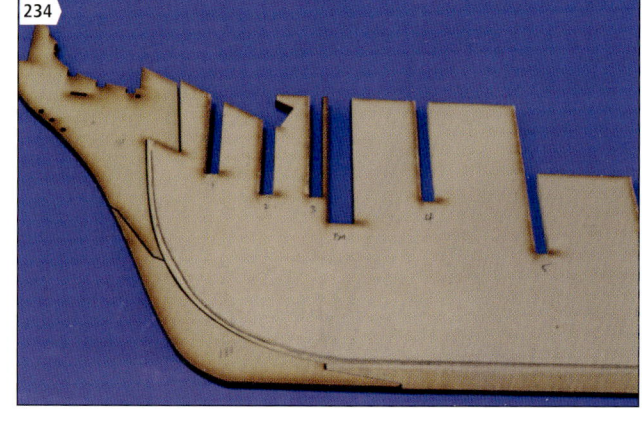

233
The bow rabbet is marked out and a craft knife is used to cut along the pencil line and a small chisel removes the MDF.

234
When the stem/knee of head and keel parts are put against the false keel you can see how the rabbet is formed along the length of the hull. The rabbet went a little wayward caused by a slip of the knife but the error is of no practical consequence.

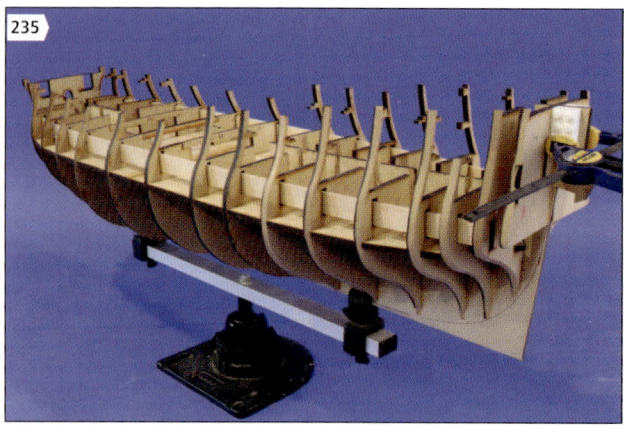

235
The hull framework under assembly.

236
The bow required a filler block.

237
Blocks of balsa were placed into the open bow area and traced all around to mark the shape. The blocks were held in a vice and carved using a shallow gouge and finished with a wood rasp.

238
Roughly shaped filler blocks are glued in place and final shaping carried out *in situ*.

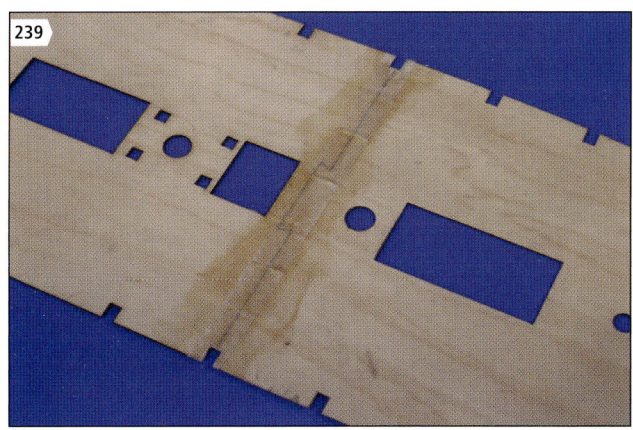

239
False upper gun deck parts are designed as two halves that must be assembled end to end. A strip of tracing paper was glued along the bottom of the joint to reinforce it.

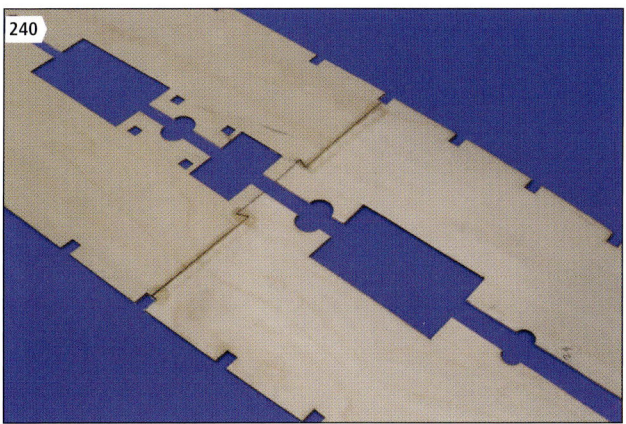

240
The assembled false upper gun deck is split into two lengthwise to aid assembly into the hull.

241
The false upper gun deck is glued in place using a combination of tape, clamps and lead weights to hold it against the bulkhead tops.

Assembly of the Hull Framework

The bulkheads were test fitted again to ensure that their bottoms met the rabbet. The bow and stern bulkheads were pre-bevelled using a bench mounted oscillating spindle sander. Beware that it is easy to remove too much with power tools, and ensure that the shape of the bulkhead is not changed. Like the *Speedy*, the bulkheads at the bow and stern are closely spaced together. One at a time, starting from the bow and working back, the bulkheads were glued into their respective slots. This kit uses a thick deck piece to lock all of the bulkheads at 90° to the false keel (Figure 235). The kit also supplied a thick strip of wood (I cut mine from a scrap piece of 1/8in thick ply) that feeds through the bulkhead slots for strength and to prevent the hull warping over time. This strip also represents the lower gundeck. Holes are drilled into the strip later to accommodate a dummy gun barrel that protrudes from the hull if the lower gundeck lids are modelled open. Once the glued-up framework has set, all the bulkhead bevels are checked with a strip of wood and faired. The bow area required a filler block to support the planking as it rounds the bow. This was made with scrap balsa shown in Figure 236 to 238. The keel and stem parts were attached to the false keel with glue and dowelled in place for a strong joint.

The Upper Gundeck

The first deck to be added to the framework is the false upper gundeck which comes split into forward and aft halves (Figure 239). A sheet of wax paper is laid onto a flat surface. Wood glue is applied to the edges of the parts and the assembly laid upside down on the wax paper. Wipe away any excess glue that oozes out of the joint. Lay wax paper over the assembly and weight down to ensure it lies flat. When the glue has cured, remove the top piece of wax paper and reinforce the joint with a strip of tracing paper. The thinness of the tracing paper does not add any appreciable thickness to the deck, even if the reinforced joint falls on a deck beam. On test fitting, the false deck was found to be difficult to slip over the bulkhead extensions. The solution was to split the deck lengthwise into right- and left-hand halves (Figure 240). In this way it was much easier to slide the false deck into place around bulkhead extensions as opposed to having to go over them.

The kit instructions indicate that the two false deck halves should be planked *prior* to final fitting on the hull framework. In a word – *don't*. The reason is that water in PVA glue used to plank the deck will curl it, making it hard to lay down neatly over the framework. Moreover, a fully planked deck can't be pinned down flat because that would leave unsightly holes in your planking. Thirdly, when both planked halves are fitted to the framework it is very difficult to get a nice neat join along the centre. The human eye and brain look for consistency and flowing forms, and any variation from that will stick out like a sore thumb. As such, it is best to glue and pin down the false deck to the framework before commencing deck planking. In this way the most visible parts of the planking down the centre of the deck will be neat and clean because the planks will cover the joint. This is at the cost of it being a little fiddly to plank the area closest to the hull sides because you have to manoeuvre your fingers around the bulkhead extensions.

Test fit the false deck and ensure that it lays flat. If any bumps

242 Only the centre of the deck is planked. The openings mark the location of the bitts, capstan and masts.

are detected, sand the top of the bulkhead until it does. The false decks are attached by brushing a generous amount of PVA onto the bulkhead tops and sliding both halves of the false deck into place. Move the deck around until both halves meet neatly in the centre and then pin them to the bulkhead tops. Start the pinning at the centre and move outwards across the bulkhead. Use weights to ensure full contact between the false deck and the top of the bulkheads. Weights can be anything from fishing sinkers to empty jam jars filled with water (1 litre of water weighs 1 kilogram). Tape and clamps can be used to pull down the deck edges onto the bulkhead tops (Figure 241).

This brings us to a decision point - how much of this deck should be planked? Many modellers will routinely plank the entire deck but a lot of this deck will not be seen because it is covered over by subsequent decks. What can be seen is just through the deck hatches or obliquely through open gunports, but because I decided to close all the gunports only a fraction of this deck need be finished and fitted out.

243 The upper gun deck area planked and all the openings cut out. Marking the deck with the shift of the butts beforehand ensured the plank ends lined up across the deck.

This meant that only the areas between bulkhead #4 to #10 will be planked, with the shift of the butts and trennels only being put in between bulkheads #5 and #9 because this area is directly visible from the openings in the deck above. Being a British ship, plank length and width is easily calculated from C Nepean Longridge's book *Anatomy of Nelson's Ships*. Given that Longridge's model is scaled to 1/48 and *Vanguard* scaled 1/72, the dimensions in Longridge's book need to be divided by 1.5. If a typical deck plank 20 feet long in 1/48 scale is 5 inches long, dividing this by 5in/1.5 yields a plank length of 3.33in or 85.5mm. The plank width using Longridge's model is thus calculated then at ⅛in or 3mm wide in 1/72 scale. A four-shift pattern is typical of larger warships, and again using Longridge's measurements the length of the first plank of each row of planking is shown in the table below to establish the correct shift.

Length of First Plank of Each Row

Plank Number	1/48 Scale Length Inches	1/72 Scale Length Inches	1/72 Scale Length Rounded mm
1	5	3.33	85
2	2	1.33	34
3	4	2.67	68
4	1	0.67	17
5	3	2.00	51
6	5	3.33	85
7	2	1.33	34
8	4	2.67	68

Note too that none of the planks will need to be joggled into the margin plank on this deck because the planked area does not extend to the curved bow where joggling will be necessary.

Armed with a bundle of planks cut from a sheet of 1/8in basswood, planking began along the centre of the deck and working outwards (Figure 242). In this area, you will likely have to plank between openings for gratings, masts, capstans and bitts. These openings will break up the shift pattern so it is simpler to lay full length 85mm planks for these rows. When you start to plank an area that has no interruptions then the shift pattern is adhered to. The plank ends are darkened with a rub of a HB pencil to simulate caulking. One tip when laying planks on such a wide expanse of deck is to draw the shift of the butts on the false deck before planking to ensure that all of the plank ends line up in a row across the deck. If you rely on just plank lengths to determine the plank butts, there will be a number that will not line up because errors will creep in and throw off the alignment. When the plank ends are drawn on the deck, you can trim the plank length slightly so its end falls in perfect alignment (Figure 243).

With the deck planked, it's time to add the trennel details. For the *Vanguard*, with the planks being just 3mm wide only a single trennel pattern will fit. The deck was lightly marked in pencil with transverse lines falling along the shift of the butts (Figure 244). Drill a small hole in the centre of the transverse lines (0.75mm dia.) in each plank, and where two planks meet, a hole at each end (Figure 245). Traditionally, the holes are plugged with slivers of bamboo drawn to the correct diameter through a drawplate or with a trennel

SEMI-SCRATCH DOUBLE PLANK-ON-BULKHEAD

244

Transverse lines are drawn across the deck where the plank butt ends meet and holes are drilled for the trennals.

246

The deck is sanded allowing the dust to fill the holes drilled in the deck. A soft brush was used to gently brush away any excess sanding dust on the deck.

247

A coat of matt acrylic polyurethane brings out the trennal and seam detail. The different colour of the wood planks is also highlighted, making for a realistic looking deck.

245

A close up of the deck drilled out for trennals.

cutter. Sharpened birch toothpicks are also an option. The pointed ends of round toothpicks are inserted into the hole with a little glue and snipped off. Wooden trennals are a must for larger scale models (1/48 scale and up) or those of the Admiralty variety in keeping with the style of model.

For smaller scale models like *Vanguard*, you can fill the holes with coloured latex wood filler used in furniture or hardwood floor repair that will contrast slightly against the deck. However, I use the 'sand and seal' method. Once all of the holes are drilled the deck is sanded smooth. The key is not to vacuum up the sanding dust but instead leave it on the deck and let it fall into the holes. The sanding dust is next compacted into the holes with your fingers and a soft brush is used to gently remove the excess dust from the deck (Figure 246). The deck is then wiped over with a damp cloth where the water helps fix the dust into the holes, shrinks the holes by swelling the wood fibres, and raises the wood grain over the deck. Once the deck is dry you will be able to feel the raised grain with your finger and see how the trennel holes have swelled closed. Any empty holes can be filled by sanding the area again and pushing in the dust. The deck can now

248

The inner bulwarks are planked and painted red. A waterway made of pre-painted strip wood is glued to the bottom of the bulwark against the deck.

be sealed with a clear matt acrylic polyurethane coating or a clear sanding sealer that will: 1) soak into the filled holes that darkens the dust slightly to provide a nice subtle contrast to the rest of the deck; and 2) stiffens the grain on the deck ready for final sanding (Figure 247). The inner bulwarks are planked next and once again pre-paint the lowest plank the interior colour, in this case 'red ochre' (Figure 248).

Forecastle and Quarterdeck

The next deck to be installed is the combination forecastle and quarterdeck. This is a one-piece part that has a large rectangular hole in the centre. The sides of the rectangle are a gangway between the two decks called the 'Marines Walk'. In this case, the false deck is provided in four parts: a port and starboard side split into fore and aft pieces. A triangular tab and cut-out system is provided to help you align the deck, but despite these alignment aids, having a piece in four parts is a source of misalignment, and this is increased if there is any slackness between the tabs and cut-outs. It is best to assemble the false deck into separate port and starboard halves before fitting each to the hull as before with tracing paper reinforcements. The deck beams are glued to the bulkheads (Figure 249) to support the deck.

Test fit the port and starboard halves of the false deck to the deck beams and trim the slots as necessary for a good fit. The tops of the deck beams might need some sanding to ensure the false deck lies flat and smooth across their tops. Check that the holes for the masts or other fittings are aligned between the two decks. Once the fit of the upper deck is to your satisfaction, mark the centre of the deck beams on the false deck. Drill small holes, just slightly smaller than the brass nails used to hold the deck down at the deck edges (Figure 250). Do not glue it in place now because there is still much work to be completed on the upper gundeck first. We are just test fitting the forecastle/quarterdeck parts to make its installation easier later on and to double check what is visible on the upper gundeck below through the Marine's Walk.

Gunport Patterns

The gunport patterns (Figure 251) are like those we used on *Speedy* except that they are larger and more complicated to fit. As before, the patterns are soaked in hot water for a few hours and when pliable are offered up to the hull. It is recommended that the patterns are fitted from bow to stern and keep adjusting their location on the hull until their positions are correct from the plans. Pick a few of the gunports to serve as reference points and continually check their location with the decks and any other convenient landmarks like a bulkhead edge. Once satisfied you have located them in the correct position, mark the lower edge of the pattern on the bulkheads to serve as a reference point. The wet patterns are tacked in place with pins that will hold them tight against the bulkheads. Drive in the pins all the way. Most instructions say the pins should be pushed in only about halfway so they can be pulled out easily later. However, the reality is that you often have to drive the pins home to keep the pattern or plank in place. The hammered-in pins are easily removed using an old pair of pointed plastic sprue cutters. The pointed tips make it very easy to get below the pinhead by digging into the wood just enough to raise the pin to be pulled out completely with a pair of pliers. Leave the patterns on until dry and once they are removed from the hull framework they will be moulded to the hull's shape. The moulded patterns are glued to the bulkheads and held in place

249

The quarterdeck beams fixed in place. Similar beams are fitted under the forecastle.

250

The quarterdeck/forecastle false deck piece is temporarily pinned to the top of the deck beams. The cut-out area defined by the Marine's Walk is known as the *waist* of the ship.

251

The gunport patterns are moulded and glued in place to the hull. At the bow the patterns had to be slit to relieve some bulging that prevented the pattern from lying flat against the filler blocks.

with pins using the same holes, ensuring they go back in exactly the same spot until the glue dries.

It is not unusual for a gunport opening to fall on the edge of one or two bulkheads. If this is correct (some kits will note this or show it on the plans) the bulkhead is usually chiselled out to accommodate the gun barrel later; or the gunport can simply be modelled closed. If you are unsure this is correct, double check with kit plans that you had not simply located the pattern a little too far forward or backwards. In many instances the gunport patterns might be a little overlong so the modeller can adjust the length that suits the peculiarities of his or her hull, and may need a little trimming or shifting to get the patterns to locate properly. The gunport patterns on my model were laser-cut by myself to replace those missing from the kit. Despite the care I took, my patterns were not quite the correct size and at least one curved edge needed to have a few slits cut into them to get them to lie properly on the framework.

The permanently affixed gunport pattern represents the first half of the hull's first planking. In a full kit, the remainder of the hull is planked with basswood or lime strip. My gift of parts contained no planking but I did find in my workshop a quantity of 5mm wide by 2mm thick tanganyika strips scavenged from modeller friends who did not want to use it on their kits. This is a fairly hard wood and a little brittle but does bend nicely after being well soaked. The strips were thickness sanded to 1.5mm to match the thickness of the gunport patterns. When I ran out of tanganyika I used some scrap basswood (Figure 252) to complete the planking. I am a bit of a magpie and I think this wood has been in my shop for over 15 years.

Our primary goal with the first planking is to sheath the hull framework with as few bumps, hollows, and gaps as possible. This will be hard on a ship like *Vanguard* because her curves are all very severe with a bluff bow, high transom, and pronounced tumblehome. These curves, unlike the fairly straight hull of the *Cutty Sark* and *Speedy* require the planks to be bent and twisted to a much greater degree. This bending and curving is induced by soaking the planks in very hot water and bending them on a heated planking iron. CA glue is not suitable for a damp plank so it is necessary to fix the planking with PVA wood glue held in place with pins that are removed once the glue has cured and the wood dry.

The first plank under the gunport pattern will require little tapering but will need a broad curve bent into it to fit around the bow. The plank end will slip into the bow rabbet and I hold the plank securely while glue and pins fix the rest of the plank to each bulkhead. The same plank is laid on the other side of the ship. The next plank is offered up and by eye you can see where the planks need to be curved. Induce the curve and test fit the plank to ensure it seats easily against the one above, and apply glue to the back of the plank and edge and tack in place. Wipe away any excess glue on the surface, and wherever you can, use your fingers to smear glue across the planks on the inside to ensure they are firmly glued to the bulkhead and each other.

In general, when planking a hull this size, multiple shorter pieces of wood that join at a bulkhead are much easier to taper, bend and fix than longer or whole pieces as we used on *Speedy*. As you work down the hull, the degree of taper increases at the bow but at the stern, especially when they start to run under the counter, the planks will splay outwards (Figure 253). Let the plank run its natural course to the rudder post and the resulting triangular gap is filled with a stealer.

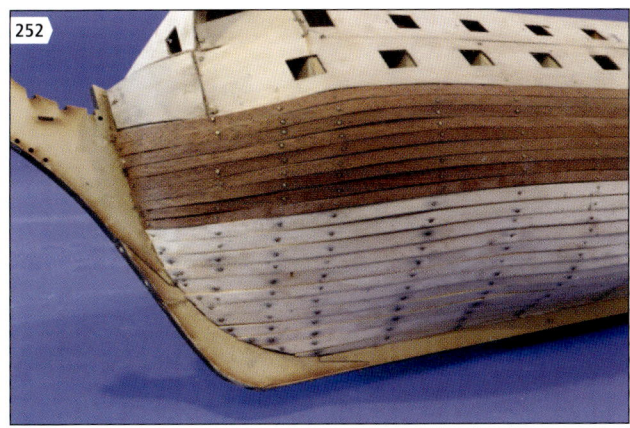

252

The rather messy first planking around the bow area. Being semi-scratch-built I used whatever wood I had on hand to plank the hull. The planks were glued and tacked down with pins to ensure they lay right against the bulkheads. The rabbet cut into the false keel has paid dividends because the planks fit neatly into the stem and keel. There is a nasty bump to the planking suggesting that a bulkhead was cut to the wrong size or shape somewhere. When I ran a plank along the bulkhead this problem did not show up so I am really at a loss as to the cause of the problem.

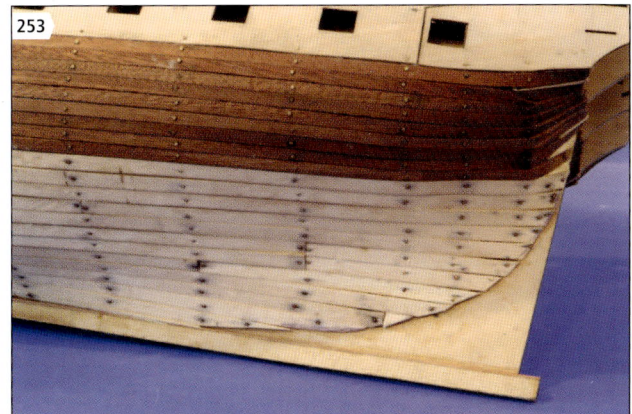

253

A view of the first planking at the stern. The planks were taken just to the bearding line instead of all the way to the rudder post to reduce the amount of sanding and problems experienced on *Speedy*. There are significant gaps in the planking as it rounds up under the transom, and the wood does not flow smoothly but rather at an abrupt angle. In retrospect, the bulkheads in this area should have had greater bevels cut into them.

The first planking can look quite rough when completed. Despite our best attempts, you will find gaps between planks, some of the tapers will be greater on some planks than the other, and even different numbers of planks on each side might be used to close up the hull. There will be pins sticking out, glue marks, and dips where the planks sag between bulkheads, or bumps because a bulkhead was not sufficiently bevelled. It can be quite a discouraging sight but don't

254
The first planking has been sanded down and any dips filled with two-part automotive filler. From this perspective the complex and beautiful lines of the ship can be appreciated.

let it get to you. With the hull carcass fully dried it is ready to be sanded. A hand-held random orbit sander makes quick work of smoothing down the planking. Again, the key is not to over-sand and look for obvious hollows caused by planking that has sunk between bulkheads. These dips are filled with two-part automotive filler, and when cured faired into the rest of the hull with the power sander (Figure 254). You will know when the hull is smooth and all hollows are filled if a long thin strip of wood lies flat along the length of the hull.

Wales

The location of the main wale's lower edge is plotted from the plans. Unlike *Speedy*, there are no handy etched marks to denote the location. Pick landmarks, such as the bottom of gunports and if there are no convenient landmarks in which to measure, create some. For example, drill a little hole through the first planking at some known point, say the top of a bulkhead, or at the location of the false deck. These little holes will give you a known datum point on the plans to

255
A wooden batten helps locate the main wale.

measure from. It will not be unusual for the plan to yield a slightly different location for the wale than you find on your hull. Move the wale location marks around until it 'looks right' when viewed from all angles. Use a narrow piece of masking tape to align the marks and keep adjusting the tape until it all looks correct. Take a break and when you've finished your tea and biscuit, have a look again with a set of fresh eyes and adjust if necessary. Once you are entirely satisfied, take a strip of wood to act as a batten (Figure 255). Soak and bend the wood to follow the tape and tack onto the hull. The width of the wale (top edge) can now be marked and beware that the wale is sometimes narrower at the bow and very gradually widens to the stern so check the plans to see if this is the case on your model. Note too that the *Vanguard*'s wale does not follow the sheer of the gundeck and so the gunports will be cut through the wales.

Marking, Cutting and Lining Gunports

The hull is now ready to be pierced for the gunports. Many kit designs, especially older ones, do not provide a gunport pattern like the *Speedy* or *Vanguard* kits and the entire hull framework is simply planked over. In this case you have to locate and mark each one of the ports from the plans. However, this is a little more complicated than marking the wale despite using the same general method from datum points. This is because the gunport must also sit in a particular relationship to the deck the gun sits up on. If the gunport is located too high in relation to the deck, the gun mounted on its carriage will not fit, and if the gunport is located too low we are faced with the same result. An additional consideration is the thickness of the deck planking. If the deck has not yet been planked then the thickness of the plank to be used must be included in the calculation.

To locate the gunports in relationship to the deck, datum holes were drilled out at the level of the deck so you know exactly where the deck lays when looked at from the hull exterior. The gunport lining itself is made from 1mm thick strip so the opening for the gunport must be 1mm wider all around than shown on the plans because they only show the finished dimensions. After marking in the location of the gunport opening in pencil, cut the opening by chain drilling (start at the four corners) and cut away with a sharp scalpel. On *Vanguard* all of this work has been done for you by the gunport patterns. This hole in the hull planking (or gunport pattern as appropriate) exposes the backside of the inner bulwark planking that will also need to be cut through. This work takes finesse because you must ensure: 1) the inner bulwark opening is square and the same size as the opening in the hull planking, 2) is directly in line with the hull opening and not angled upwards or downwards, and 3) not to splinter the wood and damage the inner bulwark planking. This is accomplished by taping a spirit level to the body of the drill to check the tool's orientation. Position the drill so that the bubble is level (Figure 256). To minimize damage to the inner bulwark opening, cover the inner bulwark with masking tape before drilling. The tape will hold the wood in place when the drill breaks through (Figure 257). The edges of the ports are cleaned up and trued with a wide flat file. The file used should be of high-quality crosscut pattern with both a safe (smooth) edge and a cutting (serrated) edge on the other side. The cutting edge can be used to clean up corners, and when the smooth edge is up against another edge it causes no damage if you are trying to clean up one edge of the port only. A spirit level can be taped to the file

SEMI-SCRATCH DOUBLE PLANK-ON-BULKHEAD

256
A spirit level is attached to the top of the rotary tool with double faced tape. The level will ensure that the holes drilled through the inner bulwark are square and level on both sides of the hull.

257
The four corners are drilled out to locate the gunport. Chain drilling between the corners will make cutting the gunport out easier. Tape was applied to the inner bulwark before drilling to reduce splintering when the gunport is cut out.

or sanding stick handle to ensure each stroke of the tool is straight and level (Figure 258).

The linings are installed by fitting the sides first and then the tops and bottoms. The wood stock used for the lining should be slighter wider than required so it overhangs the inside of the inner bulwark and the outer hull (Figure 259). When gluing in the lining don't be mean with the glue. Make sure they are glued in solidly and when dry, sand the overhangs of the sills flush with the planking and fill any gaps with wood filler and sand smooth. If the ports require an inset sill, they are installed the same way except that the front edge is set back and the back side is allowed to overhang the gunport. This overhang is sanded back flush with the inner bulwark. The method I described for linings and sills is a little tedious because each of the four sides are installed individually. To speed up the job and ensure greater uniformity of the gunports, you can glue up four lengths of wood (say about 1ft in length) into a square tube whose inside dimensions are the finished size of the gunport. Slices can be cut

258
The gunport is trimmed out and a flat file squares up the openings.

259
The lining is added to the gunports. These gunports do not have sills. If sills are required, they are put in after the second planking and are set back from the hull side by 1mm.

260
The linings have been trimmed flush with the inner bulwark and outer hull. A flat file will square up the openings, and some filler will be required to correct any gaps.

from the square tube and glued into the gunport opening which fits a full lining and/or sill in one go. Either way, once the linings have been installed the ports may look a little rough, but your main concern is that they are all square and the same size (Figure 260). Paint and the second planking will cover up the filler.

STERN GALLERIES

Stern galleries are a critical part of a large ship. Despite being complicated at first glance, careful construction and forward thinking make building the galleries one of the most enjoyable aspects of the model. The mantra when building the stern galleries is 'test, check, test, recheck, and bevel!'

The *Vanguard* kit contains several laser-cut parts that make up the structure of the galleries. They may be pre-cut, but they still require repeated test fitting, bevelling and shaping for everything to come together. A start is made by temporarily pinning in place the stern gallery facia (Figure 261). The facia will need a little gentle bending to accommodate the curve of the stern. Your hull may show a little difference from the plans so be prepared to move it around a bit until its placement looks correct. You may find that one side is a little high

261

The stern gallery facia is test fitted and tacked (not glued) into place. The facia must lie along the hull sides and transom neatly, if not, sand them until it does.

or low in relation to the main wale location. It is not fatal issue, but one to be aware of that will have to be compensated for somewhere else such as modifying the depth of the side galleries later. Again, it is all about keeping your eye open for these issues and thinking about how to compensate for them.

The next task is to locate the quarter galleries on each side of the ship (Figure 262). The side, or quarter, gallery formers are often thick pieces of ply but in the *Vanguard* they are made of three pieces of 1mm thick ply that are laminated together with glue. This is actually helpful because building up the formers in layers takes a lot of the guesswork out of the angles and makes cutting in the bevels a lot easier and less prone to over- or under-sanding. Begin with the first former, the one that forms the middle of the lamination which is first offered up against the hull and stern facia. For it to fit snugly up against the facia, where it touches the facia must be bevelled to accommodate the fascia's angle. The side against the hull is also bevelled to accommodate the slope of the hull side. Being a thin piece of ply a few swipes from the sanding stick cuts in the bevels

262

The first layer of side gallery formers are test fitted and glued in place.

263

The top and bottom layers of the side gallery formers are glued in place.

264

Side gallery formers are bevelled, ready for the side galley facia pieces.

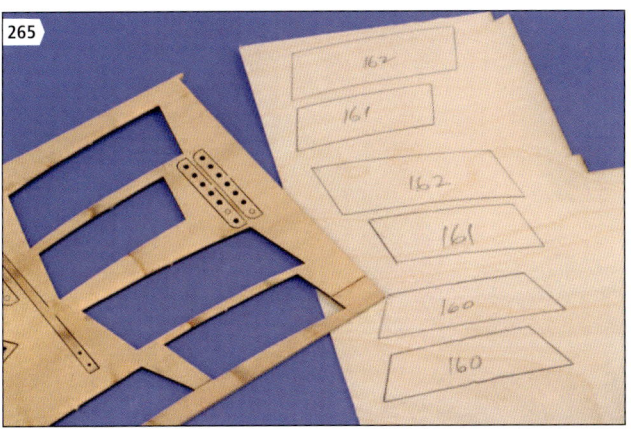

265
The kit-supplied side gallery fascia snapped at the window frames when they were bent to the curves of the side gallery formers. The kit's cut-outs were used to trace out new parts on flexible thin ply.

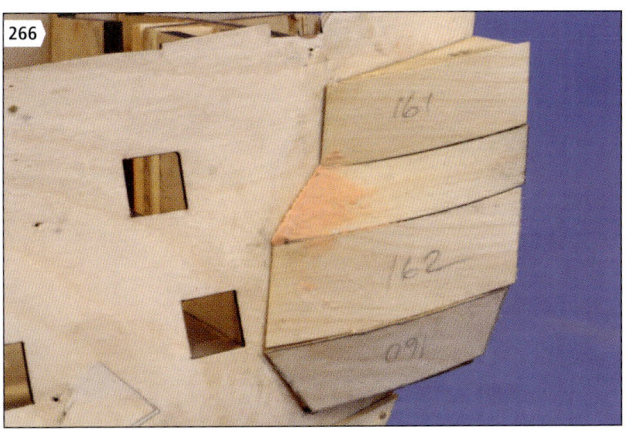

266
The scratch-built side gallery facias were attached to the side gallery formers and hull. A little two-part automotive putty was required to refine the correct outline of the side galleries.

with ease. The former can now be glued to the hull but not to the facia. Repeat the process with the top layer of the side gallery former. Lay it on top of the middle piece, sand in the bevels and glue to the hull and to the previously installed former. Given the slope of the stern facia, the front end of this former will sit slightly further back in relation to the previously installed former, and the side slightly inset. Repeat again with the bottom former, and glue into place (Figure 263). Note too that the front end of the bottom former will sit a little ahead of the middle former and the side will sit outboard and together these thin formers have now established the angle of the front and side of the formers to be faired by sanding (Figure 264). If your side gallery former is a single thick piece of wood, it must be bevelled all in one go. Fit it like it is the middle slice of the side gallery. You could use a kit-supplied thick former as a pattern to cut three copies out of thin ply so they can be laminated as described above and avoid any risk of over- or under-sanding.

The quarter gallery formers are skinned with shaped pieces of thin ply. Be aware that there will be a lot of trimming of the ply parts *in situ* to get them to fit because the parts supplied are often just flat blanks that have to be curved – often in two dimensions – and bevelled to fit. If your parts don't fit as well as you like, you can always cut a new one from scrap wood to have another go. On the kit parts I received, the side gallery facia were laser-cut from brittle 1.5mm walnut ply that did not take too kindly to being soaked and curved around the side gallery formers by snapping in two. The carrier sheet for the kit parts was used to trace out new pieces from 1mm flexible birch ply sheet. I did not cut the windows into the facia before fitting because the original parts snapped on the window frames (Figure 265). The new fascia was then soaked and curved to fit the formers and glued in place (Figure 266). Without the pre-cut windows the part bent a lot more smoothly and fitted the formers neatly with no obvious bumps or kinks. Any gaps between the fascia pieces were filled with a little wood filler and sanded smooth.

Second Planking

With the side gallery fascia in place, the hull shape defined, and the location of the main wale marked with a batten, it is finally time to start the second planking. Although the double planked design helps the modeller lay neat planking, on a large hull a great deal of careful fitting and shaping of planks lies ahead and when you take your time, it can become a very relaxing process. Embrace and immerse yourself in that feeling and remember that planking is not just a mechanical process, but also an emotional one that comes with the shaping and bending of natural materials. When they lay neatly on the hull, capturing each curve, and fitting just right you will get a sense of pride and accomplishment that no other activity can impart. And when they don't fit, solving the problem is equally fulfilling.

Preparation for the second planking is as important as actually laying the planks. The first consideration is whether or not you are painting the model. If you are building an unpainted model, the planking will have to be prototypical in nature, which means laid in scale lengths and widths; having to start at the keel because this is where planking of real ships always begins; and you can only really use a nice hardwood, such as pear, cherry, maple or box. If you are painting your model, you have a lot more options because paint covers up a lot of simplifications and model making expedients. On a painted model, it's up to you to use scale planking if you wish but it is not necessary as most of the joints will be hidden. Where the planking begins can be at the keel or just under the wale, and the choice of wood is wide open. Personally, I prefer to use a hardwood because it takes paint well, or a softer wood like bass or lime because it is simply easier to cut and bend and readily available in pre-cut strips. These choices represent the extremes of the continuum and is dictated by the materials to hand, experience of the modeller and what overall effect you are trying to achieve. The walnut typically provided in kits is my least favourite because it splinters when cut, has a coarse grain, and I find it hard to bend unless well soaked and bent with heat.

The decision to paint and weather the model released me from having to use scale planking and instead I opted for easy to handle 1.0mm thick by 5mm wide planks cut to 6in long. Planking would start under the wale simply because it is easier to start the planking process with a couple of rows of pretty much untapered planks. Starting from the keel would have meant shaping a *garboard*

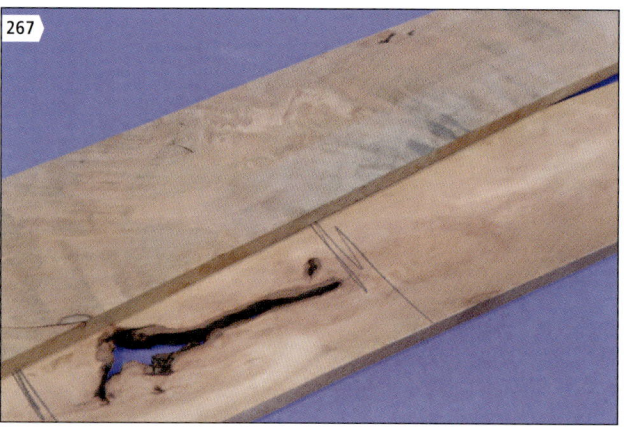

267

Some well dried pear for the second planking. The wood stock (6in wide by 1.4in thick) was left over from another project and was heavily figured rendering it useless for a bright finished model but more than adequate for a model that will be painted.

268

Wooden planks cut for the second planking. The planking is not to scale.

269

The planked lower transom.

plank (the bottom-most plank that fits into keel) and planking upwards whereas I find it easier to work downwards. Finally, the choice of wood was whatever I had to hand. In my shop I had several boards of heavily figured pear that would be covered up under a coat of paint (Figures 267 and 268).

The first area to be planked is the lower transom under the stern galleries (Figure 269). Examine and familiarize yourself with the shape of the area to be planked. The area has a gentle downwards curve, and is pierced for the rudder. With a tick strip, measure out the depth of the area to be planked and see how many 1mm by 5mm wide planks will fit there. It won't be a round number (in my case 5.8 planks, so 6 planks, slightly trimmed down will cover the area nicely). A strip of 1mm by 5mm planking was trimmed to 4.8mm on the table saw. The first plank is laid starting at the top of the transom as a full-length piece. It has to be soaked and bent to follow the curve of the transom. Cut the plank over-length and allow to overhang the sides of the transom. Once satisfied with the degree of curve, put a few dabs of thick CA on the back and apply to the hull, pressing down over the length of the plank to further spread the glue. Repeat with the next plank and when you get to the hole for the rudder post, you can start to lay the planks in two pieces just slightly overlapping the hole. Continue planking until the area is completely planked over. Some white glue can be thinned down with water and brushed into the joins between the planks and allowed to dry solid. The ends of the planks are then trimmed off to the side of the hull, and the hole of the rudder post trimmed and sanded out.

If your model is to be bright finished, trim as above but next mark out the location of the trennels. These locations are marked in pencil - make sure the lines follow the location of actual ship's timbers. Once satisfied, drill a hole for the trennel and plug with a piece of cut down bamboo skewer dipped in glue and cut flush. Continue this work until all the trennels are installed and once dry, sand down the area smooth. Under a coat of oil the beauty of the wood and trennels will reveal themselves.

270

A tricky area to understand on a large ship of the line is how the hull planks meet the transom. The side planks run past the transom planking but the planking that curves under the stern is cut flush as shown. A small stealer will need to be fitted into the remaining triangular space.

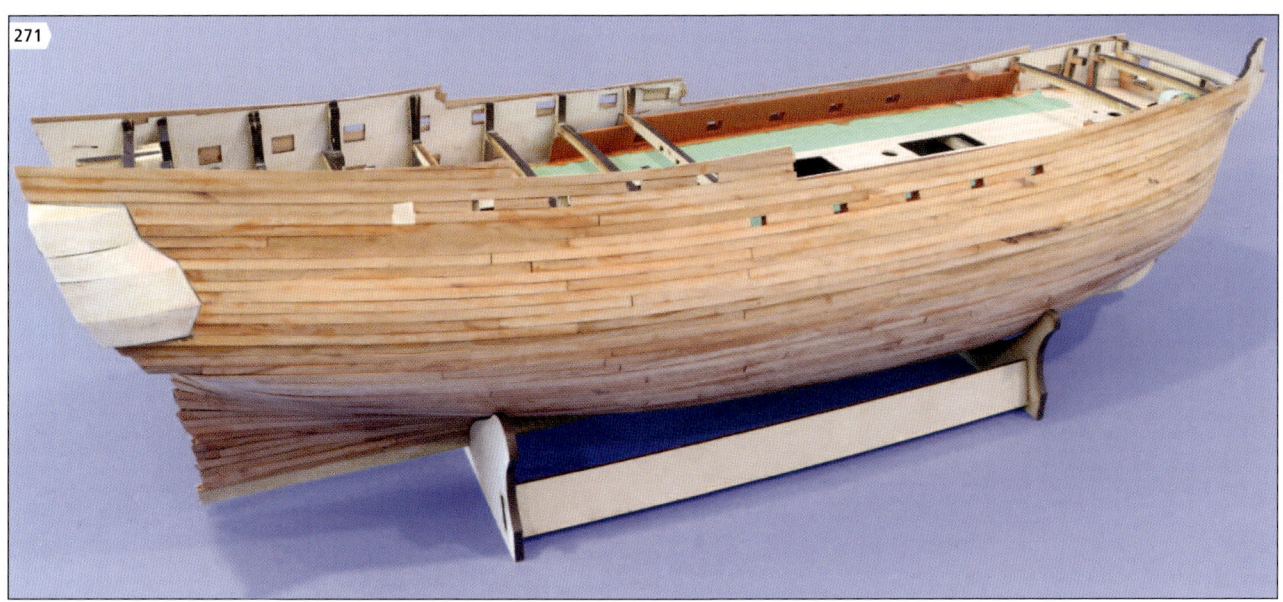

271
The second planking completed. The planks were taken right over the gunports because I am modelling the ports closed. For the open gunports, the planking was taken to just over the opening, allowing some space for a cutting tool to get inside to trim out the planks and square the ports.

PLANKING THE HULL SIDES

With a tick strip placed around midships you can get an idea of how many 1mm by 5mm planks are required. The first plank is fitted under the main wale batten and was laid from bow to stern and the remainder of the planking needs little additional comment. A couple of areas that need careful work is where the hull plank meets the transom (Figure 270) and, unique to my model which has all the gunports are modelled closed, the planks can run right over the gunport openings. *Vanguard* has a few unlidded gunports in the waist and the planking was laid between them, allowing the planks to overlap the ports but leaving enough space to get a knife and file into for final sizing (Figure 271). The second planking continues right up to the quarter galleries. The plank ends are cut and bevelled to fit snugly against them. A modelling trick I use on a painted model is to stop the planking just shy of the side gallery. Masking tape is laid around the gallery and the gap filled with two-part automotive filler (Figure 272). This filler closes the gap and provides a very neat joint to the quarter galleries.

272
Note how the planks were taken to the side galleries. Normally one would take the planks right up to the edge and bevel the ends to obtain a tight join between them. Alternatively, tape is laid around the side gallery to define the shape required. Two-part automotive filler is applied and when it just starts to harden the tape is peeled off leaving a clean line. If you allow the filler to fully cure before removing the tape, the tape will tear and be very difficult to remove (if at all).

273
Spackling compound was used to fill any slight gaps in the second planking. The model was taken outside and a power sander used to smooth off the hull. For this operation I donned a N95 dust mask and a shop coat to keep the dust out and off of me. After sanding, any dust was swept up and the area is washed down with a garden hose to keep the dust from getting into my neighbour's lungs.

274

The main and upper wales are added and spackling compound was used to fill any gaps. The rudder post has been attached and faired into the hull planking. A groove was cut into the rudder post as we did on *Cutty Sark* to accommodate the rudder's rounded-over front edge.

275

The side gallery windows were laid out with tape. Chain drilling started the opening and the window squared up with a sharp knife and file.

As before, a power sander will make quick work of smoothing out the wooden planking and any filler used to fill in gaps (Figure 273). As always, use a finer grit of paper and handle with a light touch. Pay particular attention to the area of the ship's side above the waterline because this area is in full sight and may require a little more remedial work. Under the waterline your focus should be on a smooth and flowing surface because it will form the base for the copper plating to be added next. A smooth and bump-free surface is key to a neat copper job.

The planks forming the wales are added (Figure 274) and any other openings should also be cut, such as the side gallery windows (Figure 275). The rudder post itself can be fitted and faired into the planking. At this point just the two gunports on the quarterdeck cannot be cut to size because it has not been completed. These ports will be addressed once the inner bulwark planking is finished (Figure 276). For multi-deck wooden sailing ships, building and painting happen at the same time and each deck, with all of its associated fittings, planking, cutting of ports happen in stages, one at a time like building a layer cake. A few coats of sanding sealer were applied

to the hull above the waterline and sanded smooth to start to build up an even and hard surface for paint that will come later on in the build. The upper gundeck's inner bulwarks were smoothed off and given a finish coat of red paint (Figure 277).

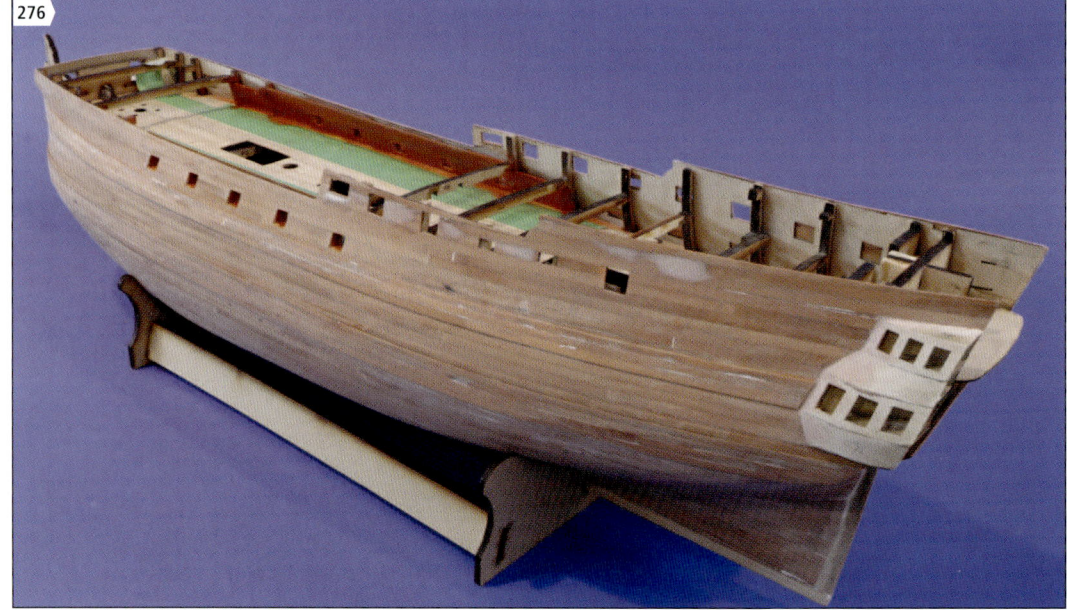

276

The second layer of planking sanded with most of the openings cut out.

SEMI-SCRATCH DOUBLE PLANK-ON-BULKHEAD

277
The inner bulwarks and gunports were given a final coat of red paint. The hull received a coat of non-filling sanding sealer to prepare the surface for paint.

278
Coppering the bow. On a bluff bowed ship the degree to which the plates want to sheer away from its row can be quite pronounced.

COPPERING

The waterline is marked as before and the hull just above the coppering is painted black. Remember to adjust the waterline at the bow and stern to overcome any sag caused by the curve of the hull. The *Vanguard* kit includes handed etched copper plates complete with nail head detail. The process is the same as *Speedy* and coppering follows the same rules. However, *Vanguard* is a much larger hull so as you lay a few rows of plates, stop and lay a strip of tape along the top edge of the previous row to see how far the next row will want to diverge upwards (Figure 278). The tape will delineate any areas that will have to be filled in later but mostly the tape will help ensure that the rows of copper will lay gracefully in a gentle sweep up the hull. It takes practice but you will over time and experience gain a sixth sense as to where the rows of copper will want to diverge. When the coppering was completed (Figure 279), the line of copper at the waterline was overlapped with a thin batten of wood.

279
The *Vanguard*'s coppering complete and any gaps touched up with copper paint. The size and shape of the hull made coppering time-consuming and at times a mind-numbing task. The copper is quite shiny and needs to be weathered.

WEATHERING THE COPPER

The weathered finish choice on *Vanguard* means that the copper plate must receive a significant patina. As we did before, a coat of matt clear polyurethane varnish was sprayed over the copper and allowed to dry. This will remove any shine and provide a tooth for the patina process. A wash of black and burnt umber oil paint was brushed on (Figure 280). A few coats were necessary to get the deep brown colour that was pleasing to my eye. Copper also turns green when exposed to salt water so I decided to add a 'verdigris' colour that ranges in shade from a bright green to a dark green. The simplest way to add this colour is with artist's verdigris oil paint. Verdigris and black oil paint are squeezed out on a palette and a little Liquin is mixed in (Figure 281). A wide soft brush picks up some of the verdigris and maybe a little black and this is daubed then brushed out over the hull (Figure 282). The key is to really brush the paint out so that you are left with a transparent green sheen over the copper (Figure 283).

280
A heavy wash of ivory black and burnt umber artist's oil was applied. After drying the wash was a little too heavy to my eye and a soft cloth wrapped around my index finger was used to wipe some of it off.

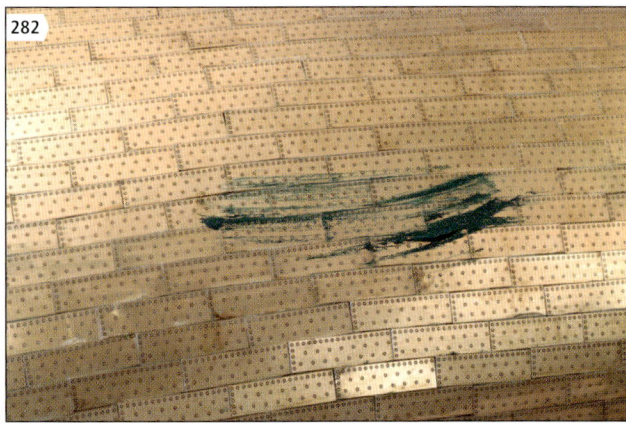

281
Verdigris and ivory black artist's oil colour is roughly mixed with a little Liquin oil paint medium.

282
The paint mixture is dabbed onto the hull.

283
The paint is brushed out with a wide soft brush leaving a green hue to the copper. You can add more or less verdigris and black as you desire. Keep it patchy to mimic the way Mother Nature works.

284
The completed verdigris finish. Compare this to the verdigris finish shown in Figure 179 achieved with patina solution.

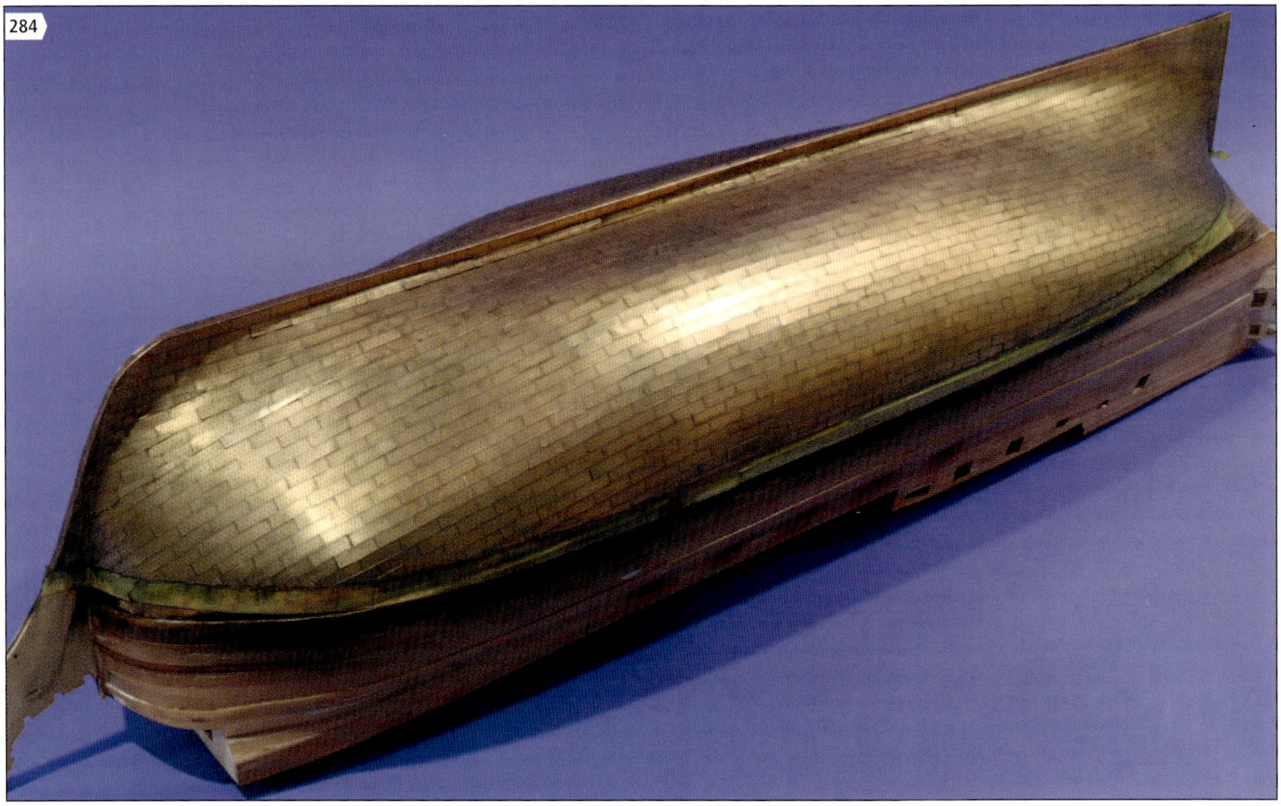

285
A close up of the verdigris finish at the bow. A coat of matt varnish dulls the copper to a realistic finish. The off-white specks on the copper plates are 'salt stains'. Overly thinned enamel polyurethane with white spirits has a tendency to dry chalky. I deliberately brushed this over the hull and allowed it to dry chalky to create the stains. Do this sparingly for the best effect.

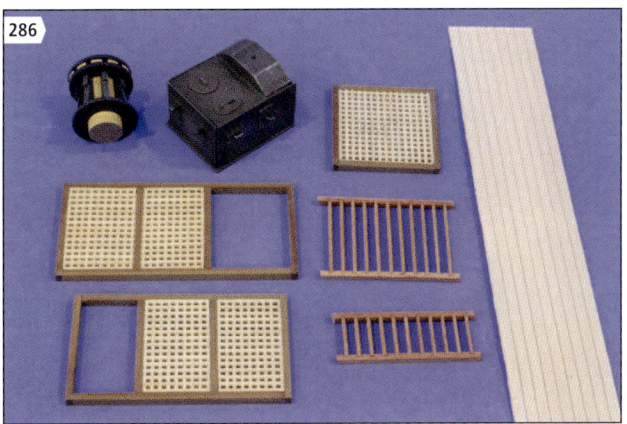

286
A few fittings made up and painted for the upper gun deck. Scale ladders and gratings were purchased so that a 1/72 matelot's feet would not fall through the gratings holes and the companionway ladder rungs were spaced so he can actually climb them without falling. Some scribed planking was used to line the foot of the companionway openings.

The verdigris and black mix should be concentrated around the copper at the waterline because that is where sea water and oxygen would mix and hasten the patina process on actual ships (Figure 284). When satisfied with the look, set the hull to dry out and protect the hull finish with a coat of matt varnish. One interesting aspect of enamel-based polyurethane like Humbrol Matt 49 is that when it is thinned out with ordinary household paint thinner, it dries clear but sometimes with patches of white (hence why a lot of people turn to acrylic or water-based varnishes – they dry clear). Ordinarily, this patchiness is unwanted but in this case, I deliberately used heavily thinned Humbrol Matt 49 to get the white patchiness to resemble salt build up and corrosion on metal (Figure 285).

COMPLETING THE UPPER GUNDECK

We now return to the upper gundeck. The process of building a multi-decked sailing ship is to build the hull to a certain level, lay the deck and fittings such as capstans, ladders, bitts and whatnot and the process continues with the next deck until all the decks are completed. The fittings are built up and painted as per the kit instructions. In my inherited kit, all of these parts were found and were duly assembled and painted (Figure 286). Fixing them to the deck required using brass pins so they were firmly attached to the deck. Should they come loose in future you would never be able to get them back in place with another deck in the way.

The first of the ship's guns need to be added at this time. The kit provides laser-cut wooden carriages and white metal barrels that are assembled and painted as outlined in the instruction booklet. Unfortunately, very few of the guns were found in my inherited kit. What I did have in my scrap box was a set of fully painted and assembled guns and carriages from the plastic 1/100 scale Heller *HMS Victory* kit (Figure 287). I scavenged these from a half-built model found at a jumble sale over 20 years ago and put them away in my scrap box. I repaired them, touched up the paint and gave them all a wash of dark brown in keeping with the 'weathered' finish I wanted for the model. The gun carriages – without barrels – were glued in place on the deck (Figure 288). The barrels would be mounted to their carriages later because at this point the barrels would have stuck out from the gunports making them vulnerable to damage as the rest of the outside hull was detailed and painted out. I also decided not to add any rigging to these guns simply because they would not be seen.

QUARTERDECK AND FORECASTLE

The next layer of the shipborne cake is added – the forecastle and quarterdeck. The respective false deck is now fixed permanently to the hull (Figure 289). One of the most interesting features of the quarterdeck is that screen bulkheads are fitted (Figures 290 and 291). The screens are built up in layers consisting of a base panel to which detailed panels are fitted and then the decorative elements such as

287
Plastic guns salvaged from Heller's 1/100 *HMS Victory* kit are a little undersized but I decided I could live with that.

288) The fittings and gun carriages (sans barrels) are fixed to the upper gun deck. The quarterdeck and forecastle deck beams have been painted black. The closed gunport lids can be seen glued to the hull.

289) The false quarter and forecastle deck is fixed permanently to the hull beams. Through the opening in the waist you can get an appreciation for how little of the upper gun deck can be seen.

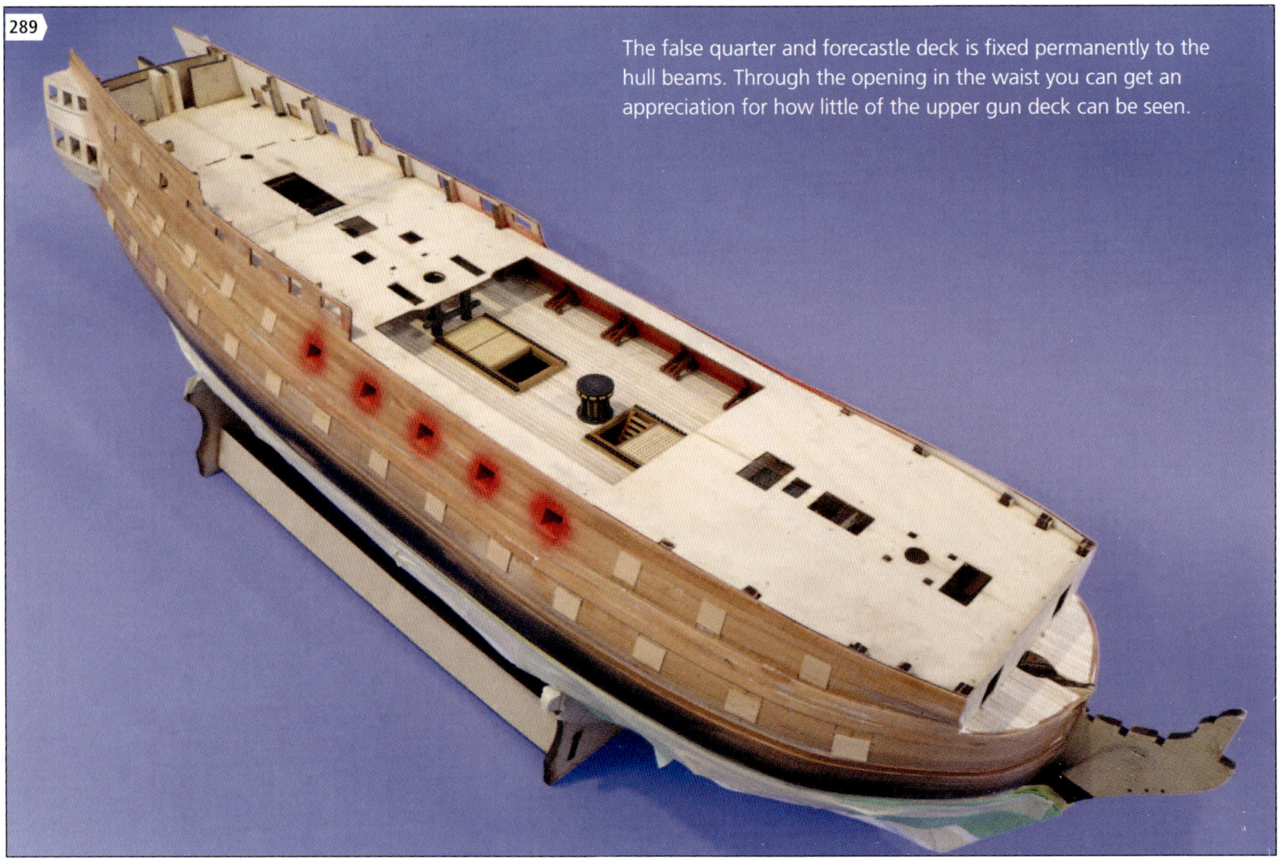

SEMI-SCRATCH DOUBLE PLANK-ON-BULKHEAD

290

The quarterdeck screens are painted and assembled before the deck is planked. The pillars are raised off the false deck by 1mm so the deck planks can slip underneath them. The pillar details were highlighted by a wash of black artist's oils.

291

The finished stern gallery screens. Scribed decking was used to plank the balconies.

pillars and window frames attached. The natural temptation of a modeller would be to paint and build these screens up as one unit and fix to the hull as a single unit. Don't! The screens have to be bent slightly to fit into the hull and this bending will cause the layers of detail to fly off with a soul destroying 'ping'. Instead, you build up each layer *in situ* on the hull. Pre-paint all the parts and install them on the ochre painted base, then the black painted panels, then the ochre painted pillars and then the white painted window frames.

The quarterdeck and forecastle decks are highly visible to the eye and so properly planking the deck is required (Figures 292 and 293). I used a four-butt shift in this scale; the plank lengths were 120mm, 90mm, 60mm, and 30mm. A proper waterway was fitted against the bulwarks and a long single plank called the 'king plank' was first laid down the centre to keep all subsequent planks in line. On this deck the curve of the hull at the bow requires that the plank ends be joggled into the waterway. The deck was trennelled and sanded as described earlier. A light coat of tung oil wiped on and when dry rubbed down with #220 paper and fine steel wool to remove the yellowish cast of the oil and make the decks a little whiter. If you look carefully at my deck some of my planks are out of place because I miscounted the shift and fitted the wrong size plank. No need to worry – if anyone notices, just call the affected plank a plank used to repair battle damage! The quarterdeck and forecastle inner bulwarks are planked and painted red (Figure 295), and the ports cut out and lined as before (Figure 296).

DETAILING THE HULL SIDES

In this phase of the build the main tasks are: 1) gunport lids, 2) decorative strips and mouldings along the hull length, and 3) steps and fenders. In real life, the gunport lids would fit flush into the hull and one method to portray them would be to scribe their outlines into the second planking. This would be tedious to do and wood is not a great material to scribe with fine lines. It is much easier to 'fake it' and cut gunports out of thin (0.5mm) strips of wood milled down from pear, and glue them to the hull. They would stand slightly proud of the hull but certainly look the part (*eg*, Figure 295).

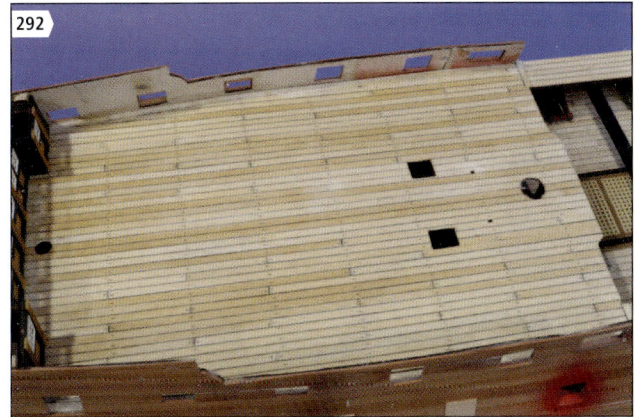

292

The quarterdeck and Marine's Walk is planked. The inner bulwarks are planked next.

293

The planked forecastle. The deck planks are nibbed to fit into the waterway.

294

The beakhead platform is planked and the decorations added. It is possible to model the beakhead bulkhead doors open to afford a view of the upper gun deck if desired, but that would entail fully detailing the entire length of the deck. This is an example of early forward planning that needs to be decided before construction of the model begins.

295

The quarterdeck gunports and other openings were laid out with tape and opened up. The ports on this deck level do not require lining. Gunport lids have also been marked out on the hull and glued in place. The side galleries have also been given a coat of black paint.

Many kits today come complete with decorative wooden mouldings laser-cut or cast in white metal. My inherited kit of *Vanguard* was missing most of the laser-cut kit mouldings and the only option was to make them from scratch. There are several methods such as scraping out your own using a profiled scraper shown in the tool section of Chapter 3. In the past you had to make your own scrapers out of steel by filing the correct profiles onto a piece of steel from an old hacksaw blade. The other option is to build up the correct profile using shaped styrene strips (Figure 297). If the model is to be painted what the mouldings are made of is irrelevant. Our goal is to find an easy way to make them.

The *Vanguard* has one set of flat but quite intricately shaped mouldings that were unfortunately missing from my inherited kit. However, what was in the box were the laser-cut carrier sheets for the parts, and with a little ingenuity the carrier sheet (Figure 298) could be used as a mould to make new ones out of two-part epoxy putty. A sheet of kitchen cling film paper was taped down on a flat surface. The edges of the cut-outs were rubbed with beeswax as a form of mould release agent. The carrier sheet was laid on top of the cling film and the whole given a liberal dusting of talcum powder to act as a further release agent (Figure 299). Make sure the edges are coated with talcum powder and blow away the excess. A ball of A+B putty is mixed (in this case Apoxie Sculpt). Roll out snakes of putty to fit into the cavities. Note that the mixed putty is quite sticky so roll the snakes in talcum powder first. Place the snakes into the cavities and sprinkle more talcum powder on top. With a dowel – also coated in talcum powder – roll over the snakes to push the putty into the mould (Figure 300). Remove any excess that squeezes out and allow it to cure. Removing the mouldings takes a bit of care and

297

Decorative side mouldings were built up using wood strip and half-round styrene strip. In the photo you can see that some of the gunport edges need more attention with filler and file.

296

The quarterdeck gunports are opened and painted.

298

The laser-cut carrier sheet that could be used to mould new decorative mouldings.

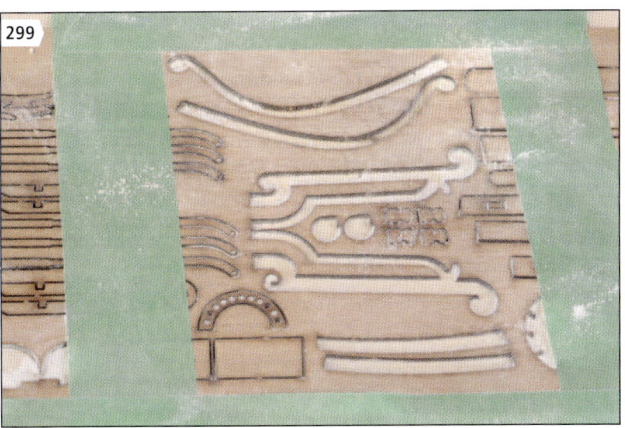

299

The mould was heavily dusted with talcum powder as a release agent.

finesse. Mine stuck to the wooden moulds and I had to break away the wooden carrier sheet to free them. The parts may snap, but can be glued back together using CA. In the end, I got the parts required and I did not have to laboriously saw them out of wood or plastic sheet. Set them aside for installing on the hull later (Figure 301).

The hull fenders were added next. The kit supplies laser-cut parts to the profile of the hull. Let's face it, my hull contours are not nearly as precise as the fender's profile. Even if your hull is better, fitting the fenders to the hull sides is difficult because they have to be notched to fit around the wales and side mouldings (or the mouldings cut away). A simple way to overcome this difficulty is make the fenders up in two laminated layers (Figure 302). Plastic strip or wood is glued in between the wales and side mouldings, and then another strip of plastic (or wood) is glued on top of that to form the fender itself. Any gap between the laminations is plugged with a wipe of filler. What could have been a tedious job was completed in about 10 minutes. The side steps were also made of plastic strip shaped to the correct profile.

300

A+B putty is pushed into the mould and rolled flat. The putty is allowed to cure overnight.

301

The putty casting is removed, sanded flat, and fixed to the hull. The casting is quite fragile. A bit of automotive glaze and spot putty filled any gaps.

302

The fenders and side steps built up from styrene and wood strips.

303

Primer shows up all of the flaws that need to be repaired by filling and sanding, or sanding smooth. Several rounds were required to correct all the little and not so little errors unveiled. Typical flaws are shown.

304

A coat of yellow ochre is sprayed onto the hull and shaded with slightly darker and lighter versions of the base colour. The colour coat revealed a few more areas that needed some corrective work.

Painting the Hull

The hull was sprayed with a coat of sanding sealer and rubbed back with #400 wet and dry paper, then polished with a rub down of extra fine steel wool. Any visible blemishes are corrected by rubbing down or with filler. Mask off areas you don't want covered in paint, such as gunport openings and spray on a coat of primer. I used an off-white or sometimes a tan yellow colour paint that with my eyesight makes spotting blemishes much easier (Figure 303). These blemishes were corrected and the area re-primed and checked again. When all corrections are completed, an overall light coat of white primer is applied to the hull to give a consistent base for the colour coats. Let the primer cure and the hull is ready for paint.

My style is to vary the shade and tone and display some weathering, but this time a little heavier than what I usually use to give the paintwork depth. The first colour to go on is the yellow ochre (Figure 304). This was applied in thin coats with an airbrush until a solid colour was obtained. Each coat was allowed to dry for two hours before the next one went on. The yellow was shaded by adding a little black to the yellow ochre and this was sprayed around the gunports, along the wales, between and around any mouldings. Once dry, the yellow was highlighted with a mix of yellow ochre and white, focusing on areas of highlight, such as between gunports. The paintwork looks a little garish and the shades are brought together with well thinned overspray of the yellow ochre base colour.

The paint was allowed to cure for 24 hours and masked off using Tamiya yellow tape. The black stripes were sprayed on with an off-black paint (Figure 305). Shading was applied with pure black paint, and a little white was mixed into the black for highlights. For the highlights, a zenithal lighting technique was used by angling the airbrush downward so that only the tops of the black areas received the highlight. The point is to paint the highlight where a light source, placed above the hull would strike it. Once the shade and highlights were allowed to dry, a thinned coat of the off-black base colour was sprayed overall to blend them in and create soft transitions between the shades. It takes a bit of practice not to obliterate the shades, but the nice thing about airbrushed paints is that the coats are thin and you can always respray. Allow the black paint to dry and remove the masking tape.

305

The areas that would remain yellow ochre were masked off and a coat of off-black was sprayed onto the hull. The black was shaded with slightly darker and lighter versions of the base colour. Once again, this work revealed a few more areas that required some remediation with putty and sandpaper.

Repairing Damaged Paintwork

On a hull with so many protrusions, nooks and crannies to paint, handling the model, missed spots, overspray, paint seeping under the masking tape, and the inevitable glue drips will all damage the paintwork (Figure 306). The best ingredients for successful paint repair include:

1. Letting the damaged paint dry hard (this is the hardest part as the error keeps looking at you and it tries to draw you into fixing it before the paint is really dry) and gently sanding down the error.
2. Spot masking, which is really about protecting areas around the

306

Some common paintwork flaws. At the top, some yellow ochre paint was pulled up by the masking tape and the demarcation between the side gallery and wale was not straight. Sanding back the flaws and respraying in light coats will correct the errors. The key is not to try to cover up the flaws in one coat but rather several very light coats.

307

Extensive re-masking and repainting corrected all the flaws in the paintwork. The key to success is to spray paint at a low pressure to prevent overspray, light coats, and allowing each coat to dry fully before spraying another coat or sanding back. Where I wanted a hard line between colours I used Tamiya yellow tape because it seals nicely. To protect from general overspray, inexpensive green painter's tape is lightly tacked to the surface. When blending colours with an airbrush the aim is not to inadvertently create a hard edge. Holding a piece of card in my hand just off the surface prevents a hard edge being formed.

damaged paint from overspray. The key here is not to create a hard masking line where the new paint will stand out from the previously painted areas (Figure 307).

3. Setting the airbrush compressor to a low pressure setting so just a little paint is sprayed at a time.
4. Not pulling too far back on the airbrush trigger and releasing too much paint at once. You have to build up the repaint repair in layers, allowing each layer to dry before applying the next.

The final touch is to give the entire hull a thin wash of lamp black and burnt umber wash. This wash is more like a glaze or 'filter' as used by plastic modellers to weather armoured fighting vehicle models. When applying the wash, it is tempting to lay the hull on its side as you would when making a model aeroplane so that the coverage is even. On a ship, the hull should sit *upright* and the wash applied. In this way the wash flows into the nooks and crannies that mimics the effects of water and grime washing down the hull to define the line of the wales and other hull fittings. Any excess wash can be sopped up with a brush to avoid streaks and the next day any unwanted stains removed with a cotton bud moistened with white spirits. I applied three coats of washes, letting each dry overnight before I achieved the weathering patina that I found pleasing to my eye. The yellow ochre areas were carefully rubbed over using a makeup pad pinched from the female family members very lightly moistened with white spirits to remove some of the wash. This has the effect of brightening up the overall paintwork and leaving the wash largely in all the nooks and crannies. Once everything was painted to my satisfaction, the hull was given another coat, a satin polyurethane to seal and protect the weathering, which helped blend all the shading, repairs, and provided a consistent sheen to the model.

DECK FITTINGS

A ship's deck is covered with fittings and they are fun to make. There are a few tricks to making them easier to assemble, as well as making them look a little more realistic. One of the most prominent features are the gratings. Reference works show how the grating's coamings were built with lap joints but if you are painting them, then simple butt joints will do. The most important feature is the gratings themselves. Kits and scratch-builders alike use a form of the comb method (Figure 308). When the gratings are assembled, what to look out for is whether or not the resulting square holes are to scale. Often the holes are too large and a 1/72 scale matelot's foot would fall into the holes breaking his ankles. Ouch!

The ship's wheel is made up of etched brass components that give a delightfully delicate look. It is painted to look like varnished wood by priming the item in a light tan or white paint overall. A mix of burnt umber and burnt sienna artist's oils are mixed together with a

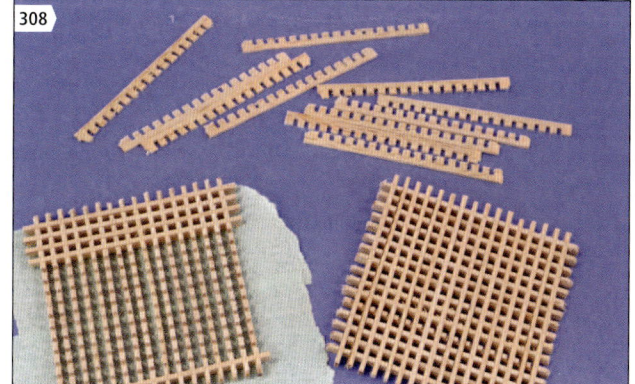

308

Assembling hatch gratings is fiddly. Building them over a piece of tape sticky side up holds the combs in place and makes the job much easier.

309

Illustrated is the binnacle and wheel from Amati's 1/64 *Pegasus* kit showing how a few extra details such as lashing the binnacle down to the deck, to painting the ship's wheel in shades of brown to look like wood is quite effective. The same details and painting can be applied to the *Vanguard*'s fittings.

310

The fittings have been fixed to the quarterdeck area.

311

A view of the waist.

312

The forecastle's inner bulwarks have been added and painted.

little Liquin medium and the paint streaked over the part. The paint is semi-transparent and is brushed out to give a wood grain effect. The wheel has decorative brass insert around its circumference and this is easily represented by scraping the paint off the raised area allowing the brass to show through. Nothing looks more like brass than brass. Tiller ropes can be added around the barrel that feed into holes drilled through the deck. The binnacle is made of up laser-cut walnut which is easy to assemble. It is detailed by adding glazing from Micro Kristal Kleer, lashings to the deck, and a small disc of plastic painted brass can be placed inside as the compass. A small air vent can also be added from plastic rod and painted brass (Figures 309 to 312).

Poop Deck

The final layer of the cake is the *poop* deck. The deck gets its name from '*la poupe*' which is the French word for stern and it goes on the same way as the other decks. The subdecks are fitted and planked over as before (Figure 313). On this deck, the planks are nibbed into the waterway, and the length of the planks to create the shift of the butts would be 30mm, 60mm, 90mm, and 120mm respectively. The decks as laid were also a little too pristine for my liking and the brightness of the wood was toned down with a few light washes of grey paint. In order to know when to stop weathering, you have to think about what a ship at sea would be doing. For example, decks would be regularly scrubbed and swabbed so they would look used but not filthy. On the other hand, the outer ship's sides would show a great deal of weathering from beating back and forth across the high seas and would not receive the same attention from the crew as the inside areas of the ship. Damage would be repaired and painted over (by an unfortunate matelot slung over the side of the ship), and the paint used mixed from colours on hand in the ship's stores leading to a patchier looking exterior. As such, having relatively pristine inner areas and a more weathered outer hull would be perfectly acceptable (Figure 314).

Stern Gallery Decorations

The stern gallery decorations are a major focal point of the model and it pays to take some time to really bring the feature to life. The kit provides the decorations as hefty castings of white metal and these must be gently bent to fit the stern galley facia. These parts may be

SEMI-SCRATCH DOUBLE PLANK-ON-BULKHEAD

313

The completed poop deck.

314

A view of the fully painted hull sides. All of the effort was worth it!

provided in resin and to bend them they are quickly dipped in hot (not boiling) water and gently bent. Once the fit is satisfactory, it is cleaned up and primed white. My approach to painting the decorations is to bring it alive with dramatic shading and highlighting. My method is a simplified variation of what model figure and wargame painters do to bring their miniatures to life on the tabletop.

The background is painted dark red (Vallejo 7078 Carmine Red) as the first shade (Figure 315). The red base is highlighted with a brighter shade (Vallejo 70908 Vermillion) that is painted in the centre of areas of dark red base and a second highlight is painted in the centres of that (a mix of Vermillion and Vallejo 70845 Sunny Skintone. Do not use white to create a lighter shade of red because white will turn it pink).

The yellow ochre areas are painted next (Figure 316) using Vallejo 70872 Golden Brown darkened with a little Vallejo 70941 Burnt Umber. Highlights on the figures and filigree are painted in with a dry brushing of Golden Brown and Vallejo 70953 Yellow. The cherubs are painted using the Andrea White paint set base colour (a stone grey colour) that is highlighted with progressively whiter paints in the set (Figure 317). At this point the stern gallery has a great deal of depth from the shading and highlighting, but the figures and

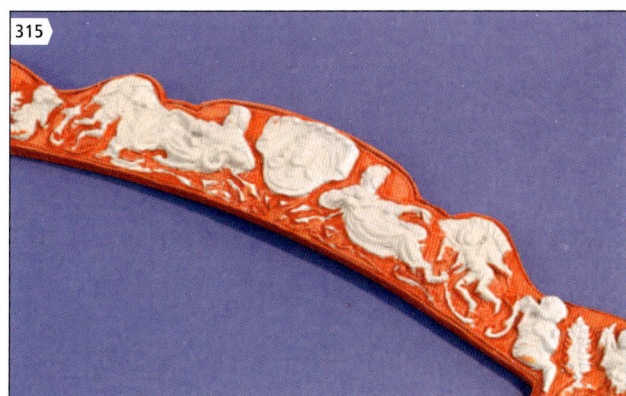

315

The red background is painted and brought to life with three shades of red.

cherubs still lack a little definition so there is one more step.

A gloss clear coat was applied next to seal in the colour coats. When thoroughly dry, give the stern gallery a coat of Army Painter Dark Tone (Figure 318). Army Painter is a heavily pigmented polyurethane varnish that seeps into all the crevasses of the casting

316

The yellow ochre areas are painted in and shaded.

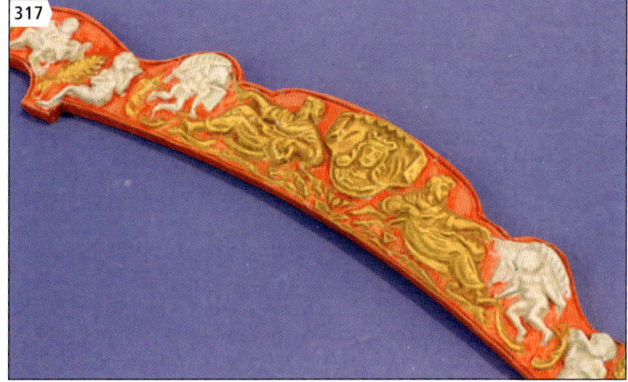

317

The white cherubs are painted in and highlighted. A coat of gloss varnish protects the paintwork.

318

The Army Painter Quickshade is brushed on and the excess removed. This varnish is a highly tinted enamel based polyurethane varnish designed to quickly shade wargame figures. It is applied over a gloss finish because it causes the product to roll off it into the nooks and crannies and not stain raised areas. Its brown/black colour gives the paint a nice patina in keeping with the period.

319

The completed stern galleries. Still a little paint touch-up to do here and there.

320

The biggest challenge was carefully bending metal parts to fit the curves of the side galleries.

and creates instant outlining and blends all the colour together. It's pretty alarming when it first goes on, but after letting it settle into the casting for a few minutes, remove the excess with a brush and allow it to dry. As it dries the paint shrinks and you are left with a beautifully shaded stern gallery. A coat of satin clear takes away the shine and it is ready to be fixed to the stern facia. If you do not have access to the colours I used, you can substitute any paint brand (*eg*, Games Workshop paints) but whatever you use I highly recommend that you use an acrylic paint. The reason is that acrylic paint when dry cannot be lifted by subsequent brushing over by an enamel-based paint, and are not affected by washes made with white spirits. In the place of Army Painter, wargamers also use a home brew mix called 'The Magic Dip'. This is acrylic gloss floor varnish mixed with dark brown acrylic paint. It is painted on and it settles into the cracks and crevasses quite well. I suggest some experimentation before you use it. I practiced all the various techniques on miniature figures, and now have quite a nice collection of Napoleonic wargame figures.

With the galleries in place, it's time to add all of the remaining stern and quarter gallery decorations (Figures 319 and 320). Despite being a kit with highly engineered components, some will simply not fit your model. Small variations in your build may be the culprit, or possibly the components themselves are not well produced. For example, the white metal double beaded rails provided are of uneven section and do not lie as neatly as one would like. It is not uncommon for parts not to fit precisely and you must be mentally prepared to do a lot of fettling and shaping. Moreover, sometimes despite your careful assembly, there is simply not enough room for the parts and you may have to leave them off. This is just what happens so don't get discouraged. This is not a sign of poor workmanship on your part at all. It is part of the experience and on your next model you will be more aware and better able to spot and prevent errors to minimize surprises at the end.

THE SHIP'S HEADWORK

Like the stern and quarter galleries, prepare yourself for a lot of test fitting and slow and steady work. There is a lot of geometry with angles and curves in three dimensions that have to be taken into

321

The incorrectly placed roundhouses were chiselled off and reattached in the correct place. The three hairpins are the first parts to be added to the head. On a large and complicated ship like *Vanguard*, mistakes are common.

SEMI-SCRATCH DOUBLE PLANK-ON-BULKHEAD

322

The cheeks and decorative rail are fixed in place. The hairpins have to be bevelled so the cheeks seat against them. The decorative piece is an A+B putty casting made to replace the missing wooden part.

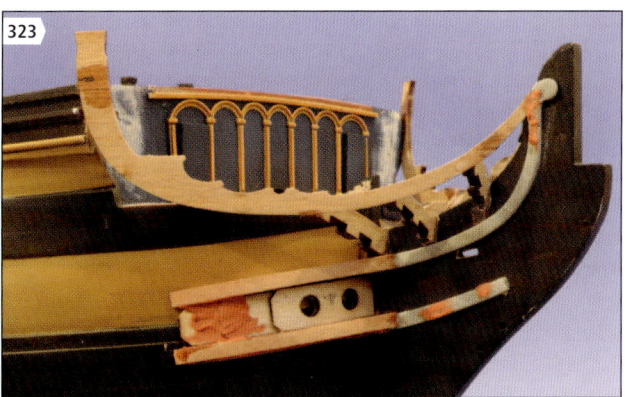

323

Hawse holes and more decorative rails are fixed in to the hull. As you build up these parts, always ensure that the parts flow harmoniously together and are symmetrical on both sides of the hull. Automotive glaze and spot putty is used to correct any gaps and flaws.

324

Additional rails added and the work painted. The figurehead was painted in the same way as the stern galleries, finished with a dip in Quickshade. Just visible on the prow is a lead sheet cutwater. As always, a lot of touching up to do here and there.

325

The gratings and seats of ease were fixed into place and the roundhouses repainted.

account as each part is fitted. The components themselves are very delicate and initial test fitting often makes you wonder if they will all fit together. Let me assure you they will, and it takes a good mental attitude to tackle this fascinating area. Mistakes do happen, and do not be afraid to remove and rebuild a part. For example, after beautifully painting the roundhouses and planking the beakhead deck, I noticed I had located them incorrectly. After recovering from the shock, I had to chisel them off, repair all the paint work, fix the planking and glue then into the correct place (Figure 321).

The most intricate head work begins with gluing in the hairpins. These three parts hold the cheek pieces. The fit of the cheeks is the most critical as their position will determine the ultimate location of rest of the parts. Where the cheeks join the hull may need some bevelling to sit properly (Figure 322), and the hairpin ends require bevelling. Tape them in place and fit the shaped grating that sits within them to ensure that the angles are correct and they seat properly. Once you are happy with the siting of the cheeks, tack them into place and look at the head all the way around. Make sure the cheeks are symmetrically placed, sit at the correct angles, and are not too low or not too high on the hull. Only then commit the glue.

The decoration to the stem is added, and in this case the home cast A+B putty castings. The kit-supplied hawse hole patterns were too short but was useful to set the spacing and angles, but once fixed in place an extension was fashioned out of wood and faired in place with putty (Figure 323). Each additional part added to the head was test fitted a multitude of times but eventually it all came together. Always ensure that as each part is added, the spacing is correct and most of all the parts flow neatly into one another. You will likely find slight differences between the port and starboard sides, but as long as the work looks symmetrical, do not spend too much time fussing over perfection which does not exist in the world of handmade ships and models of them. The paint is touched up and the figurehead can be added (Figure 324). The gratings are added, as are the seats of ease that complete the headwork.

RAILINGS AND BARRICADES

Most of the rails that are fitted on the top of the bulwarks were

326

The railings are made up of several parts to take account of the curves and shape of the bulwark tops.

327

Balustrades and railing are fitted and painted black.

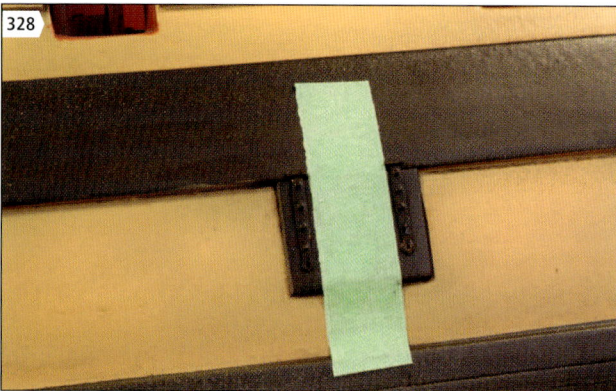

328

A piece of tape is used to space the gunport hinges

329

The gunport lids are rigged. A jig was used to drill the lanyard holes to ensure correct spacing. The lanyards themselves are pieces of thread inserted into the lanyard hole and the other end is tied to an eyebolt fitted to the gunport lid. To get the thread into the hole, its end was dipped in CA and pulled straight. The CA will stiffen the end like a needle and it is easily inserted into the hole.

fashioned as shown in the previous builds. It is also advisable to paint the underside of the rail black before fixing to the top of the bulwarks. The *Vanguard* also has some delicate railing around her poop deck (Figure 326) that must be built up in place. The thin pillars that sit on top of the bulwark rail must be pinned in place and not just glued. Balustrades that sit fore and aft of the waist are a challenge because they must be curved to match the camber of the deck (Figure 327). They are best assembled on the model so the wooden parts can be bent and any slots adjusted to accommodate the deck camber. Pre-painting them before permanently attaching them to the deck is advisable.

Gunport Hinges and Lanyard Holes

Gunport hinges and lanyard holes are small details but they are very important ones because they draw the eyes to the sweet lines of the hull. The gunport lid hinges are photo-etched parts provided in the kit (Figure 328). Some of the hinge pieces were missing on my inherited kit so replacements were made with just strips of black paper and dots of white glue to represent the bolts. Over each gunport are a pair of lanyard holes that are drilled using a jig to ensure they are evenly spaced and in the correct orientation to the gunport lid (Figure 329). A simple jig takes but a few minutes to make out of scrap plastic card. When drilling a hole in a painted surface do not forget to touch up the hole with paint to cover up any of the newly exposed whiteness of the wood. Even flowing a little black/brown wash into the hole will do.

On a large ship of the line, one of the most fiddly bits (at least for me) to finish off the headwork is the cathead. This is a beam located on both sides of the bow and angled forward at roughly 45° to support the ship's anchor when raising or lowering it. It is fiddly because some of the side mouldings must be cut away, the beam end angled and it is supported by a knee that is joined to decorative rails to be bent and fitted against the hull (Figure 330). Once again, slow and careful work will get the cathead, knees and mouldings into place, but gaps are inevitable. These are best filled with some white PVA glue with the excess wiped away. The glue is painted over when dry.

Channels and Deadeyes

The channels that hold the deadeyes (Figure 331) are laser-cut pieces that were cleaned up and any fittings such as eyebolts were added

SEMI-SCRATCH DOUBLE PLANK-ON-BULKHEAD

330
The decorative railing has been cut away and the cathead, cathead knee and its decorative rail glued in place. White glue was used to fill any gaps.

331
The main channels and deadeyes fitted to the hull. The channels are pinned in place and iron knees are fitted underneath them to take up the strain of the rigging. The deadeyes are stropped in the most realistic way with three-part chain plate irons. Can you find my error? If this was to happen on your model, how would you deal with it? Every modeller has their own approach.

332
The string method is used to set the angle of the chain plate irons to the hull.

and the whole assembly painted off the model. The real challenge is fixing the units to the hull without messing up any existing paintwork. The inside edge of the channel is drilled in at least two places to accommodate a brass pin. Corresponding holes are drilled in the hull to take the pins and provide a solid attachment to the side. However, getting the corresponding hull holes in the correct location is a real challenge. Invariably, one of the holes will be slightly off to one side preventing the pins from fitting. The natural response is to re-drill the hole a little way over, but often the drill bit slips and falls back into the previous hole and you make a mess. You may be tempted to drill a bigger hole in the hope that the pin slips in, but that leads to a sloppy fit and often the edge of the hole shows despite most of it being covered up by the thickness of the channel. The best way to overcome this is to drill the hole of the first pin only. The channel is then offered up to the hull with the first pin in place, and the hull is marked exactly where the second pin is located and the second hole drilled.

The care taken in positioning all of the external elements, such as mouldings and rails on the hull sides, will now pay dividends because the locations of the channels are often determined by them. If the rails or mouldings are a little too long or short, or too high or low on the hull, the channel will also be too far forward or back, or too high or low. This problem manifests itself when you attach the deadeye strops and chain plate irons themselves – they are just too long. On my model, the channels were slightly off so that in one place the chain plates themselves fell in front of a gunport! The only way I could correct this was to 'fake' it by leaving one section of the offending chain plate iron off. Don't despair – mistakes happen and you adapt and find a solution. The chain plate irons themselves are raked and the string method helps set the angle (Figure 332).

GUNS

The guns can now finally be glued down to the deck. Because I received the remnant of a kit, a number of fittings were missing, such as the carronades so these guns do not appear on my model. Of course, one could find some aftermarket fittings to make up the shortage, but I decided to fill the spots with long guns I had in the spares box (Figure 333). Is this wrong to do? It can be argued that it is not entirely out of the bounds of reality as many ships of this time

333

The forecastle guns are fixed in place and a simplified breeching rope was fitted. The guns are a little under scale, but look the part. Being a semi-scratch-built/kit bashed project, the modeller has many options to build everything at their discretion. My motivation was simply to rescue an abandoned model as economically as possible and serve as a test bed for learning new techniques, such as laser-cutting.

334

Brass and white metal castings combine to create the ship's lanterns.

underwent armament changes over its lifetime in spite of official establishments or in accordance with the preference of the Captain at the time, or what was available in the dockyard when fitting out.

I decided only to fit the breeching ropes to the guns simply because I did not have enough blocks to properly rig the other tackle. Given the small scale of the model, I also did not fit ring bolts into the bulwarks to take the ends of the breeching ropes and instead decided to simulate them with a knot representing the seizing of the breeching rope through the bulwark ring bolt. The middle of the knotted breeching rope was glued to the cascabel of the cannon and the knotted ends glued to the deck right up against the bulwark. A little thinned white glue was soaked into the breeching rope to shape it to hang naturally. This modeller's simplification looked well enough and saved a lot of small-scale work that might have stalled the project to be put away on the ignominious 'shelf of doom' for another day.

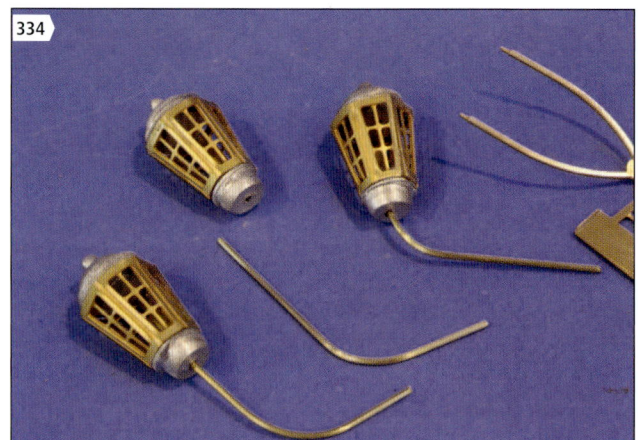

335

Painted and detailed lanterns are fixed to the stern galleries.

SEMI-SCRATCH DOUBLE PLANK-ON-BULKHEAD 117

336

336

Vanguard carries several boats and each is constructed as miniature double plank on bulkhead kits.

337

The ship's boats were test fitted to the boat skids in the waist of the ship. Fitting all the boats would almost entirely obscure the work put into the upper gun deck so a decision was made only to complete two of the largest ones.

FINAL DETAILS

The time has come to finish the hull by fitting the final details. There are a lot of little things to add, each taking time and care to get right. The details include: lanterns, ship's boats, anchors, anchor cables, ladders, booms, and cleats. Modern kits now provide the lanterns as delicate brass-etched pieces that are folded up and glazed as opposed to the brightly gilded solid heavy metal castings often found in older kits (Figure 334). The etched brass route is better in that the lanterns are hollow and can be fitted with a light emitting diode (LED) if one wanted to illuminate them. On this kit the etched parts are folded up and the white metal top cap is fitted. On my model the lanterns were painted gold and then dipped in Army Painter to shade them, and they were glazed with Micro Kristal Kleer. Brass rod stems are added to the lantern bases and the stems are attached to the hull (Figure 335). Measure carefully their location on the stern galleries and use a new and sharp drill bit to cut the holes. At this point of the build you want precision and a new and sharp bit is much less likely to skid across the surface of the hull ruining your hard work.

Ships Boats. The kit's boats are miniature double plank-on-bulkhead kits and are pretty much constructed in the same way as the main ship's hull (Figure 336). The only difference this time is that there are five of them to build. Although the boats are designed to be double planked, I opted to simply do one layer of planking because I planned to paint my boats, and then cover the interior with tarps as befits a stowed boat. I also decided to only build two of them because I wanted the lower deck to be open for viewing (Figure 337). The completed boat shells were sanded to shape and detailed with a keel and stem. A ball of A+B putty was rolled out

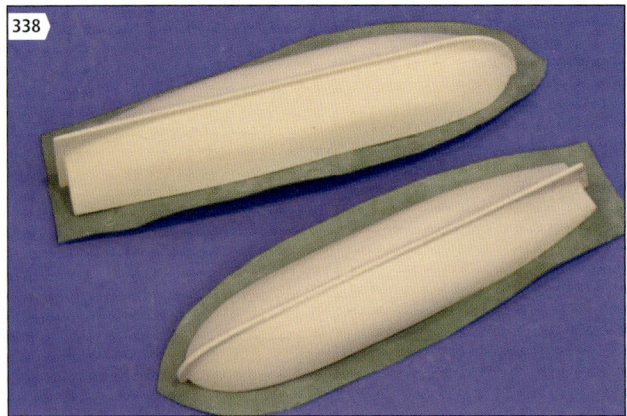

338
The boat shells were painted white. Rolled out A+B putty was used to make the boat covers. The covers were cut oversize and draped over the sides allowing realistic folds to be sculpted in.

339
Boat covers were painted a tan or light canvas colour. Note how the putty was allowed to sag inwards and letting a few bumps show up under them giving the impression that the boat is full of stores.

340
Two ship's boats were mounted onto the boat skids and lashed down with thread.

341
Sandpaper taped to a flat surface was used to sand in the tapers for the anchor stocks.

and allowed to dry for about an hour. The boat was laid on top and the putty cut about 1cm all around the boat (Figure 338). The boat was turned right way up allowing the putty to hang over the sides and was folded to hang realistically as if gravity were really playing a role (Figure 339). The tarps were painted a canvas colour and fixed to the boat skids and lashed down (Figure 340).

Anchors. Ships carried many anchors and kits typically include one-piece cast metal shank and flukes. Stocks are provided as pre-shaped wooden parts or are easily made from wood strip that fit around the stocks. It is a little thing, but the underside of the wooden stock is tapered and that is easily made by sanding the stock on a piece of sandpaper taped to a flat surface (Figure 341). The metal parts of the anchor are painted black and the wooden stock is made from a dark coloured wood like walnut or pear, or stained a dark colour. Anchor stock reinforcing bands are strips of black cartridge paper. The ring was bent from brass rod and painted black. A nice touch is to wrap the ring in black thread called 'puddening' (Figure 342).

Stand

The kit-provided stand is of the cradle type that is laser-cut from wood. A pet peeve of mine is that when these stands are used the builder has done little to finish them properly. The laser-cut char marks still show and at best, perhaps a coat of stain or oil has been used to treat the wood. The model you have built deserves a nicer stand and just a little more effort makes all the difference (Figure 343). At the very least after assembling the stand, all of the gaps should be filled and sanded smooth, primed and any blemishes

342

The anchor stocks were detailed with black paper bands and a thread puddening added to the ring. The whole assembly was lashed to the hull.

343

Vanguard is placed on the black lacquered stand which gives the model a period feel.

corrected with putty and re-primed until the surface is flawless. The stand should be painted black or brown and the look we are going for is a lacquered black or a polished wood finish found on Admiralty models of the period. For *Vanguard* I sprayed the stand black, rubbing down between coats. After the final coat of colour, it was sprayed with a gloss clear lacquer finish by Tamiya, and a coat of wax (fine furniture wax or carnauba wax for cars) was applied and polished and buffed out by hand to a deep gloss. The cradle edges were lined with felt. A nameplate can be added but it is important to keep with the period feel of the model, so use a typeface typical of the time, like the name on the stern of the ship. Don't use a modern font, it just looks odd. The ship's name should look something like this: *Vanguard* not Vanguard.

Stub Masts

To keep a period feel to my model I decided to add *stub masts* (Figures 344 and 345). Stubs masts are simply the lower part of a mast that is fitted to the hull to show where the masts are positioned.

344
The mizzen and main stub masts.

345
The forecastle and bowsprit stub masts.

They are used in Admiralty models and an option if you just want to show off the hull, or you just don't feel like rigging right now, or don't have the space to display a fully rigged ship model. The mast stubs are made from suitably sized dowels and if you fit them it is important that the height of the stubs follow the sheer of the hull and that their ends are cut off at an angle. The plans will show what details to add, such as racks for boarding pikes, mast bands from rope or metal.

Prior to detailing out the mast stubs they were stained dark walnut but for some reason I could not get a nice even finish to the wood. The grain pattern was heavily emphasized and just looked out of scale. The way to correct this was to overpaint the dowel with oil paints. Burnt and raw umber oil colour was mixed with a little Liquin medium. The oil colour was brushed on up and down the dowel, and with a clean soft brush, brushed over to create a more uniform finish. Oil paints have enough density to cover up the grain but remain transparent enough to allow some wood to show through yielding a much more uniform and in scale appearance. Once the stub masts were detailed, their tops painted red and inserted into the hull without glue – I may wish to build complete masts and rig the model in future.

Vanguard – Fini?

After placing the model on the stand, sit back and enjoy your creation. Think about what you could have done differently. For me the list includes:
- Fully rig the guns with breeching tackle.
- Add handrails and stanchions to the ladders.
- Make rolled up hammocks and fit them into the hammock cranes that line the waist.

- Use more in scale fittings like the ladders.
- Add more fine details, like fire buckets.
- Fit a few more of the ship's boats.

I was gratified that I was able to take an incomplete box of parts to create a model inexpensively using stock materials, often leftover scraps, and odds and ends found in my workshop. Building this model taught me a lot about new technologies such as laser cutting, and I didn't have to go out and buy one of my own. Instead, by joining a makerspace that has all the tools, and most importantly, friendly and freely available expertise to use them, a new dimension was added to my model making tool box. Most importantly, being part of a makerspace community gave me the feeling that nothing really can limit my creativity or my choice of subject.

8: Plank-on-Frame Modelling
French Naval Lugger *Le Coureur*

Our final construction type is the fully framed or plank-on-frame hull. These models in some ways represent the epitome of wooden ship model building because each of the frame timbers are cut out, shaped, and assembled like the original ship. In the not too distant past, plank-on-frame models were virtually all scratch-built to drawings that drew out each and every part – or you lofted out each component yourself. These drawings were attached to wood stock and cut out using a fret saw, shaped with chisels and assembled in elaborate jigs to hold all the parts in the correct place. These models took years to build and were a real testament to the skills of the builder. All of the deck beams, knees and planking was done to scale, and fastened together using trennels in the correct scale and patterns. Beyond the ship's frames, all of the ship's decorations such as figureheads and the elaborate carvings were all individually sculpted. I am a very poor carver so was always put off attempting one of the more elaborate and beautiful ships.

Today, there are several kits to make up a plank-on-frame model that serve as an ideal introduction to fully framed models. The skills you learn on one of these kits are a stepping stone to building one from scratch and creating the freedom to then build whatever ship you would like in future. These kits are designed using CAD and cut using lasers and CNC milling machines. Even the carvings are provided beautifully milled out of solid blocks of wood from 3D renderings. These innovations have spread to the more mundane tasks such as hull and deck planking that use CAD to spile and cut each plank with a laser. Specially designed jigs are included that ensure accurate placement of parts but it also ensures the geometry of the hull timbers stay true. Presently, most of these kits come from China, Russia and Japan and are cut from fine hardwoods such as box, pear or cherry (Figure 346). Added to all this are a host of specially designed cast brass, resin, and etched brass details.

These kits are designed to be built in much the same way as a scratch-builder would do. Work begins with laying the keel timbers, adding the stem and rudder post and all of their supporting timbers. The frames are constructed next, futtock by futtock, and each is fixed to the keel. The deck beams are installed, followed by planking the

346

Some of the contents of CAF Models 1/48 scale *Le Coureur* plank-on-frame kit.

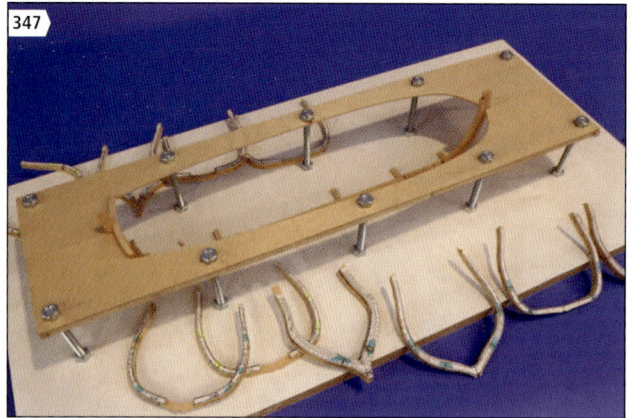

347

A typical home designed and built jig. This jig is for a model of *La Belle* from the Jean Boudriot monograph. Nuts and bolts are used to adjust the height of the hull template which is set at the waterline. Unlike other jigs, this one is not notched to hold the frames. Instead, as each frame is attached to the keel a length of wood cut to the space between the top timbers of each frame and glued to the jig ensures proper spacing.

348

A Harold Hahn style jig. Hahn-style models are built upside down with extensions added to the top of each frame that fit into the notches in the jig. This jig is for a model of the colonial schooner *Chaleur*.

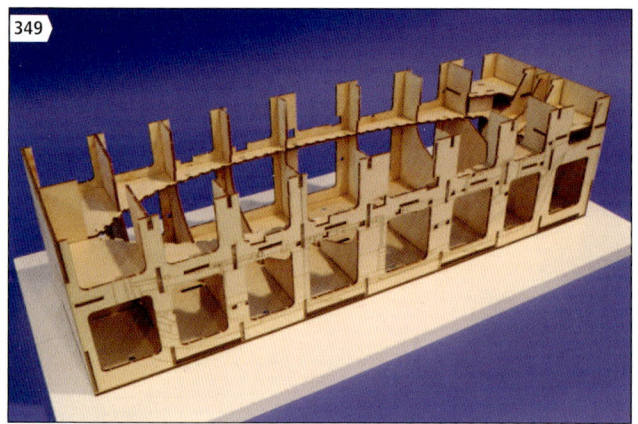

349

CAF Models' jig for *Le Coureur*. It is constructed of several laser-cut pieces of plywood whose assembly must be checked for squareness. The tolerances of the laser-cutting is quite tight and some tabs and slots may require relief with a touch of a file. The base of the jig is screwed down to an inexpensive melamine faced shelf found at any DIY home centre to keep it flat.

interior of the hull (called the *ceiling planks*), the decks, and hull. The only difference from scratch-building is that all of the parts are provided ready cut for you to fit. These kits save you a lot of effort and especially cost that would otherwise have meant you having to find supplies of timber, and buying power tools to mill it all into usable pieces. Despite the huge amount of prefabrication, these kits are not easily assembled. The parts are raw materials and they require a great deal of skill to properly fit them. Indeed, being so precise as befits a CAD designed product, the joints often leave little room for error and the tolerances are very tight – and having so many parts to assemble usually means something will go awry.

The purpose of this chapter is to introduce you to some of the basic skills required for fully framed models. The model we are to work on is the French naval lugger *Le Coureur* that served during the American Revolutionary War. She was built at Dunkirk and launched on May 1776 and was captured by the British cutter *Alert* on 17 June 1778. The British took *Coureur* into the Royal Navy under her existing name, and she was captured again by two American privateers *Fortune* and the *Griffin* in June 1780. *Coureur* was recaptured the next day by the 14-gun sloop HMS *Fairy*. The model is from a kit by CAF Models of Shanghai, China and developed from draughts of the ship obtained from the National Maritime Museum in Greenwich, and with reference to the ANCRE monograph of the ship. The primary wood is North American cherry which has a warm brown tone to it.

Considerations:
- Plank-on-frame and built upright like a real ship.
- The hull is clinker planked which means that the frames will be more difficult to build as they will have to be notched so the planks can properly overlap at their edges.
- All planks for hull and decks are laser-cut to precise size and have trennel marks laser-etched.
- Laser-cutting char. The model is designed to be bright finished so the laser-cutting char will be visible on some surfaces. This charring will have to be removed.
- A custom designed building jig is included that will be a great help in construction and will hold the parts in the correct spaces and places.

THE BUILDING JIG OR MODEL SLIPWAY

The building jig is the most important component of a framed model. The jig holds all the parts in place and in the proper relation to one another. When scratch-building a framed model, the builder typically designs a jig that works for them. Figure 347 and 348 show

PLANK-ON-FRAME MODELLING

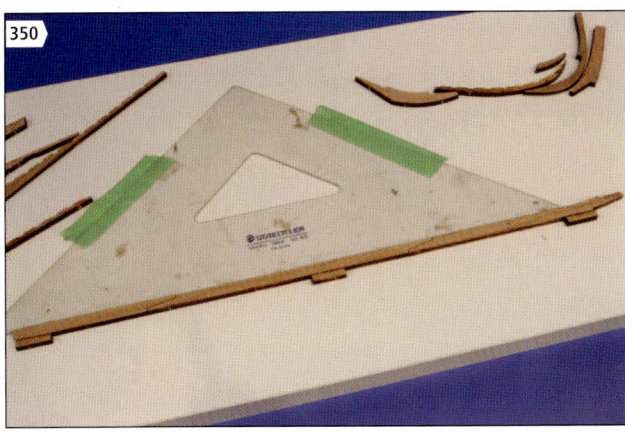

350
Keel assembly. A straightedge is used to ensure the keel runs true. The tabs located on the bottom of the keel parts are to help locate the keel into the assembly jig. They are removed after construction of the entire model is complete. The tabs were found to need a little filing down to fit into the jig.

351
Stem parts for *Le Coureur* (bottom). Note the laser char marks that must be cleaned off the edges and the side faces. Above it is the scratch-built boxwood stem for *La Belle*. The complexity of the actual construction of the stem post can be appreciated and illustrates how many kits simplify these parts by combining them into a single part generally called the 'stem post' which is not technically correct. You can easily identify the rising wood, apron, inner and outer stem post, knees and other individual components. Each must be painstakingly cut out, shaped, and assembled.

examples of jigs that are commonly used. The CAF kit provides an elaborate jig that must be assembled (Figure 349) that is cleverly designed to not only hold the keel, stem, stern and frame assemblies in place, but also provides positive locations for deck beams and other structural timbers. The jig must be assembled accurately and is screwed down to a flat piece of wood to prevent any warping or distortion.

A few observations on the CAF Models jig. The jig is designed with knock-out panels. The panels can be removed to afford a better view of the interior so you can see how each part, such as the keel, is sitting within the jig and check if the frames are properly seated on the keel. When you remove the knock-out panels, do not throw them away because they will have to be glued back into the jig to help construction. For example, the knock-out panels have a number of square holes cut into them. A drawing of the ship's interior has been laser-etched onto the sides of the jig and each of the square holes corresponds to the levels of each of the ship's decks. Once the frames are in, sticks are slid into the holes and where they cross a frame marks the exact point where a deck beam or clamp is located. Without these knock-out panels put back in place, measuring the location of the decks becomes a lot more difficult.

KEEL, STEM AND STERN ASSEMBLIES

Up until now, the ships we have built have keel, stem and stern assemblies that include all of their constituent timbers as a single part called the false keel. In framed models, you will actually shape the timbers and assemble them. The parts are laser-cut in thick wood and separating them from their sheet takes a bit of effort. Cutting away some of the excess wood around the part makes extraction easier. Assembly begins with keel parts and getting this dead straight is important. Any bend here will throw the entire model out of shape and the parts will not fit. Figure 350 shows the keel parts being glued together against a straight edge to keep it straight. The parts for the stem (Figure 351) are assembled onto the keel (Figure 352), followed by the rudder post and supporting timbers (Figures 353). All of the mating faces were gently cleaned with a file to ensure a neat fit.

In a laser-cut framed model most of the burn marks will be removed as a natural part of construction or are covered up when another part is glued on top. However, they will be very visible on some faces, such as the outside of the keel, stem and rudder posts. You will have to keep in mind where the char will be visible and remove it completely before assembly. On the keel, stem, and stern assemblies the burns were removed by gently kissing each component against a power disc sander fitted with fine sandpaper.

352
The assembled stem. The laser char marks were gently sanded off the sides after assembly. CAF Models has cleverly included a CNC cut rabbet milled into all the laser-cut parts for the keel, stem and stern assemblies. The rabbet may need a little cleaning up with a file but it that is child's play compared to cutting a full rabbet by hand.

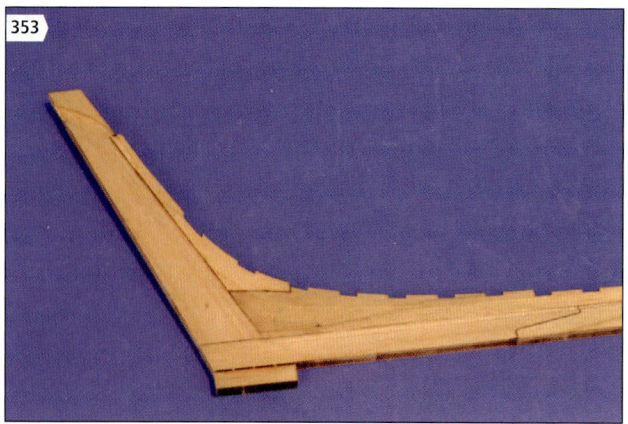

353
The assembled stern post.

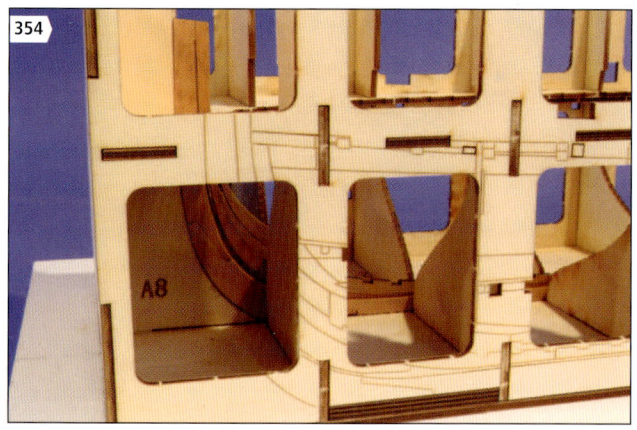

354
The keel assembly is fitted into the jig. The jig needed a little sanding and trimming to allow the assembly to fit easily.

The key word is *kissing*, so just the char and no more is removed. The process is greatly facilitated by using a sanding disc that is very slightly dished outwards that limits the surface area being sanded at any one time. On concave surfaces a fine sanding drum powered by a rotary tool can be used to similarly 'kiss' the wood to take off the char. A firm foam-backed sanding stick works well on any face of the part. Some modellers have reported success using a soft wire brush spun in a rotary tool. I have yet to try it but whatever tool or method you use, practice and experiment first.

The completed keel, stem and rudder post assembly is test fitted into the jig (Figure 354). The jig may need a little dressing with a file to have the assembly slide in and out without stress. The jig tolerances are very tight and it was very difficult to put the assembly into place. In this case the jig was modified slightly by filing bigger notches to allow the assembly to slide into place. The lesson here is that the jig, not the ship parts should be modified to fit. How can you tell which part is correct and which part is not? In this instance, the ship part matched the plans exactly, and the jig part was slightly off. Even computer designed parts and cutting still need the human touch.

Stern Timbers

The stern timbers are erected first and this is a complex set of shapes. Careful study of the plans and familiarity with the parts is essential. Construction of the stern timbers requires you to visualize in three-dimensional space what the assembled stern framing looks like. Don't make a start until you have this visualization clear. The complexity of this area has been taken into account by the designer who has cut some of the parts in three dimensions using CNC milling in order to create the angles and notches that is impossible to do with a laser cutter, which only cuts in two dimensions (Figure 355). The other challenge is the order in which parts are assembled. In this case, starting assembly with the centre timbers and moving outwards is the best approach (Figures 356 and 357). The value of the jig really comes into its own because it is designed to hold the parts together in the correct relationship to each other.

Frames

The ship's frames are the meat of the project. The kit has drawn out each frame on the plans and the wooden parts are built right over it. Let's have a look at the frames. *Le Coureur*'s framing is quite a bit

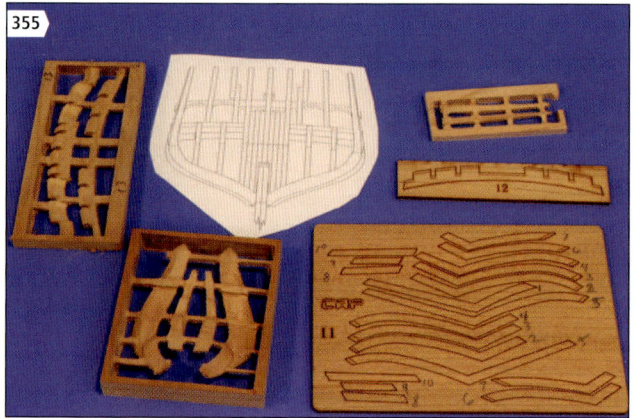

355
The complicated parts for the stern timbers are provided as a mix of laser and CNC milled parts. The laser-cut parts feature lines indicating where bevels are to be sanded in. You can use these marks to guide the start of the bevels before assembly. After all of the components have been assembled the final fairing can be completed. The stern framing is the most complicated area to build because the timbers do not lie in two- but three-dimensional space, requiring complicated angles and bevels to be cut. It is vitally important that you understand the shape of these parts before any cutting and gluing anything together. Personally, I had a difficult time understanding the geometry so I scanned the parts into a graphics programme to create a 3D drawing of the assembled timbers that could be rotated 360° to get that understanding.

PLANK-ON-FRAME MODELLING

356

The stern timbers fitted into the jig beginning with those in the centre and working outwards.

357

All of the stern timbers assembled into the jig. Despite the extensive prefabrication, all of the parts required a lot of fine tuning to get them to fit into each other. The slots in the CNC milled parts require widening and despite my careful fitting, a few gaps existed between parts. These gaps were filled with a mixture of sanding dust collected up from the work bench mixed with a little PVA glue. The dust being the same wood as the rest of the model helps ensure that the repair is a reasonably good match to the rest of the wood. When the model is finished I will give it a coat of tung oil that will help blend in filler with the rest of the wood. The pencil marks seen on some of the timbers denote where they will be trimmed back after the hull is removed from the jig.

358

Typical hull frame parts. The bottom slice of the frame is made of three parts, and the top slice is a single part called the *half futtock*. On this frame the bevel marks are clearly shown for the notched and un-notched parts of the frame. Laser-cutting has left the edges of each part a little jagged and this must be smoothed out with a file.

different from other ships in that they are what we will refer to as the 'half-futtock design'. This means that each frame is not made up of two fully overlapping slices but two partial slices. One slice is missing its centre, and a second slice is that missing centre. This piece we will call the 'half-futtock' (Figure 358). Each complete frame looks like it is missing a tooth. The frames were originally designed in this way to keep the structure light. The ship's frames are further complicated by having notches cut into them to allow the planks to overlap along their bottom and top edges. Clinker planking imparts greater strength to the hull and improved water-tightness. For the model, however, this means that each one of the notches has to be laboriously filed out, and that the notches will have to be filed out at an increasing angle as the frames change their shape towards the bow and stern.

Each of the frame's components are cut from their sheets only as you need them. The kit parts have the basic notches cut into them, and the bevel lines for each notch are etched on their front and back. The bevel, like the bulkheads in plank-on-bulkhead models, become much more acute going forward and aft. When you study the plans, on the midship frames the notches for the bottom and top slice of the frame fall pretty much on top of each other and there is little bevelling of the frame and notches required. When you look at a bow frame the notches on the top and bottom slices of the frame are now offset, and this offset grows the further fore or aft you go. The offset has to be filed way to create angled notches. The char on the inside and outside edges of the frames will get removed when you bevel a frame after assembly. However, the top and bottom tips must have the char removed before assembly, especially on the half-futtock piece because its top and bottom ends are visible. Gently kissing the tips on a disc sander will quickly remove the char and also square them up. If you were to use a file or sanding stick you will likely sand an angle onto the tips because it is almost impossible to hold the sanding stick perfectly square to the rest of the part without a jig or fixture like a True Sander.

Assembly of the frames themselves is quite straightforward but requires attention (Figure 359). Start with a midship frame and sequentially assemble the next frame aft, and the next frame forward. In this way, you will get a good sense as to how the shape of the hull changes, and the bevels required. The frame drawing is taped to a flat surface and the drawing covered with rubber cement. Each part of the bottom slice is placed over the plan ensuring that its placement on the plan is accurate. After the rubber cement is dry, the half-futtocks are glued on top. The parts have some laser-etched lines on

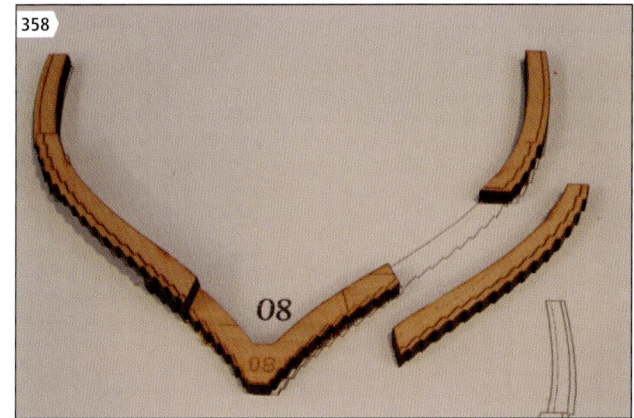

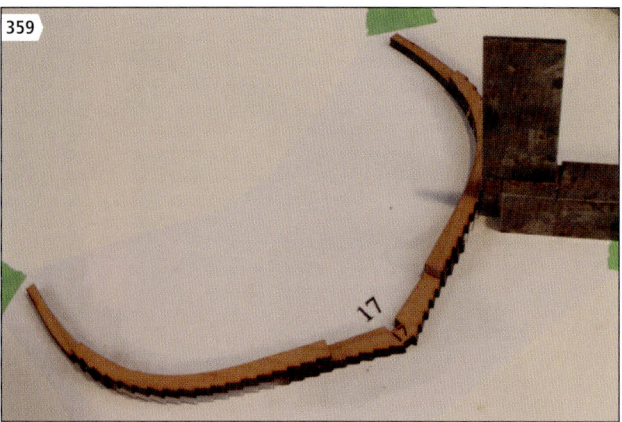

359
Assembly of a frame. The three parts for the bottom slice of the frame are temporarily glued to the drawing with rubber cement. The half futtock is glued on top. A set square is used to check that the half futtock is in the correct location.

360
A close up of how the set square is used to check the positioning of the half futtock.

363
The front face of the same two frames after bevelling.

361
All of *Le Coureur*'s frames assembled.

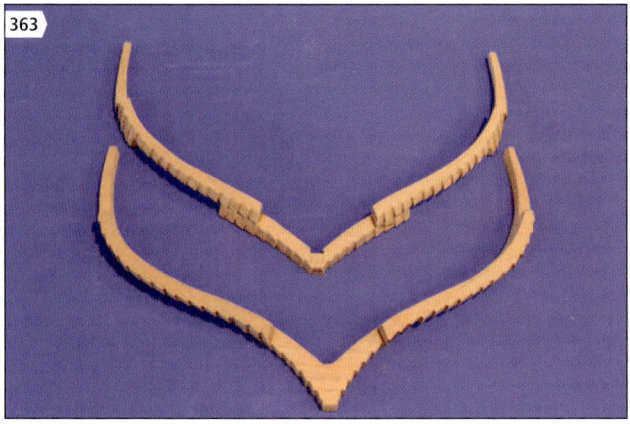

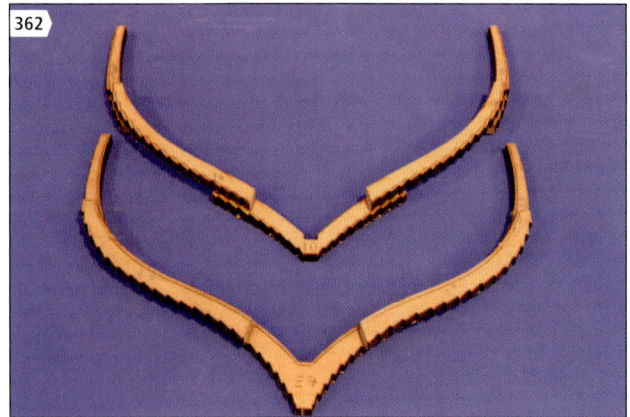

362
Two frames ready for bevelling. The frame at the top of the photo will require more bevelling than the one underneath it.

them to guide placement but you cannot entirely rely on them. Instead, rely on the drawing. Accurate placement of the parts over the drawing is assured with the aid of a small set square that checks that the top edge of the half-futtock lines up exactly with the frame outline drawn on the plans (Figure 360). Once the part is in place and the glue starts to set (if you weight a freshly glued joint the parts may slip out of place), lay a flat square of wood over the frame and a weight. This will ensure the top and bottom slices are firmly joined. The frame is peeled off the paper and any residual rubber cement on the frame can be rubbed off with your finger. Continue gluing up all the frames and set them aside for the glue to dry (Figure 361).

The frames will now have to be bevelled and shaped (Figure 362). This job is quite a lot of work and I suggest you get some good quality needle files because there are a lot of notches to shape. Start again with a midship frame. With the midship frame examine the notches; on this frame they can be filed out smoothly with little problem. Clamp the frame into a bench vice and file them out until the laser char is gone (Figure 363). As you progress towards the bow and stern, the frames will require a greater bevel and these are marked on the parts and plans. The notches too will start to take on an angle. The offset to the notches increases and that extra wood will have to

PLANK-ON-FRAME MODELLING

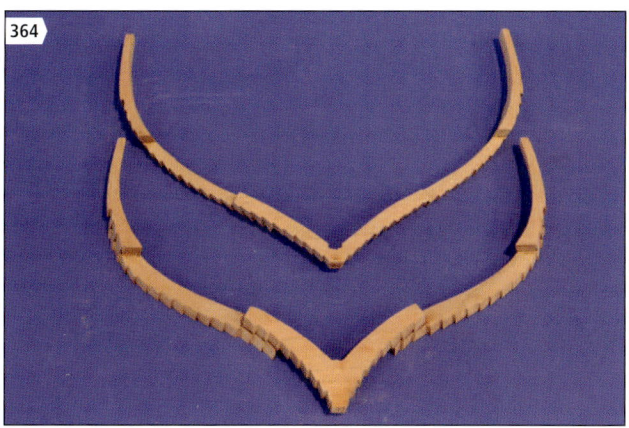

364
The back face of the same two frames after bevelling.

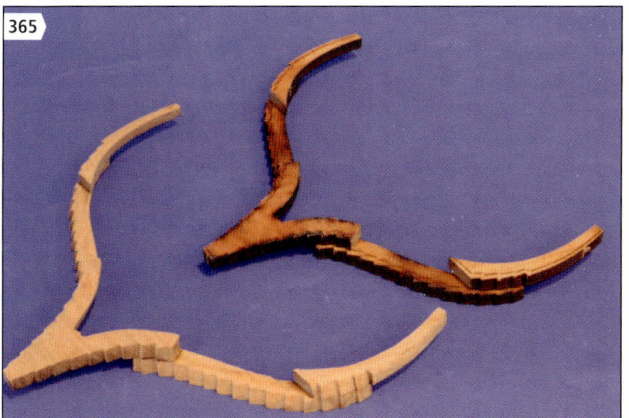

365
A side view of one frame before bevelling and one after.

be filed away (Figure 364). This offset becomes quite large and takes a great deal of effort to get the angle correct while not changing the geometry of the notch (Figure 365).

This filing all takes time and care to get it right, and there is still the matter of bevelling the inside of the frame and the un-notched outside areas. On the inside of the frame the correct bevel is best worked in with a sanding drum. Using a power tool to cut in the bevel requires a lot of care and a light touch. The drum must be held at an angle to cut the bevel with the front tip of the sanding drum while not allowing the back of the drum to touch the back edge of the frame. Use the laser char as your guide here – by leaving a little outline of laser char on the frame's back edge ensures you will not gouge the back and change the shape of the frame. The bevels are completed with a sanding stick, and the frame's front and back faces are sanded to remove any char. This is all very painstaking work and accuracy is key. If you get the bevel wrong the planks won't lie flat and if you don't file the notches correctly, the planks won't line up and not fit the frames at all.

As you complete each frame, install them onto the keel with their tops (known as *top timbers*) put into their respective slots in the jig (Figure 366). Glue should be applied only to the notches on the keel and do not glue the top timbers into their notches. I found the fit very tight in places and the jig notches could do with a little relieving with a file. As you add frames to the keel assembly, you can check the frame's installation and that the correct bevels have been cut into them through one of the knock-out panels (Figures 367). When all the frames have all been installed (Figure 368) the four-part keelson is installed to lock all the frames in place (Figure 369).

After the frames are installed, the installation of the various decks is next. This process begins by gluing back the knock-out panels in the jig and then the measuring sticks are threaded through to help locate the decks (Figure 370). The first parts to go in are the *deck clamps* that are attached to the inside of the frames to act as a ledge for the deck. These clamps are glued into place underneath or above the measuring sticks as indicated in the plans so they are located precisely within the frames (Figure 371). The clamps have notches for the deck beams, and then the decks are planked directly onto the beams. In this kit the decks planks are fully cut and detailed with the proper shift of the butts. The trennels are etched in to the planks as well, and you can drill out these marks and insert pegs cut from a sliver of bamboo for a truly authentic finish.

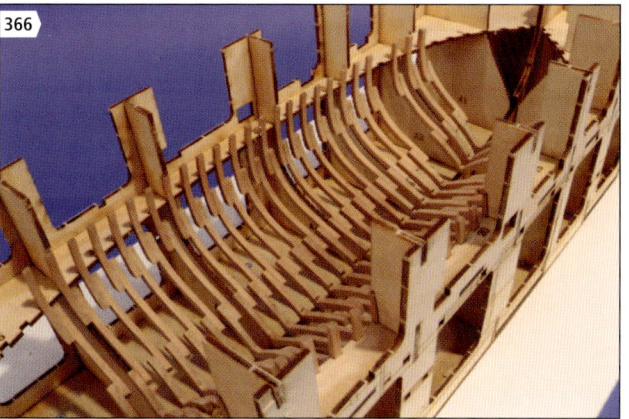

366
The frames being installed in the jig.

367
A view of the frames and their seating on the keel through the jig.

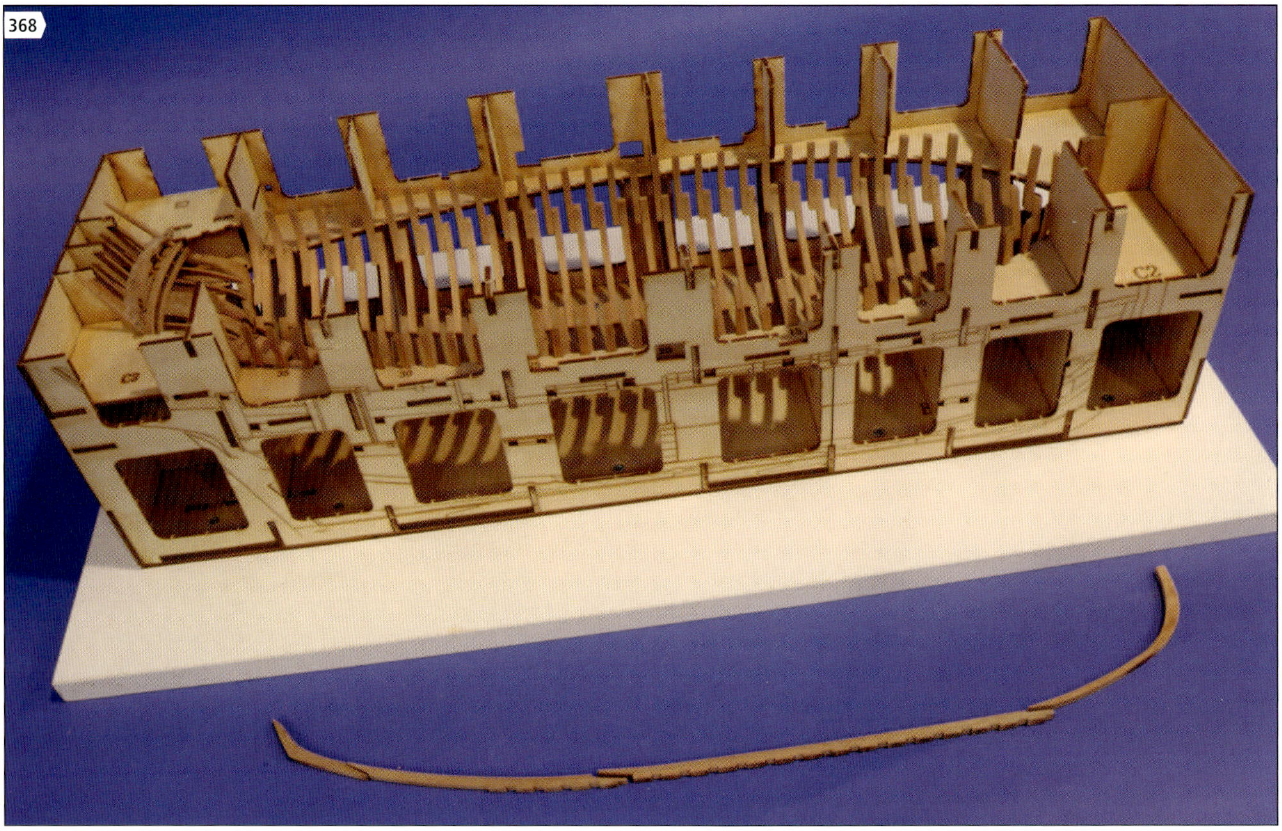

368
All of the frames have been installed and the keelson is installed on top of them to lock them in place. The keelson is in four pieces that are cut with authentic scarf joints where they connect.

369
The keelson at the bow is shown in place. The keelson at the stern looks similar. After gluing in place, a hole was drilled through the scarf joint and a trennal made from a sliver of bamboo skewer was inserted to strengthen the joint. In reality, the keelson was also fastened to each frame with a bolt, and the location and pattern of the bolts is shown in Jean Boudriot's drawings of the ship for you to reproduce if you want greater accuracy and detail. A number of modellers use brass rod to represent the metal bolts to differentiate them from wooden trennals. My method is to use slivers of bamboo dyed black.

But before you go any further it's time to make some decisions. A model in frame is constructed just like the real ship, and as such you have a multitude of ways to finish the model. At one end of the spectrum you can leave off a lot of the hull and deck planking to show off all the frames, beams, clamps and knees. This is just how many models in frame are built where emphasis is put on the framework. You can choose to plank parts of the ship's interior, such as the ceiling planks that form the floor of the ship's hold, and/or plank over some of the interior decks that show off how a ship's timbers were sheathed. With this kit you can also fully build out the different cabins, which ranges from planking the bulkheads between the different compartments, and so on. The designer even includes bedding cast in resin to fit to the cots.

At the other end of the spectrum you can plank over all of the decks and hull. If you choose this route, you will cover up all of the frames and any interior work. This approach is common in scale aircraft modelling where the cockpit and cabins are fully detailed and painted but hidden away when the fuselage halves are put together. The builder often says 'I know it's there and that is all that matters to me'. Nevertheless, glimpses of the interior work will be seen through hatches and gunports and these fleeting glimpses (imagine lighting up the cabins with LEDs, perhaps via a model

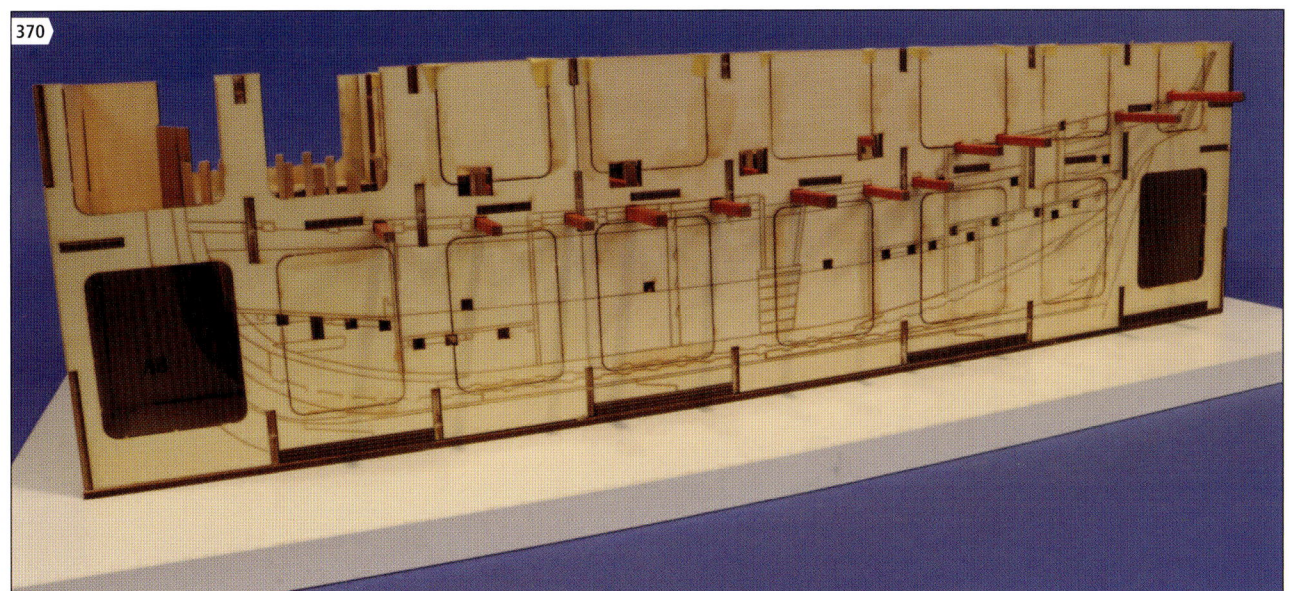

370

With the basic hull framework in place in the jig, the next phase is to install the deck beams, clamps, and pillars. The jig's knock out panels are reinstalled and measuring sticks (painted orange for visibility) are threaded through to precisely locate the deck levels on the frames.

371

An interior view of the jig with the measuring sticks inserted. The deck clamps, a type of sill that runs along the inside of the hull frames, are built up against the measuring sticks to guarantee that they are fixed in exactly the correct spot.

372

The hull planking omitted from part of the hull to show off the hull frames. (Photo courtesy of Tom Cao)

373

The clinker style planking flow into each other and become edge to edge at the bow. A real planking challenge. (Photo courtesy of Tom Cao)

374

The bevelled notches are shown to good effect. (Photo courtesy of Tom Cao)

lantern hanging from a beam or a model candle set on a cabin table) make it seem less like a model but more an impression of the real thing into which you are getting a peep of another life and time.

Another option would be to plank much of the hull but to leave some of the planking off in some areas to permit a view of some of the framework timbers, or to show the ship under repair. You could also plank one side of the ship and leave the other side unplanked. The choice is yours. The kit's designer, Tom Cao built his model to show off the clinker planking, but left off enough of the hull and deck planking to show the interior frames and compartments (Figures 372, 373, and 374). The model is designed to be fully rigged with a lugsail and sailcloth and rigging materials are included.

375

A highly accurate cross-sectional model of the whaler *Charles W Morgan* from Bluejacket Shipcrafters. (Photo courtesy of Al Ross)

376

A view of the interior framing and planking on the *Charles W Morgan* cross-section. You feel like you are really inside the ship! (Photo courtesy of Al Ross)

377

CAF Model's cross-sectional kit of *Granado*. This kit shows the unique nature of British framing practice of the time. This style of timbers is rarely reproduced except by highly skilled scratch-builders. (Photo courtesy of Tom Cao)

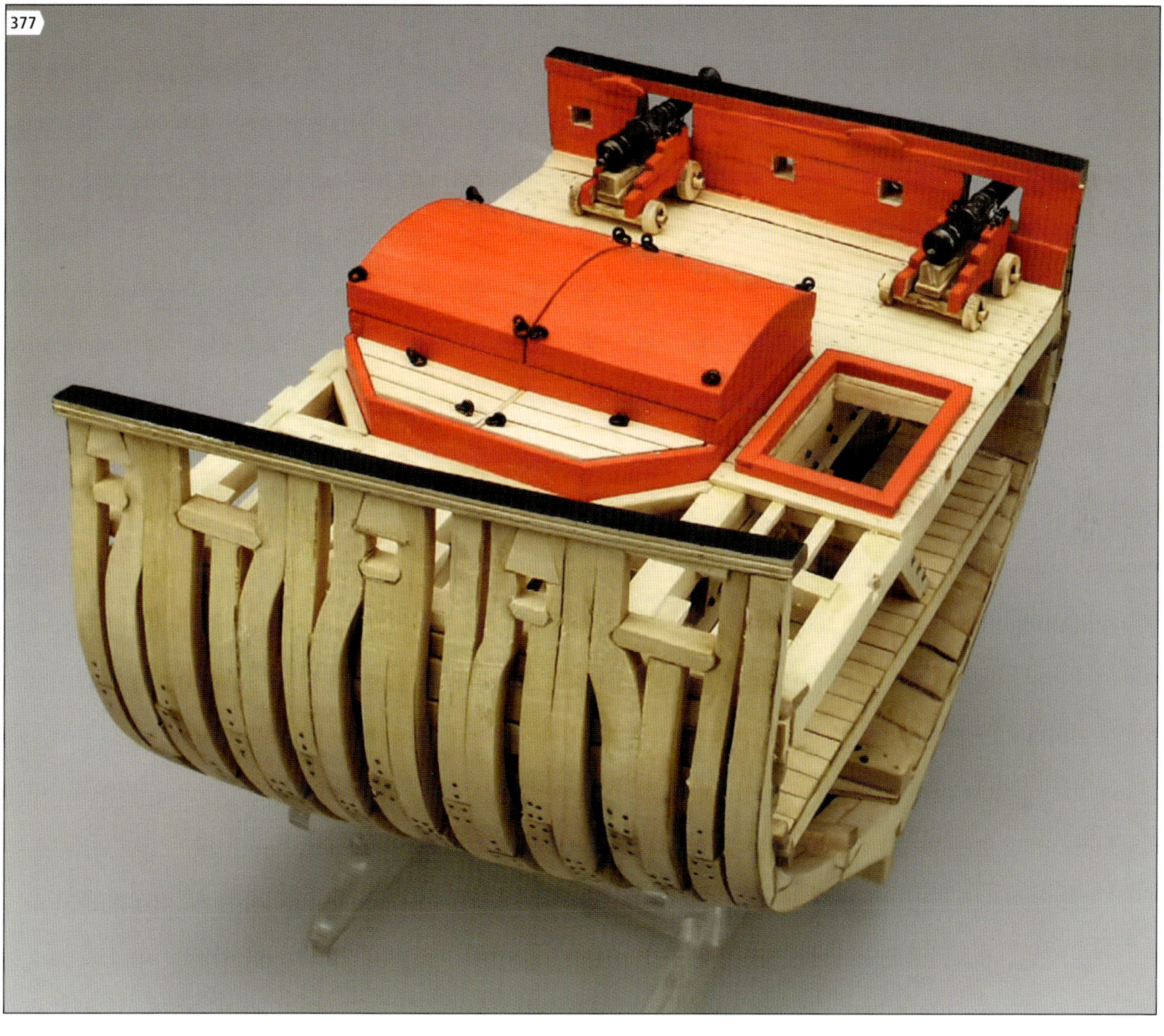

CAF also offer figures of French sailors for this model and these can be painted up and added to the decks creating quite a stunning display.

To be honest I have not yet decided how I will finish building my model so I will leave the build here while I think about what I want. If there is any message you take from this partial build it should be that this form of model requires a lot of careful and precise work, and that, most importantly, it is essential to be able to visualize parts in three dimensions. The stern timbers illustrated are an example, but there are other areas that that are quite perplexing such as the cant frames that make up the bow. In plank-on-bulkhead models we used a filler block to represent these frames, but on a framed model, they have to be built up slice by slice. Their shape is complex in that each frame can be visualized as a slice from a peeled orange. The side of each cant frame is shaped like a wedge that when fitted against each other form a curved surface. On my first attempt at building them I thought the term 'cant' frame was very apt because I 'can't' get them shaped correctly. Designers have devised clever jigs and CNC cut parts to build up this notoriously difficult area of a framed model so check the reviews of a kit to see how the bow framing is tackled.

With this brief overview of *Le Coureur* I hope I have given you the flavour of one of these remarkable new styles of kit. Please be aware that this kit is more difficult because of the clinker planking than other kits that use regular smooth sided frames, such as *Enterprize* shown in Chapter 2, that does not require angled notches being filed out. If you are not ready to build an entire ship in frame, another option is to build a cross-sectional model. This type of model only recreates a segment of a ship, say the length of four or five midship frames and everything that is found in this section. Cross-sectional kits have been around for quite some time and most often they focus on a midship section and include a mast to build up. Other kits focus on the stern or bow areas. However, be careful in your selection as most available cross-sectional kits *do not* feature prototypical framing. They are designed more as a cutaway model to show what is inside a ship. The focus of these models are items like cannons, ladders, pumps, ballast and barrel stowage and few representative beams and knees. Any framing or structural elements are not portrayed accurately. What you want to look for are kits that feature prototypical framing.

At present, there are only two cross-sectional kits that were designed from the outset to feature building up the frames, beams and decks in a prototypical manner that would make a great introduction to plank-on-framed models. The first is by Bluejacket Shipcrafters, who have recreated a section of the whaler *Charles W Morgan* (Figure 375). This large-scale cross-sectional (1/2 in = 1ft) was designed by Mr Al Ross that shows merchant style framing and features a detailed tryworks used to render whale oil from the blubber. At 1/24 scale, the large size of the model makes it easier to build the frames and planks and to replicate all of the small fittings such as bolts and other fastenings (Figure 376). The accuracy of the kit is impressive: even the tryworks are built up from individual bricks like the real thing. The second kit is a cross-section of the bomb vessel *Granado* that precisely recreates British naval framing (Figure 377); it includes one of the main mortars and the massive bed on which these guns were mounted. This kit shows the unique nature of British framing in which some of the timbers have a distinct curve to accommodate gunports, and that each futtock is not the same thickness. When the futtocks are assembled you get the correct stepped appearance. As discussed above, you can decide how much planking to add to the frames and decks of these impressive models (Figure 378).

If you are trying your hand at scratch-building a framed model for the first time, there is nothing to stop you building a cross-sectional yourself. The monographs by Jean Boudriot are a great place to start because each frame and its components are drawn out in full, including the location of beams and knees, which are also the subject of separate drawings as well. It is just a matter of selecting a section of the ship to build and using the drawings as your pattern. At any rate, this new breed of kit puts the fully framed model within the reach of model makers of different skill levels who just do not have the tools and resources to do it all from scratch; they also provide the instruction and hands-on experience to build a ship like the real thing.

374

378

The *Granado* cross-section has been planked on one side and the frames left open for viewing on the other. On the planked side, the shift of hull planks and trenail pattern is clearly reproduced. Any bright finished model should reproduce these details. French and British shipbuilding practices, for example, often differ in these small details, so you must strive to represent them accurately. (Photo courtesy of Tom Cao)

9: Masts and Yards

Masts, yards, rigging, and sails provide the motive power for a ship to cut through the waves. They are also a focal part of a model that captures all the romance and grace of a ship. When it comes to ship models there are many different ways to represent them. Here are three general approaches to consider: stub masts, bare poles, and fully rigged.

The stub masts as we fitted to *Vanguard* in the previous chapter is one way to give the impression of rigging without having to do any of it at all. There are good reasons for displaying a model with stub masts, the most practical being space because full-height masts do take up a lot of room. There are also precedents for this type of display. Models were built not so much as a hobby but as a way of showing the Lords of the Admiralty the new design of a hull. The focus was on the hull lines and any innovations in its shape to make the ship sail faster or provide a more stable gun platform. In contrast, the basic elements of rigging, which was carried out by a master rigger, followed established dimensions and principles so did not need to be displayed. Innovations tended to lie with the hull, and captured ships from other nations were studied intently and lines copied, whereas differences in rigging were minor in comparison.

Bare poles is the way most models are shown (Figure 379). All of the masts, yards, booms and standing rigging are shown *but no sails*. The running rigging that controls the sails is often omitted or their lines are included but knotted to the block that leads it to the sails. In this way, all of the lines are shown. The argument for this type of display is that by omitting the sails, you get an unobstructed view of the hull details you worked so hard on.

The fully rigged model is one that shows all of the masts, yards, rigging and sails on the model. This is the most authentic way of displaying a sailing ship model but given the considerations noted above, this type of model is fairly rare. Fully rigged models are typically found on scenic models that show a ship under sail in the ocean with a crew working the sails (Figure 380). This is the most popular way to display miniature models because there is no concern about space. On large scale dioramas such models are impressive and really capture the essence of a ship at sea where you can see how each rope does something and is straining under the pressure of the wind (Figure 381).

379

The brig *Speedy* sporting rigging but no sails – a bare-poled model.

380

381

380

The small scale of many plastic or resin kits make them great candidates for a scenic model under full sail. Langton Models 1/300 *Victory* was given this treatment. This kit was designed as the ultimate wargaming model that is highly detailed and ready waterlined. The model was fitted with a full crew of sailors to work the sails and Marines and officers on the deck.

381

Large-scale models under full sail. The French lugger *Le Coureur* under pursuit by the British cutter *Alert*. The *Alert* is entirely scratch-built starting with a carved wooden hull and *Le Coureur* is a heavily modified kit by Mamoli. Figures are 15mm wargame items. The diorama is large being 44in long by 22in wide by 18in high so I do not think I will make any more of these. I made some mistakes in the rigging – can you spot them?

382

Speedy's mast begins as a dowel that is compared to the plan to get a sense of what work will be required. The plans give the length, diameter, shapes and tapers required. All this information needs to be transferred to the dowel. (Plan used by permission of Chris Watton, Vanguard Models)

383

The first task is to taper the dowel along its length to the correct diameter with a sanding block. Rotate the dowel with each pass to ensure an even taper along its circumference. *Perry*'s main mast is being tapered in the photo.

When it comes to masting and rigging, the methods are fairly similar across manufacturers and designers. This is probably because masts and yards in model form are really no more than dowels of wood into which tapers are cut. Most of the other major mast elements, such as the tops and the cheeks that support them are laser-cut parts that are attached to the tapered dowels. The real effort is in cutting the taper so that it is even along its length, begins at the correct point and that any flats and square sections required are positioned correctly and are square. In the case of yards, ensuring that the tapers are symmetrical on both ends is the most important task. Most of the model making innovation for masts and yards comes from a kit providing all of the specific mast fittings like hoops, rings, a mouse and highly detailed blocks as opposed to a set of generic parts. All of the information you need to make a mast and its associated parts are on the plans and the most time-consuming elements will be studying the plans, mentally untangling all the lines and ropes, and devising your plan of attack to build them.

Lower Masts

Masts are typically composed of three sections. The *lower mast* is set into the hull and ends with a platform appropriately called the *top*. The second section is called the *topmast*, whose bottom fits into the top and ends with a *trestletree*, a type of lightweight framework. The third part is the *topgallant mast*, whose bottom fits into a trestletree and ends with a cap, called the *truck*. Start work with the lower masts. Whether your model is kit or scratch you will start with a dowel of the maximum diameter (Figure 382). Some scratch-builders do not use dowels at all, instead gluing together several lengths of wood and then planing them round to replicate how real masts were made. Contrary to popular belief, masts were rarely a single tree trunk shaped into a large tapered dowel. The dowel for the mast is cut to the correct length as indicated in the plan. Remember to include the length of the mast that emerges above the deck plus the length of dowel that falls into the mast hole. Cutting a little over-length is always a good idea as you can always trim it back after it has been test fitted to the hull. Mark the bottom of the dowel with an 'M' to remind you this piece is for the mainmast, 'Z' for mizzen, and 'F' for foremast. This seems silly to do but soon you will have several dowels in front of you and it is hard to keep them straight. The lower mast usually has a gentle taper. Using the plans, mark on the dowel where this taper begins and with a sanding block cut in the taper (Figure 383). With a pair of callipers or a circle template, check the diameter of the taper along its length as you sand until the correct dimensions are achieved.

The next step is to mark out where there is a change in shape or taper (Figure 384). On the *Speedy* plans these changes are clearly marked with all diameters and shapes dimensioned, but on other plans you may need to measure each item yourself. Remember to *measure twice*. Most ships have masts that follow the same basic shapes so if in doubt you can always refer to a reference book for guidance as to what goes where. Use a narrow piece of tape to mark the measurements across the entire circumference of the mast. The tape will serve as a guide for creating 'stop cuts'. A knife blade is used score a line around the mast by rolling the mast on the workbench top with the knife edge. Just a shallow cut will do for now because the groove is just there to help guide the blade and ensures that the cuts on the masts are straight and square along its circumference (Figure 385). Starting to shape the mast means deepening the stop

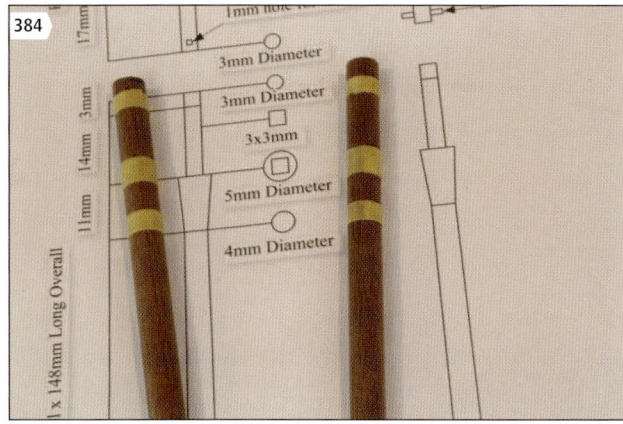

384

The location of different shapes and structures are marked in pencil and then with strips of tape to ensure visibility around the circumference of the dowel. The Vanguard Models plans are use-friendly in providing both written dimensions and shapes. Most other plans would require you to measure directly off the plans themselves.

385

Stop cuts or scores were made by rolling a knife blade along the marked lines on *Perry*'s mast. The perils of not using tape to guide the cut manifested itself as my knife blade did wander and I cut a little bit of a spiral!

cut by pressing on the blade a little more and start paring away the wood into the cut (Figure 386). The wood will fall away from the cut leaving a square edge. The shape is worked in around the mast, paring away a little wood at a time. You can continue to deepen the stop cut as you go along until you reach the correct size and shape. Finish shaping the cut with a file (Figure 387).

Some sections are squared off and again the stop cuts determine the length of the section. Lay the mast on its side on the workbench. With a sharp knife cut in a little flat. Turn the mast over 180° and cut in another slight flat. Turn the mast around again and cut in a flat on the third side, and turn it again and cut in a slight flat on the fourth side. You have now marked all four faces. With a file, held dead horizontal, file in a wider flat, turn and repeat. Keep doing this until your edges meet up. In cases where there only two flats are required the main consideration is that the flats are even on both sides. Pick a side and mark it 'S' for starboard and 'P' for port. Again, cut a slight flat on both side and gradually file in the flats to the correct dimensions. When you are all done, check the dimensions and refine any shapes as necessary. This work is all very therapeutic and although it sounds hard it is not at all.

Top and Topgallant Masts

The topmasts are similar to the lower masts, so once again, with reference to the plans, cut a piece of dowel a little over-length. Mark out the places where the tapers begin and use tape to mark the area and make shallow stop cuts. Unlike the lower masts where there is typically a gentle taper, the taper of a topmast is much greater. In these masts I find it easier to start the taper by paring them in with a knife, followed by sanding. When paring away the wood, start at the top and pare away the wood all the way around. Work your way

386

A knife is used to pare down a flat. The wood will part neatly from the stop cut.

387

A file is used to refine the flat. With the stop cut, pare and file flat method, any shape can be worked into a dowel.

MASTS AND YARDS

388
Speedy's lower masts, topmasts and topgallants shaped.

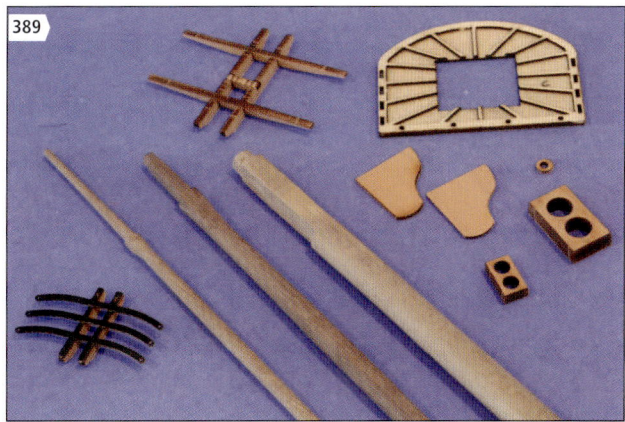

389
Speedy's mast tops, trestletrees, cheeks, caps and truck ready for assembly.

390
Speedy's mast tops fixed to the mast with the supporting cheeks. Some eyebolts have also been fitted.

391
Speedy's main top mast being fitted.

down the taper, with more wood being taken away at the top then the bottom. Constantly turn the dowel to ensure that you are taking the wood off evenly. When the taper starts to form, use a coarse sanding stick to sand the taper to the correct dimensions. Once again, the key is to rotate the dowel constantly as you cut or sand. Always use a new sharp blade when paring down the dowel and take shallow cuts. If the dowel doesn't cut well, cut in the other direction. Shallow cuts with the grain work best. The topgallant masts are made the same way. Topgallant masts are very thin and can be easily cut through or snapped into pieces while sanding, so sand the tapers in gently, moving the sanding block only in one direction.

With all the masts components carved and shaped (Figure 388),

392
Speedy's topgallant being installed.

393

Speedy's completed masts are test fitted to the hull. The masts have a rake and the tops and trestletrees are fixed parallel to the waterline.

MASTS AND YARDS

394
To taper a yard in a lathe, one end is chucked and the other end is sanded with sandpaper held in the fingers. The friction can generate a lot of heat and cause a burn, so watch the lathe speed. When one end is done, the other end is chucked, gripping the flat centre section and repeated. A piece of tape is wrapped around the dowel to minimize any chance that the jaws of the chuck damages or marks the wood.

it is time to assemble them into their full units. Whether kit or scratch-built, the next step is to make and shape the tops, *cheeks* (timbers that support the top) and *caps,* a piece of wood that fixes each mast to one another with the proper spacing (Figure 389). These items are clearly shown in all plans and the thing to keep in mind is that masts are not perfectly vertical, but generally lean backwards – the angle is called the *rake* of the masts. The amount of rake is shown in the plans and will differ for each ship and, indeed, type of ship. What this means is that the tops are fixed to the mast at an angle to compensate for the rake so it is parallel to the waterline (Figure 390). The mast caps are also put on at an angle and to do so means that the holes that are cut into them to accommodate the mast must be filed to an angle to allow them to sit properly (Figure 391).

YARDS

The yards hold the sails and are tapered like the masts but differ in that both ends are tapered and the centre section is not. On some of the yards, the centre section is round, and on some the centre section is octagonal. Reference to the plans will show how each yard is shaped. The tapers are cut as before using a knife and sandpaper, but another method is to chuck the dowel into a lathe and hold a piece of folded sandpaper to grip the dowel. Turn on the lathe and sand in the taper (Figure 394). You could also do this in a hand-held power drill but you have a lot less control and the spinning wood gets hot quickly and can burn your fingers. The wood can also whip and snap off causing injury. I prefer the knife and sandpaper method which is a little slower but you get ultimate control. If you are worried about the tapers not being round you could chuck it into a lathe to correct the shape after the basic tapers have been cut in with file and knife.

If the yard requires an octagonal shape this is best done with a flat file. Always file on directly opposite sides to get an even result. For example, if you imagine the cross section of the yard as a compass, sand a slight flat at the North position then sand another flat directly opposite at the South position. Next sand flats at the East and West positions, followed by the North East and South West positions, then the North West and South East in turn. Repeat, each time filing in the flat a little more, and after three or four rotations the edges of all faces should meet and you have an even octagonal section.

All other yards and the booms are similarly tapered and shaped. The bowsprit is built more like a mast and must be test fitted to the hull to ensure its angle is correct and that its end fits into the knighthead whose hole will have to be angled to fit (Figure 395). There are a multitude of items such as footropes, eyebolts, irons, bands that are carried by the masts and yards (Figures 396 and 397). The important consideration is which parts to put on before painting the masts, yards, booms and bowsprit and which are best added after. For the yards at least, these were often painted black so virtually all the fittings can be added and painted in one operation (Figures 398). Masts were often painted, particularly in later periods, but at many times the timber was just clear varnished. In such a case, the mast is finished first and the fittings added later. Figures 398 to 400 show several variations.

395
The bowsprit under construction and test fitted. It is critical to get the angle of the bowsprit and its cap correct early on.

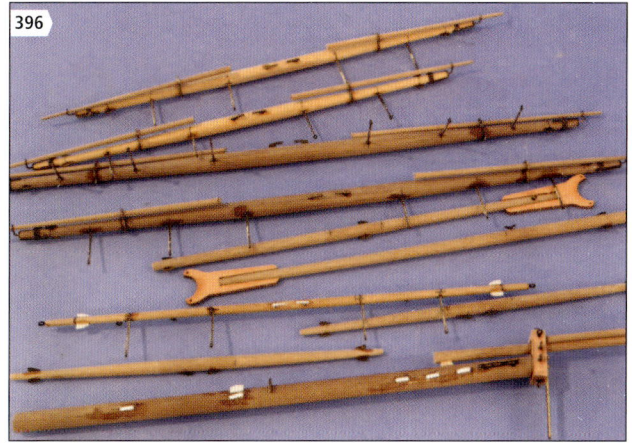

396
Speedy's yards, booms and bowsprit ready for painting with all fittings fixed in place.

397

Perry's mast, yards, booms, and bowsprit parts ready for assembly and painting.

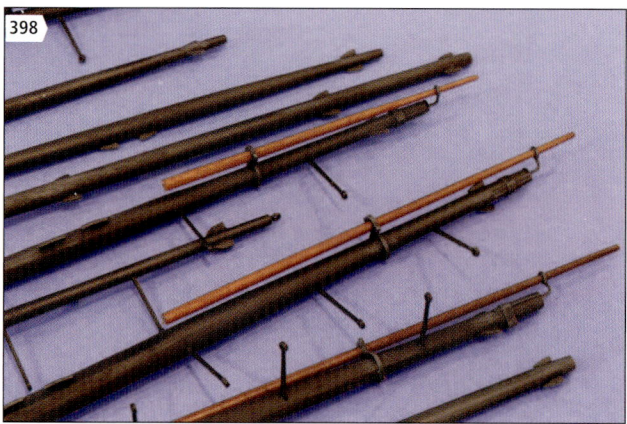

398

Speedy's yards are painted black and detailed. The stunsail booms on the ends of the yards were clear finished and fixed in place after the yards and fittings were finished in black.

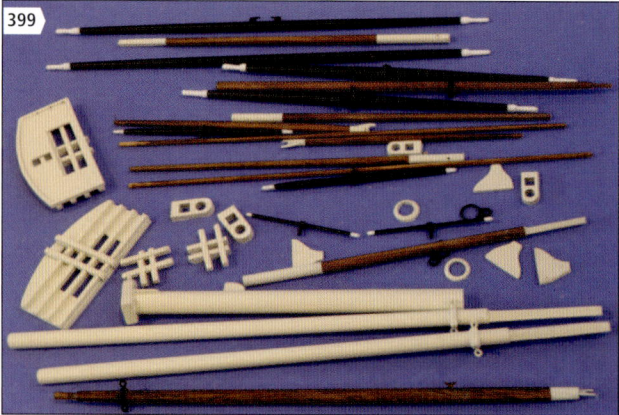

399

Perry's painted masts, yards, bowsprit and booms. Unlike *Speedy*, the mast parts were painted before assembly owing to the more complex colour scheme of this ship. Painting white is also difficult with a brush, requiring several coats to build up a solid colour. Masking and spraying with an airbrush or aerosol is much faster and yields a very smooth finish. The white tips on the yards were painted by dipping the ends in white paint. White paint is poured into a little cup to the height required and the yard dipped in. The excess paint is wicked away and the yard is held vertically until the paint is dry.

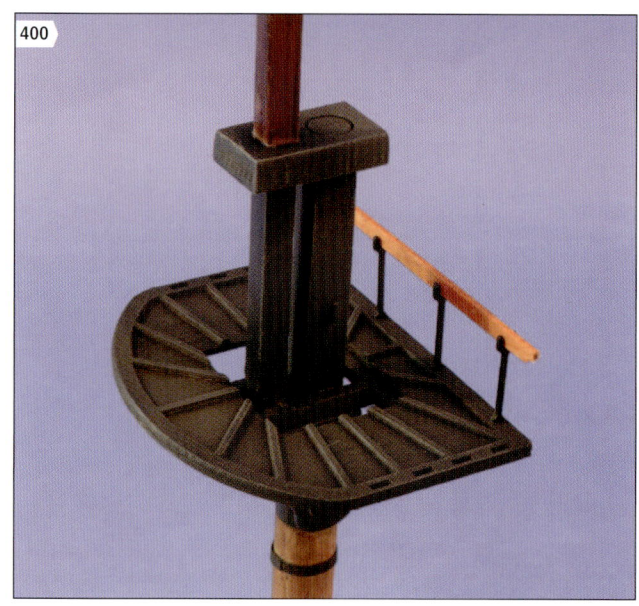

400

Speedy's finished mast top. The mast itself was clear finished with the mast's strengthening bands made of black cartridge paper. The top was painted black and lightly dry brushed with grey to bring out the details.

Preparation for Rigging

Before we can start stringing lines there is a great deal of preliminary work to do beginning with the preparation of the blocks, stropping them and attaching them to the masts and yards. The extent of this work is shown on the plans, and I would strongly suggest you check the plans against an authoritative reference to ensure that they are correct. You cannot entirely rely on kit plans because they are often simplifications of the rigging and some get it wrong altogether. Moreover, it's important to refer to an authoritative reference to get the characteristics and peculiarities of the rig correct for the ship's time period. Rigging practices changed over the centuries, and there are some national differences as well. Given the conservative nature of rigging, often the required changes are accomplished by deleting or adding lines or blocks to your model.

I won't go into making your own blocks because these days there is little need to. In many kits, the rigging blocks are pretty unrealistic and are simply square pieces of wood with some holes (often not accurately) drilled through them. I call these 'blocky blocks' because

MASTS AND YARDS

401

401
Wooden rigging blocks. The blocks to the far left are typical walnut blocks found in many kits. They bear just a passing resemblance to the real thing. The blocks in the centre are excellent representations that have been properly milled to the correct shape, have the correct scores and a representation of the sheaves inside. They are made of pear wood and can be supplied by Vanguard Models. On the far right are boxwood blocks made by the Syren Model Company. These blocks are correct in shape and details and usable right out of the bag. They are available in a large number of different sizes and types to rig your model to scale. It is wise to run a drill bit through the holes of any block to ensure they are clear.

402
Unrealistic blocks can be sanded to a more oval shape to better resemble the shape of real blocks.

that is what they are (Figure 401). New kits, and certainly those available from the aftermarket sources, provide beautifully shaped blocks whose shells are correctly shaped, with holes, grooves for strops, and even a hint of a sheave already carved in place. These new blocks are courtesy of laser cutting or CNC technologies. They are very much worth the investment and they are not too expensive given the detail they carry. In my search for accurate blocks, thanks to CAD and CNC milling these days you can find blocks in specific sizes and shapes used by the British and Continental navies.

The version of the *Speedy* kit I purchased had realistic wooden blocks included as part of the package, and the *Perry* has pewter versions. The *Cutty Sark* kit had hundreds of blocky blocks as did the *Vanguard*. Blocky blocks can still be used and you can greatly improve their appearance by sanding them to a little more of an oval shape as shown in Figure 402. Some people have created 'block sanders', which is a form of rock tumbler used to polish stones that is lined with sandpaper. The blocks are spun around in the drum mounted to a drill or motor and that smooths off the edges. Personally, this hasn't worked all that well for me and a few swipes of a sanding stick works better if a little tedious.

All blocks must be *stropped*. Stropping a block is to add a loop of rope or metal band (depending on the era) around the block so the block can be attached or *seized* to a mast or yard. The strop can take many forms, depending on the block's purpose. The strop can have a loop formed into it (called a *becket*) so that a hook or line can be attached to it; or an eye to allow the block to be seized onto something like a mast, eyebolt or yard. With reference to the plans, the blocks will be fitted with different kind of strops with one loop, two loops, or items like hooks. Stopping blocks is a fiddly procedure

404
The seizing thread – usually a thinner diameter – is laid across the two threads.

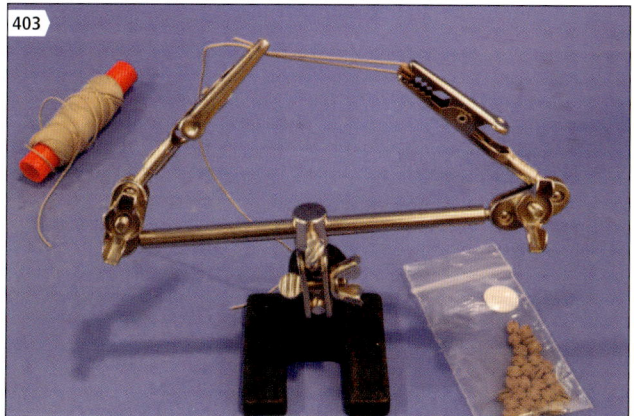

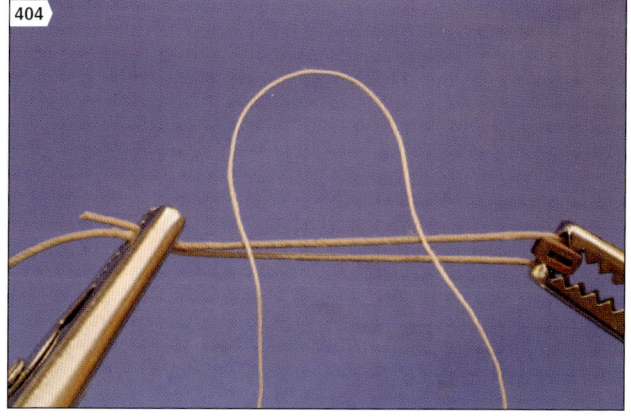

403
Stropping a block. A length of rigging thread is wrapped around a block held in the right-hand jaw. The thread's tail is held in the left-hand jaw and pulled taut.

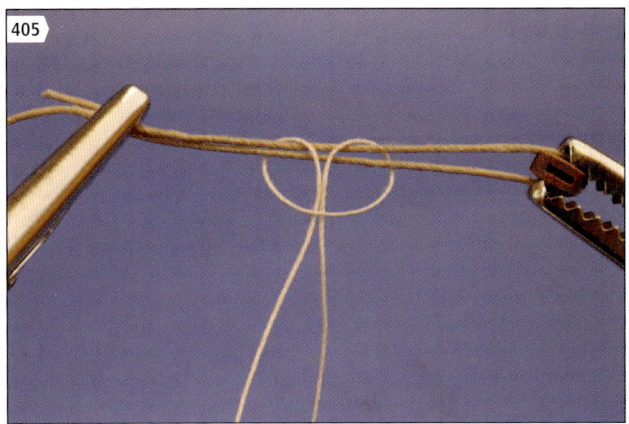

405

The tails of the seizing rope are looped around the thread stropping rope.

406

The tails of the seizing rope are pulled tight.

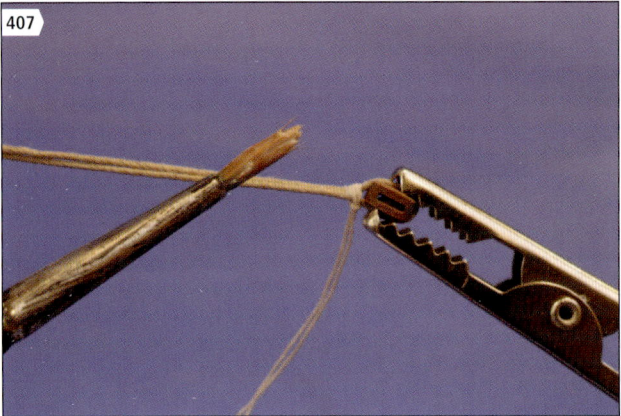

407

The knot is slid down tight against the block and a dab of glue fixes the seizing. Once dry the tails of the seizing knot are cut away.

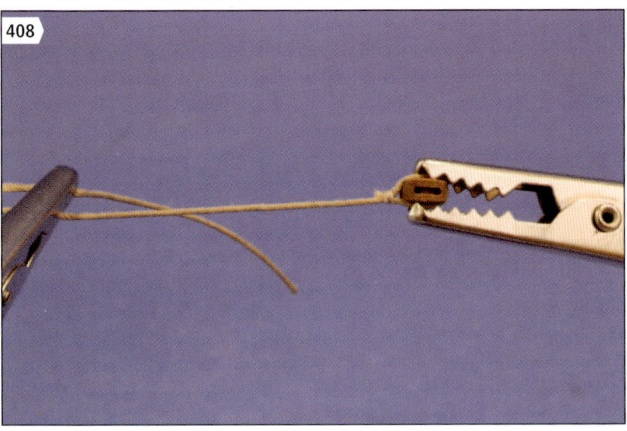

408

One of the tails of the strop is cut away and you are left with a neatly stropped block ready to be attached to whatever place it is required.

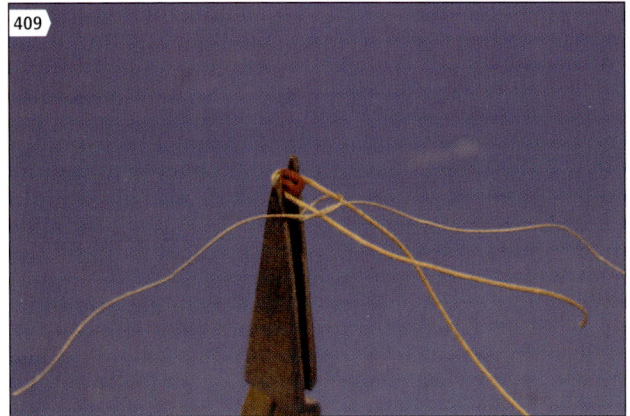

409

Another way of stropping a block. A block is held in a pair of cross action tweezers wrapped with stropping thread. A simple overhand knot is used for the seizing held fast with a dab of glue.

because the blocks are often very small, or you have to form a loop before wrapping the rope around the block and tying it off. Sometimes if the strops aren't fitted well, the blocks slip out and fall to the floor often never to be seen again. Everyone develops their own method of stropping a block but shown in the Figures 403 to 409 are two ways I use to get you started.

To add a becket a loop is first formed with a simple slip knot. The knot is fixed with glue and the ends of the line are fitted around the block and tied off at the bottom of the block, making sure the becket at the top is in the correct position. Stropping blocks and figuring out how to add beckets using slip knots (some blocks have two) takes practice. The first few blocks you will strop will be frustrating because they always seem to fall out of their strops or from your fingers. The first few will seem to take ages to do and that the job will never get done. Do not despair: after some practice your brain and fingers will work together and the job becomes quite enjoyable and hundreds of blocks are prepared in no time at all.

Following the plans, seize all the blocks to their yards and masts. The line is wrapped around the mast or yard or put through an

MASTS AND YARDS

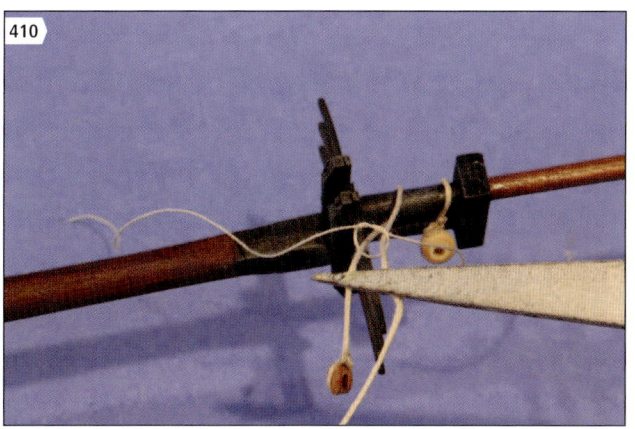

410
A block is being seized to a mast. The stropping thread is wrapped around the mast and a simple overhand knot is used as the seizing.

411
The blocks attached to a mast.

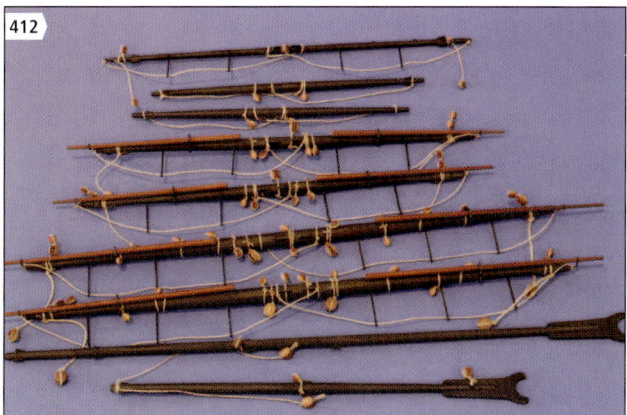

412
Following the plans, all the required blocks are seized to the *Speedy*'s yards and booms. There is a myriad of different types of stropping attached to the blocks, some with beckets, some with lines, and some in which a smaller block is stropped to a larger block.

413
Deadeyes and blocks fitted to *Speedy*'s mast top.

414
Speedy's bowsprit fitted out with its blocks and deadeyes. It must be emphasized that before attaching any block or deadeye in place that a drill bit is run through all of the holes to ensure that they are clear.

415

The *Perry*'s masts are fitted to the hull and all the blocks and footropes attached to the yards, boom and bowsprit ready for rigging. The blocks for this kit are provided in white metal and have to be cleaned up and painted before use. Some of the blocks supplied are ready stropped and have a moulded becket(s) to attach the lines. The moulded becket often needs to be drilled through, like the sheave holes, to ensure thread can easily be rove through. Bluejacket Shipcrafters offer a huge variety of highly realistic unstropped and stropped blocks with metal or rope beckets.

eyebolt and the tail knotted with a seizing which can be a simple overhand knot (granny knot). A pair of cross action tweezers are helpful in holding lines in place (Figure 410). Once tied off, the block can be slid into position and the knot fixed with glue and the excess thread trimmed off (Figures 411). As the blocks are being seized to the yards (Figure 412) this is the time to rig footropes and any other fittings. The deadeyes on the mast tops can be inserted (Figures 413 and 414). The number of blocks to be attached to the ship can be confusing, so work methodically starting at one end and working your way down. Remember to glue your knots; a little thinned PVA works well but takes a bit of time to dry, and if you are impatient, you can bind the knots with shellac that dries quickly. The use of CA is controversial in some circles. The reasons to use it is that it dries instantly and really soaks into the line. However, it makes the line where it is applied hard and brittle that can snap and the longevity of the bond is unknown. Personally, I use whatever works best at the time and I have decades-old models where CA was used on some or all of the rigging and so far no problems.

The masts are inserted into the hull (Figure 415). The height is checked and the bottoms trimmed if necessary. The rake is also checked and may need to be corrected by shaving a little wood off the base of the mast, or shimming it with slivers of wood until it stands at the correct angle. I do not recommend that the masts are glued into the hull, but packed into place. You may want to remove the mast one day to change the rig, or have to remove it to make repairs. With the masts in place, it is time to start threading the lines.

10: Standing Rigging

Rigging begins with thread. It can be made of cotton, linen or a mix of polyester and cotton. They are all, upon close inspection, a little fuzzy but this can be reduced by running the line through a block of beeswax that lays the fibre down. A ship is rigged with many different diameters of line, and this is reflected in kits by providing several thicknesses of thread (Figure 416). Kit manufacturers typically provide a few diameters but they do not reflect all the different diameters used on a real ship. You can add more thread sizes if you like and it will take research to determine how many additional sizes are required; and it is this work that makes this hobby so absorbing. Often times the thread may be only available in white, but it can be coloured with fabric dye to whatever shade you require. Model rigging thread is often provided in shades of tan or black/dark brown. The black thread represents the *standing rigging*; these are ropes that have been covered in tar for protection. Standing rigging is in effect a structural part of the ship whose job is to hold the masts in place and keep them from bending too far forward or back, or side to side under the pressure of the wind. The tan coloured thread is for the running rigging to be covered in the next chapter. *Running rigging* is the working rigging, natural untarred ropes that are heaved in and let out to work the sails.

Thread is fine for most models, but many will insist it does not look like real rope. In Chapter 3 I showed a rope walk used to spin your own rope. If your pocket book allows it, you can buy hanks of ready-made scale rope from a number of suppliers. I think scale rope is important to use on larger scale models (*eg*, 1/48 and up). In smaller scale models, thread is fine, and for miniatures, tinned copper wire or hard nickel chromium is best because of its fine dimensions, lack of hairiness, and natural sags or catenaries can be shaped into the wire to represent the effect of gravity and the weight of ropes in a most realistic way. Wire is easily painted by stretching it straight and running it through a brush loaded with paint.

The most important question on rigging is 'what order do I do it in?' It is important to note that the order we rig a model is not the same procedure a master rigger would use on an actual ship. On models, rigging usually starts at the bow and works aft. Rigging is started at the hull level and works upwards. It all starts with adding the standing rigging first, and the order I use is:

1. Bowsprit
    i. Gammoning
    ii. Stays
    iii. Boomkins
2. Mast
    i. Shrouds
    ii. Ratlines
    iii. Back Stays
    iv. Fore Stays

Bowsprit Rigging

The bowsprit is fixed to the hull and you must ensure its angle is correct. Rigging begins with the *gammoning*. Gammoning is a rope lashing by which the bowsprit was held down to the stem. For modelling purposes, tie black coloured thread with a simple overhand knot and feed the free end around the bowsprit into the slot in the head (Figure 417). The gammoning will take around eight turns or so until the slot is filled. The free end is pulled tight and wrapped around the middle of the lashing around two or three times to pinch the gammoning in – called the *frapping*. The bowsprit stays are rigged next and these stays help the bowsprit *stay* in place and prevent side to side movement. Bowsprit stays are rigged using deadeyes, blocks, or thimbles (a round hollow block) depending on the type of ship. The purpose of the block or deadeye is to provide a

416
Many types of commercially and kit supplied threads of different weights and colour. My favourite is all 100% linen thread that has the least amount of hairiness and a hard finish that looks most authentic.

417
The bowsprit has been attached to the hull and the gammoning and stays rigged. Pay particular attention to the orientation of the deadeye holes. By pulling or letting out the lanyards laced through the deadeyes the bowsprit can be tensioned. The deadeye lanyards are not black because they were untarred.

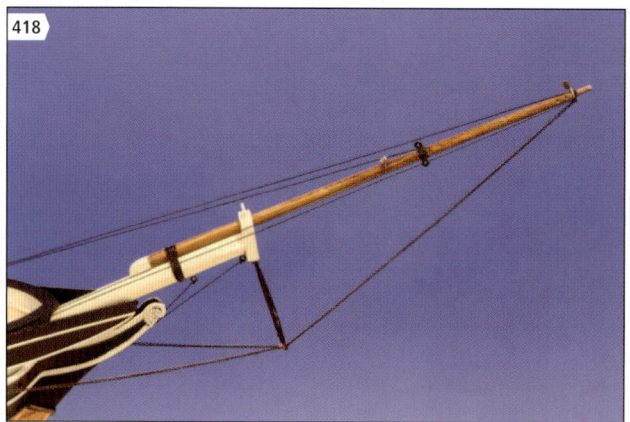

418

The bowsprit rigging on *Perry* is a little different. Coming from a later era some of her stays are chain. The principal stay is a length of chain that starts at the end of the jibboom and attaches to a martingale (also called a dolphin striker). The martingale is attached to the hull by two lengths of chain called bobstays. These stays check any upward tension put on the bowsprit and jibboom from the action of sails and rigging used to hold the fore mast upright.

means of tensioning the stay using lines (called lanyards) that can be pulled tight or let go slack to align the bowsprit or tighten up stays that work loose (Figure 418). The *boomkin* is next installed into the bow of the ship and its stays rigged. The boomkins are short spars mounted to each side of the ship to hold a block to which lines controlling a foresail were passed (Figure 419).

Shrouds

The shrouds are put up next. Shrouds are parts of the standing rigging that hold the mast upright from side to side. Each mast typically has three sets of shrouds to be rigged: 1) the lower shrouds that run from the hull deadeyes to the mast top; 2) the upper (or topmast) shrouds that run from the mast top to the trestletree; and 3) the topgallant shrouds that run from the trestletrees to the very top (or truck) of the mast. The lower shrouds are the first to be rigged and they are connected to the chain plates by pairs of deadeyes that are rove through with lanyards.

Rigging starts with stropping deadeyes to the shroud lines. I use a model making expedient that uses three knots to seize the deadeye to the shroud as shown in Figure 420. You can properly seize the deadeye to the shroud by tightly wrapping the ends of the shroud together with thread. There is a device called a 'serving tool' that holds the shroud around the deadeye, and then you turn a hand crank that wraps the line in fine thread. A spacer is made out of a bent paper clip or brass rod to help space the deadeyes pairs. The served shroud is now ready to support the mast. The end of the shroud is loosely seized to the mast so it can be tightened or let out to get the spacing correct. Once the spacing is correct the shroud is permanently seized to the mast and the deadeyes are laced with a lanyard. There is a proper order to the reeving of the deadeyes and this is shown in Figure 421. Pull the lanyard taut – but not too tight because adjustments will likely be necessary later, so don't tie off (Figure 422) until all the shrouds are on (Figures 423 and 424).

419

The boomkins are mounted to the hull and rigged. The bowsprit gammoning can be seen to good effect.

420

The shroud has been attached to the deadeye with three seizings. A shroud is a length of rope with deadeyes seized to both ends. A deadeye is attached to one end of the rope and it goes up and around the mast and back down to the same side of the ship where the second deadeye is attached. The distance between the top pair of deadeyes and the lower pair set into the channel is temporarily spaced with a bent paper clip.

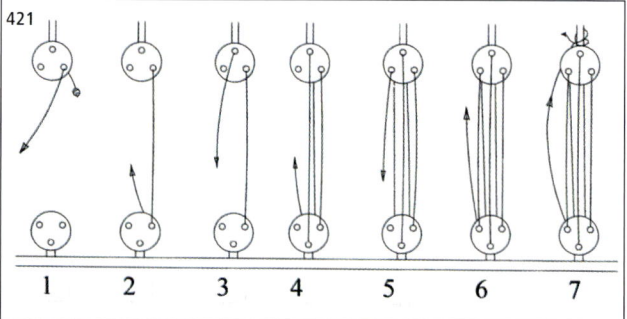

421

Lanyard reeving order. (Diagram courtesy of Vanguard Models)

STANDING RIGGING

422
The deadeyes are laced (rove through) and left loose until all of the shrouds are in place.

423
The deadeye lanyards can be adjusted to ensure equal spacing and tension on all the shrouds. The ends of the lanyards are brought up to the back of the deadeye and tied off around the shroud.

424
Shrouds set up on *Perry*. The first deadeye is slightly too high compared to the others. Those lanyards will be cut and re-laced and pulled down to the correct position before tying off.

THE TOPMAST AND TOPGALLANT SHROUDS

The upper shrouds are set up like the lower shrouds but these go from the mast top to the tip of the topmast. The first step is to put the deadeyes into the mast top (if you have not already done so) and attach a metal bar with a touch of glue to the top of the shroud (Figure 425). This bar is called a *catharpin,* a clamp used to brace the shrouds toward the masts and prevent them from interfering with the yards. Once the glue is dry, thin thread ties the catharpin to the shrouds, and it is held in place around the mast with a rope, trimmed and painted black (Figure 426). The *futtock shrouds* are fitted next. These shrouds are ropes that hold the deadeyes set into the mast top in place. The Vanguard Models kit is very accurate in providing little hooks to attach to the deadeyes (Figure 427) and the futtock shrouds themselves are tied to the catharpin. With the mast top deadeyes locked in place, the upper shrouds can be rigged in the same manner as the lower shrouds (Figure 428). The final set of shrouds to be rigged are the topgallant shrouds shown in Figure 429. This procedure is repeated for all the masts on the ship.

RATLINES

The shrouds are 'rattled down' – that is, the *ratlines* are added next. Ratlines are lengths of thin line tied between the shrouds to form a rung that enables the matelot to climb up the shrouds into the

425
The catharpins being attached to the main mast shrouds. Note that the deadeyes in the mast top will need rotating so that the holes are correctly oriented.

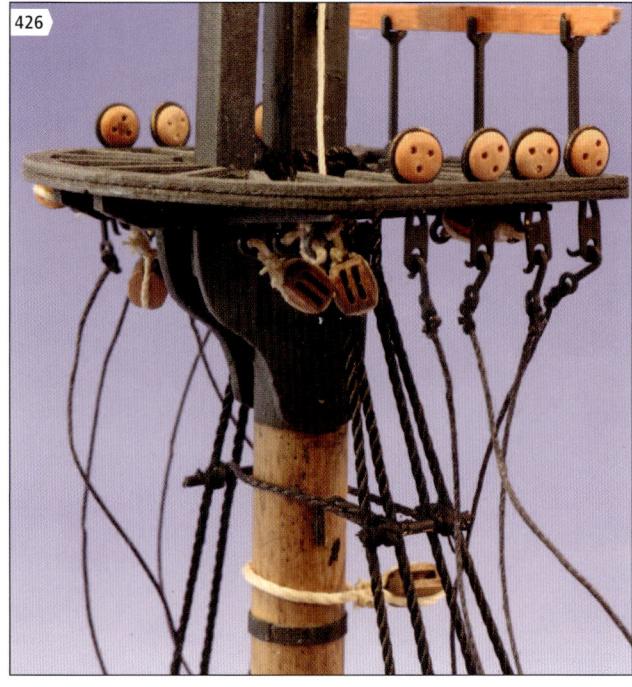

426
The catharpins are now fully rigged, the bar trimmed back and painted black. The futtock shrouds are attached to the deadeyes using hooks.

427
The futtock shrouds are tied off to the catharpins.

rigging. There are many schools of thought as to how best to tie ratlines on a model ship. The most common one is to use clove hitches to tie the thin thread around each shroud. However, I tend to focus on aesthetics. Clove hitch knots can look very large and lumpy, and when tying many in a row tends to pull the shrouds inwards. This is especially problematic on smaller scale models that use lighter weights of thread.

My solution – and this is just my way of doing things – is to choose how I tie the ratlines depending on the scale of the model. For models greater than 1/64 I will use clove hitches to fix the ratlines on each shroud, simply because the shrouds, being of thicker thread will not pull out of shape and the knots do not look out of place. On models from 1/64 to around 1/96 I will tie the ratline on with simple overhand knots to each shroud (Figure 430). On models smaller than 1/96 or so I will use a simple overhand knot on the outer shrouds and let the ratline lay on top of the inner shrouds which are then fixed in place with a dab of thinned PVA glue (Figure 431). I will use all the different methods depending on the ship and where the ratlines need to be tied. The upper shroud ratlines are finer than the lower shrouds so a simple overhand knot and glue will do (Figure 432). Miniature models don't use thread but wire for rigging so ratlines are glued in place.

When it comes to the ratlines there is a bit of a debate over what colour thread to use. Many modellers use tan thread thinking these ropes have to be untarred and flexible for the feet of the sailors who climb up them. Some authorities suggest the colour difference between ratline and shroud depends on the quality of the tar used on each part, or how many coats have been applied, or how long it's been on and weathered. Black or tan, it has been a debate and my

STANDING RIGGING 149

428

The main mast upper shrouds are installed and catharpins fitted to the top of these shrouds as before.

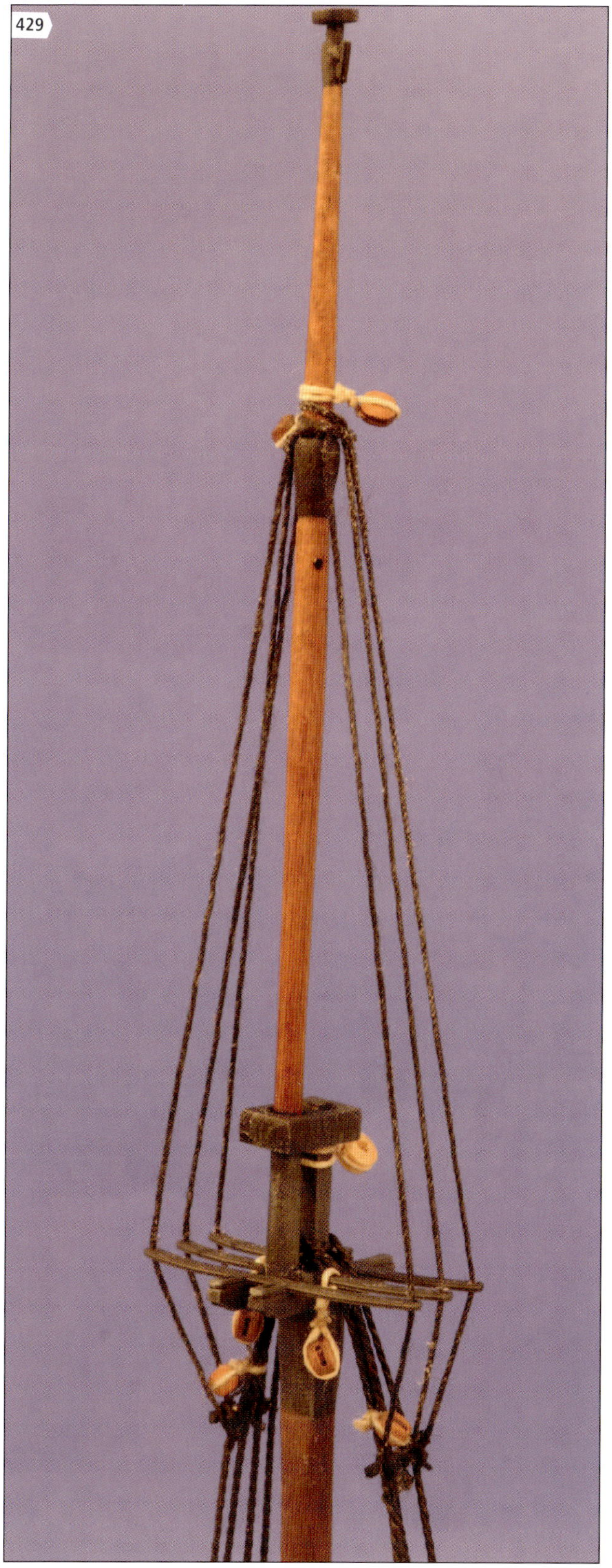

429

The topmast shrouds are rigged and tied off to the catharpins.

430

Ratlines being tied to the main shrouds using overhand knots. On the lower ratlines you can see some of the fuzziness that can occur if you don't run the thread through beeswax before using it.

431

Compared to the much larger scale of the *Speedy*, the *Perry*'s shrouds and ratlines were of much finer gauge and the shrouds were much more easily distorted as the ratlines were added. I will confess a major error here. I used the wrong gauge thread for the shrouds. The thread is far too fine. I dropped the bag of thread spools on the floor and the correct one was found under a bench a month after the shrouds were rigged. Instead of tearing it all out and re-rigging the shrouds in heavier thread, I left it as is. As a result, I was forced to use even thinner thread for the ratlines making the job far more difficult because the thin thread has no weight and does not want to lie flat. After all the ratlines were tied, they all got a coat of thinned PVA glue and while drying I shaped the ratlines to sag naturally. Some of them simply refused!

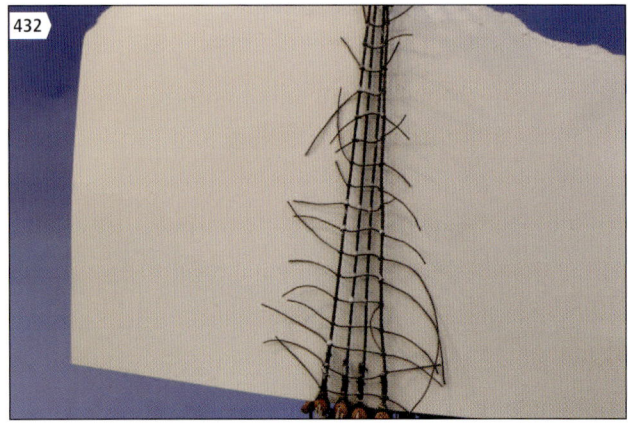

432

Speedy's upper shrouds being rattled down. Overhand knots were used on the outer shrouds and the thread was allowed to lay on top of the inner shrouds. Thinned white glue is used to secure all knots. A piece of white card is placed behind the shrouds to make the work more visible. On a large ship there are so many lines going all over the place it's easy to get confused!

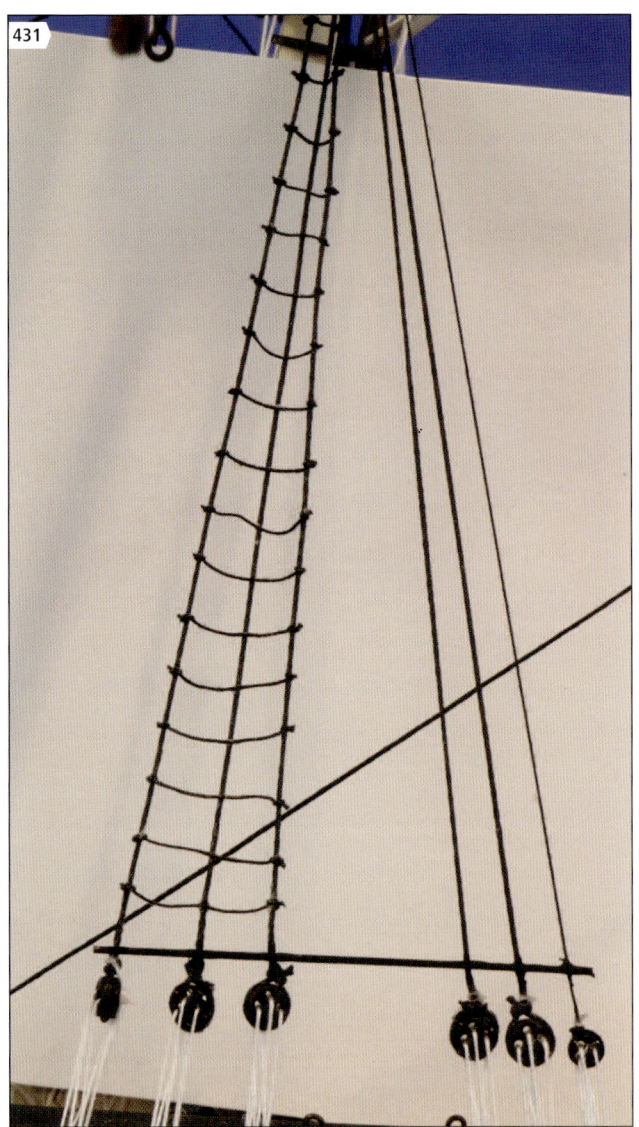

only suggestion is to use what is the most pleasing to your eye. I like black so that is what I use.

STAYS

Next up are the stays. These are the lines that keep the mast from falling forward or backwards. The first to be rigged are the *backstays* that are lines running from the mast to the rear quarter of the ship; they keep the mast from falling forward. A ship often has several backstays which can form either the standing or running rigging of a ship. We are going to rig the permanent backstays which are part of the standing rigging. There are four for each mast on *Speedy* – the topmast backstay (Figure 434), the topgallant backstay (Figure 435), the shifting and the royal backstay (Figure 436).

The forestays keep the mast from falling backwards and, like the backstays, there are several attached to each mast. Rigging starts with the main forestay and the preventer forestay (Figure 437). These stays are unusual in that each is rigged in two parts. The top part is a line that ends in a 'mouse' which is a large woven knot of rope that acts

STANDING RIGGING 151

433
The completed ratlines on *Speedy*'s main mast.

434
The main topmast and fore topmast backstays (marked with a white arrow) are rigged to deadeyes (port and starboard sides) set into the channels on the hull.

435
The fore topgallant backstay (marked by an arrow) is rigged just aft of the topmast backstay. These backstays are also rigged on the main mast.

436
The shifting (red arrow) and royal (white arrow) backstays are rigged on the main and fore mast last. With all four backstays rigged you can see how they would be adjusted on a real ship to support the mast.

437

The main (white arrow) and preventer (red arrow) forestays are set up on the main mast. These forestays are looped around a mast and into an eye. The rope is held in the eye using a 'mouse', or a large knot of rope. The mouse is represented by a large black bead.

438

The fore mast forestay (white) and preventer (red arrow) stays are rigged to the bowsprit.

439

The main topmast (white arrow) and preventer (red arrow) stays. These stays are looped around the mast and the other end of the line is rove through a block to be tied off to a bitt fastened to the deck.

440

Fore topmast stay (white arrow) and preventer (red arrow) stays. These stays are also looped around the mast and the other end is rove through blocks on the bowsprit and the line tied off to a block and tackle set fixed to an eyebolt in the bow. This set up allows the block and tackle to be pulled or let out to adjust the tension on the stays.

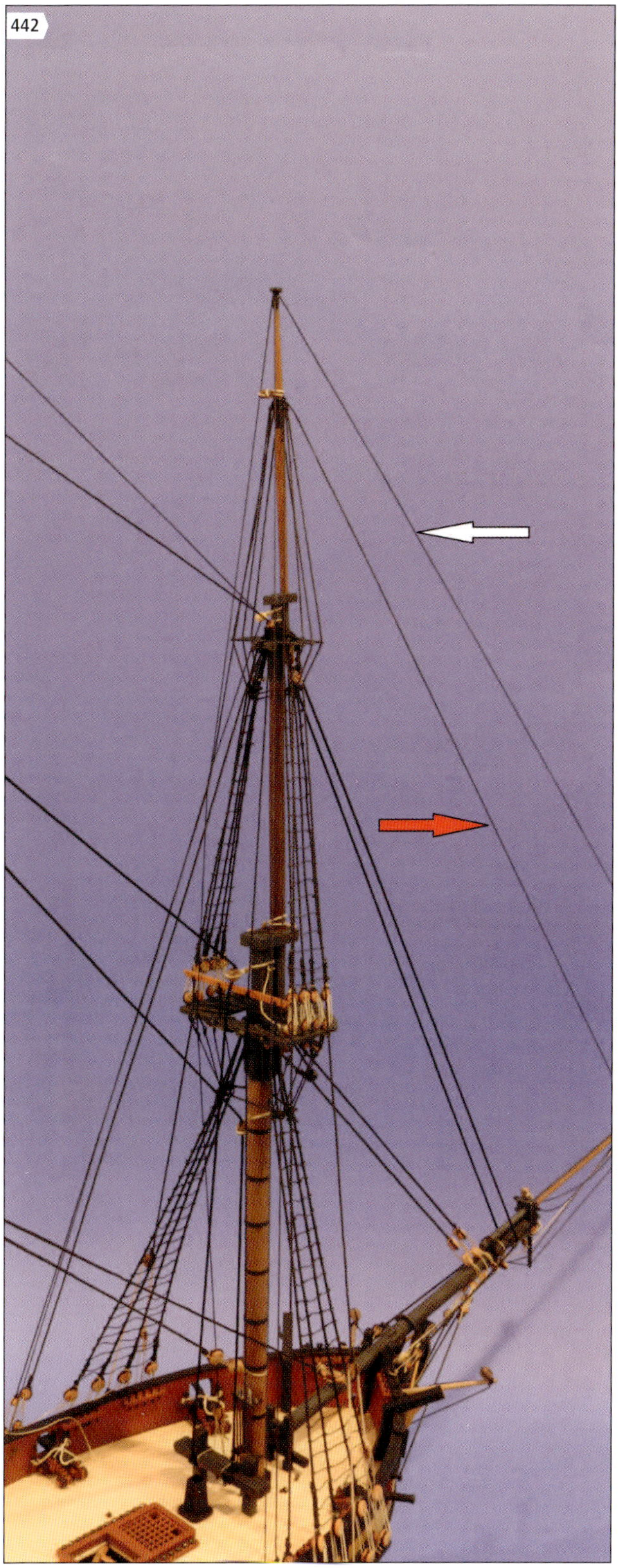

STANDING RIGGING

441

The main topgallant (red arrow) and main royal (white arrow) stays.

442

The fore topgallant (red arrow) and royal (white arrow) stays are rigged. In this photo you can see all the forestays, some of the backstays, and shrouds and when examined together as a system you gain an appreciation as to how the standing rigging works to keep the masts from falling over in any direction, and how the lines would be tensioned to adjust the rake of the masts or their stiffness. This allowed adjustments to the masts to better catch the wind and transfer the power down the mast to propel the ship forward. Sails don't just trap the wind but rather work like a crude aerofoil. The sails create high and low pressure areas to push the ship through the water and the efficiency of the sail's aerofoil is adjusted with the rigging. A ship's captain who knows the way of his ship would be able to sense this and make adjustments to get his suite of sails to peak efficiency.

like a stopper; and the bottom part is a line with an eye that slips around the mouse and ends in a deadeye. The main forestay is attached to the foremast, and the preventer stay is attached to the bowsprit. Both stays are tensioned with lanyards rove through a pair of deadeyes. The foremast also has both stays, called the forestay and fore preventer stay (Figure 438). Both of these use a mouse and eye arrangement as well and are attached to the bowsprit through a pair of deadeyes. This arrangement is repeated for the main topmast (Figure 439) and fore topmast (Figure 440), but the stays run through blocks attached to the mast or bowsprit and run along them to be tied off to a belaying pin, pin rail or tied to a deck bitt. The last stays to be rigged are the main topgallant and royal stays (Figure 441) and the fore topgallant and royal stays (Figure 442).

The real challenge to rigging is keeping the lines straight in your head and following their run. The nomenclature can be particularly

443

The shrouds, backstays and forestays rigged on *Perry*. Although a different ship, nationality, and time compared to *Speedy*, the same basic elements of standing rigging can be observed. The lines may have different names, but the principles of rigging and the purpose of each stay is very much the same. On this model I decided to rig the stays before the ratlines because of the small size of this model and required access between the shrouds. If I had put the ratlines on first they would have blocked a point of access.

challenging because it is like having to learn a new language. However, if you consider each line separately and take the time to understand what it does, you will soon find a pattern to all of this and it will become second nature to you.

11: Running Rigging

Running rigging is defined as a system of ropes to control or set the yards and sails. It is the rigging that is used for raising, lowering, shaping and controlling the sails. On a model this is usually represented with tan or natural colour threads to show it is not tarred. Installing the running rigging gets complicated simply because at this point, the model has so many lines going in every direction possible that it is easy to lose track or have one line rub up against another line (also known as *fouling*). Be prepared to string a line, then have to take it out because it becomes twisted around another line, and that the space you have to manoeuvre your fingers and tools is becoming progressively smaller and harder to do. Your best friend at this point are a few pairs of long pointed tweezers to help you get the lines where they need to go.

Rigging begins with mounting the yards and booms to the masts. Yards on real ships are supported by ropes that can raise and lower them, but leaving them loose on a model is impractical because they have no weight. Instead they must be pinned to the mast in the position you wish (Figure 444). Most modellers will pin the yards at a 90° angle to the masts, but sometimes I like to be a bit different

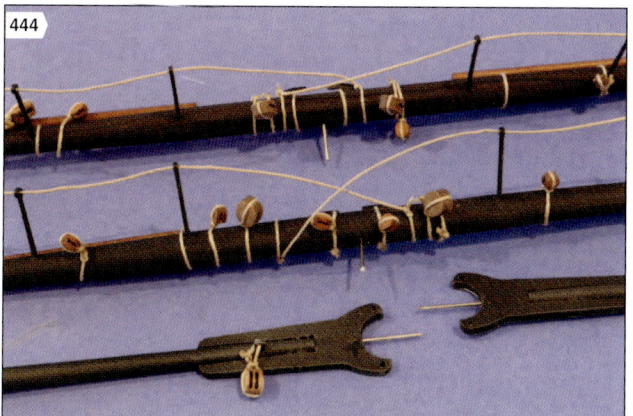

444

Brass rods are used to form a pin on the yards and booms that will fit into a hole drilled into the mast. The pins shown here are overlong and will be trimmed back so they do not protrude through to the other side of the mast.

445

The yards are attached to the masts at an angle to add a little drama and visual interest to the model.

446
Parrels can be a simple rope, beads threaded onto a rope, or an elaborate roller bearing system.

447
Parrels used in the main topmast to hold the topsail yard in place.

and swing them an extra 10 or more degrees to the mast (Figure 445). Mounting them at an angle gives a little visual excitement and allows you to see all of the detail work on the yards. Some of the yards (and booms) are held against the mast using *parrels* that allow free movement up and down the mast but will prevent a yard from being blown away from the mast (Figure 446). A parrel can be a rope, or it can be a series of beads threaded to a rope to form of roller bearing (Figure 447).

The easiest order to add the running rigging is to fit:
Yard ties
Lifts
Clews, Sheets, Tacks
Yard Braces

448
The yard lifts (white arrows) are quite visible on the fore and main masts because the ropes run from each end of the yards to a block and down the mast to a specific belaying point.

RUNNING RIGGING

449

The centre of each yard also has system of blocks and line to haul it up the mast as shown on the fore topsail yard (white arrow).

Yard Ties and Lifts

The yards need ropes to haul them up and down the length of the mast and these ropes are called *lifts and ties*. Each yard has a system of blocks to run the lifts through and by following the plan you will see where each rope goes. The lifts are attached to both ends of the yards through a system of blocks to the deck where the matelot can pull on them to keep the yards level (Figure 448). The ties are attached to the centre of the yard and through a system of blocks are used to raise and lower the yard (Figure 449). The one area where a plan is often not too clear at times is just where do the ends of the lift and ties rope go? That is, where is the rope belayed so that a sailor can quickly locate it when ordered to do so? Often on plans the rope goes into a vague location somewhere on a belaying rack and it is necessary to consult an authoritative reference to find out exactly where the lines are belayed. Newer kits will label the line with a number and belaying point with the same number, but there are often errors like finding three lines all assigned to the same belaying pin. By referring to rigging references you can get a good idea where lines are belayed, but in the absence of any information you will just have to pick a pin and hope it's correct.

450

The clew, sheet and tack lines (white arrow).

451

A bit of a test – can you pick out and identify the lines we have rigged so far? Rigging soon becomes a mass of lines seemingly running everywhere but when you systematically add each line and learn its purpose this mass of lines is quite beautiful and purposeful, and finding the clew versus a lift is quite easy. For model makers and sailors alike, it is crucial to ensure that no line fouls another. Do not hesitate to rerun a line to make sure it runs without fouling or chafing another.

Clews, Sheets, and Tacks

The next series of lines control the sails. However, because our model is bare-poled, the lines cannot be attached to the sails. Instead the line is knotted and reeved through the block nearest the sail and the line's tail (or *fall*) is threaded through its block system and tied off at the correct belaying point. There are three lines that are connected to the lower corner of each sail but because there is no sail, these lines sit tied together hanging off the yards (Figure 450). Each adjusts the sail in a different direction. The first rope is the *clew*, which hauls up the lower corners of the sail (called the clews) when it is being stowed. The second is the *sheet*, which pulls the sail down and back towards the yard below. The third is the *tack*, which leads forward and is pulled to help form the sail into an aerofoil shape as opposed to being just a bag of wind when the ship's desired course is heading into the wind. When the wind is on the starboard side, the starboard tacks are hauled forward to better catch the wind, and the ship is then said to be *on the starboard tack*. Turning through the wind is called *tacking* – when the bow comes towards and eventually past the direction of the wind, the ship has changed tack, so that the the wind blows from the other side, allowing progress in the desired direction.

Braces and Bowlines

Braces are ropes to rotate the yard around the mast to allow the ship to sail at different angles to the wind (Figure 452). They are always used in pairs. The *bowline* is a rope that holds the edge of a sail towards the bow of a ship and into the wind, preventing it from being taken aback and flapping or luffing (Figure 453). It is used when a ship is tacking to pull the leading edge of the sail forward when sailing as close to wind as possible.

Boom and Gaff

Like the yards, the main boom and gaff are pinned to the mainmast in the desired locations. The boom is rigged first because the rigging will hold it in place, allowing the gaff to be rigged without being pulled all over the place (Figures 454 and 455).

Bowsprit

The bowsprit has its own rigging and on *Speedy* it is a little more extensive because it also carried a sail called a *sprit sail* that is mounted under the bowsprit. Like the other sails and yards, many of the same lines are present and belay in racks or bitts in the bow (Figure 456).

RUNNING RIGGING   159

452

The braces are rigged (white arrows).

453

The bowlines rigged to the fore topsail yard (white arrows).

454

The main boom topping lift can be seen at the top of the picture (white arrow). The boom is pulled down to the deck via block and tackle – sometimes referred to as a boom vang to control the shape of the sail.

Rope Coils

When a rope is tied off (belayed) to a pin or tied around a deck bitt, the loose end is coiled and hung neatly. Representing these coils of rope are an important finishing touch to the model. Rope coils are easily made by wrapping thread around some pins shown in Figure 457. The most important aspect to get correct is that the coils should hang naturally and that they do not defy the laws of gravity (Figure 458). Figure 459 shows the completed rigging on *Speedy*, and Figure 460 on *Perry*. On both ships the same rigging can be found, but on *Perry*, coming from a later period, the rigging is modernized and simpler.

Sails

As we discussed in the previous chapter, adding sails to a model is really a personal choice. The biggest issue with model sails is that the fabric they are made from is usually quite coarse and the weave is

455

The gaff is rigged. The gaff tie (red arrow), vangs (white arrow), and run of boom topping lift is seen. The vangs pull down on the gaff as another way to change the sail's shape.

456

Bowsprit and sprit sail rigging.

457

Rope coils were formed by wrapping thread around pins pushed into styrofoam. Each loop was coated with thinned PVA and left to dry. When dry, they were trimmed and hung around belaying pins.

458

The rope coils fitted around the belaying pins. This photo shows a myriad of details from how lines are belayed, to how the anchor hawse has been shaped to realistically drape over the coaming, while Lord Cochrane looks on.

clearly visible and out of scale. There are many details to be incorporated into sails, such as showing how the bolts of fabric are stitched together, as well as the seams and reinforcing bands. The stitching is crucial and even the best sewing machines cannot produce scale stitches so they will always be over-scale.

Some kits today provide sail material in a fine weave cloth for you to cut up and make sails, and some kits even include pre-sewn sails, or print the fabric with all the hems, seams, reinforcing bands and

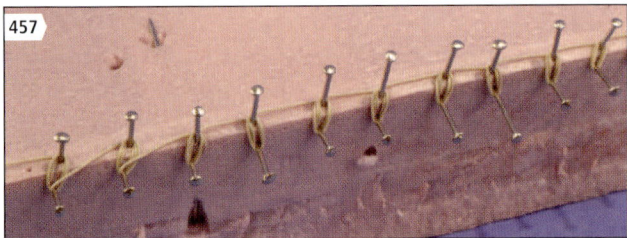

459
The amount of rigging for this little brig is quite astounding and is a credit to Vanguard Models' design to capture the look and feel of rigging characteristic of the late 1700s. The Red Ensign flag is an aftermarket cloth item from BECC. Getting the correct flag on the ship is very important. Too often the flag provided in kits is the modern versions of a national flag, and not the version flown at the time.

other details (Figures 461 and 462). As you can see from the figures, none of these really looks right. Even if the finest cloth is used, their light weight does not permit the sails to hang properly without starching and moulding them. On real ships sails are made from hundreds of yards of canvas and they are very heavy, and a real sail will hang in a way that no lightweight woven material ever can on its own.

My solution is to do what miniature ship modellers do – don't use cloth at all but paper (Figure 463). Paper has no visible weave, it can be painted and detailed with pencil, and most of all it can be moulded and shaped to hang properly. Paper sails work well on miniature models, but also on large-scale models as well. The first step is to take a sheet of copy paper and paint it over with thinned out tan coloured acrylic paints. Don't try to get the colour even, just brush the paint on with a wide brush in the direction of the paper's grain. Add a little black paint and paint it over here and there, add a little brown paint and paint it there and here until you

get an uneven finish that covers the whiteness of the paper. Allow it to dry and paint the other side. Do paint several sheets of paper at once with some being a little darker or lighter in overall tone than the other.

The dried painted paper will be a little wrinkled so flatten it with a warm iron. To make a sail, first draw its outline on the painted sheet in pencil. The plans you built your model to might have drawn out the sails so you just have to plot out the shape. If your plans don't provide a sail plan, then you will have to draw it out yourself using an authoritative reference for the correct size and shape. With the outline drawn, draw in the reinforcing bands around the sail edge, then the reef bands and reinforcing corners in pencil. This has to be done on both sides. I have an artist's light box that shines light though paper and this allows me to get the pencil lines in exactly the same spot on both sides of the paper by simply tracing as opposed to laboriously plotting the pencil lines on both sides. The last thing to draw in are the seams to represent the bolts of fabric that were joined together to make the sail, and the sail can now be cut out.

To provide more detail to the sail, cut some strips of painted paper the width of the bolts of cloth from a sheet that is a slightly different shade than the sail you are working on. These strips can be cut to random lengths and glued down to the sail. This will give the impression that different bolts of cloth were used to make the sail and provides visual interest. The reef bands are pierced with a pin or needle to produce reef points to which short lengths of thread are glued. These lengths of rope, called reef lines, are used to tie up the gathers in the sail when they are taken in (*shortened* or *reefed*) to control the speed of the ship or prevent the mast and sails from

460

Perry all rigged. It is quite interesting to see how rigging changed from the time of *Speedy* to *Perry*. The same basic elements are there from ties, braces and lifts, but the increased use of metal work and materials meant the rigging is simpler without losing functionality.

getting damaged in heavy weather. The threads are trimmed to length after the glue has dried.

The final step is to put on *bolt ropes* (Figure 464). The bolt rope is laced along the edges of the entire sail and provides reinforcement to the sail's edge. One way to represent the bolt rope is to use PVA glue to fix a heavy thread along the back inside edge of the sail. Another way is to make some wire rope. Three or four strands of tinned copper wire are twisted together in a lathe to resemble rope. The wire rope is painted a tan colour and the wire rope is glued along the back inside edges of the sail with flexible CA. The advantage of

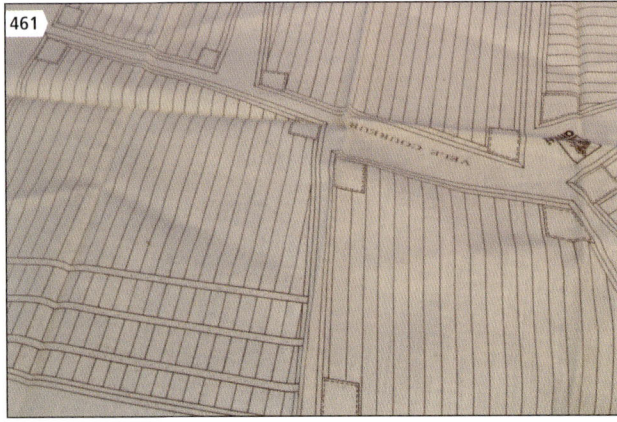

461

Kit supplied fabric sails and sail material. It all looks over scale.

462

Pre-sewn sails included in the *Cutty Sark* kit.

RUNNING RIGGING

463
Paper sails made for a 1/100 model of *Victory*.

464
Close up of wire bolt rope on a paper sail.

the wire rope is that you can bend and shape it, and thus give your sails a look that they are filled with some wind or bent to hang properly (Figure 465). Note how the wire rope is looped at the corner to provide a convenient place to tie the sail onto the yard. It is not

465
Paper sails on the cutter *Alert* showing the billowing effect you can achieve.

entirely authentic because the sail was attached (or *bent*) to the yards along its whole length but it is a convenient model making expedient.

A modified version of paper sails can be made of cloth. Instead of painting sheets of paper, pieces of the finest weave fabric you can find can be dyed different shades. The fabric is then soaked with thinned white glue (or fabric glue sold at fabric shops) and set aside to dry. The glue will provide stiffness, but also prevent the threads from unravelling when you cut the cloth into bolts. The bolts are

466

Le Coureur's fabric sails. (Photo courtesy of Tom Cao)

best cut with a rotary cutter used by tailors. The bolts are glued together by overlapping the edges of each bolt to one another to form the sail. The fabric is ironed flat and the sail cut out. Reef bands, reinforcing bands, and whatnot are glued to the sail like the paper sails. The bolt rope is a heavy thread or scale model rope that is best stitched to the sail by hand with tiny stitches. This is tedious work but the effect well worth it as shown on CAF's *Le Coureur* model (Figure 466). Having a model with sails really is the ultimate ship model but they are amongst the most difficult items to create with a scale-like appearance. Model making books on how to make dioramas and model soldier books are especially helpful for further reading because they dwell entirely on how cloth behaves and how to represent that, and the effects of scale, colour, and gravity.

The final step is to add the flags and pennants to your model. Many kits provide paper flags that are folded around its *halliard* or *halyard* (a line use to haul up a sail, flag or yard. The term comes from the phrase, 'to haul yards'). When using paper flags, take some time to give it a flutter appearance by curling it over the end of a paintbrush until it looks like it is fluttering in the wind naturally. Don't forget to paint over the cut edges of the paper for a finished and authentic effect. Fabric flags are best soaked in some hot water to soften them and given a thin coat of fabric glue before they are cut out. After they are cut out they too must be shaped with gentle curling, but be careful not to fray the edges. Most importantly, ensure that your ship is flying the correct flag. The Union Flag changed as different countries joined the United Kingdom, the number of stars on the United States Flag changed as states were entered into their union, and Canada flew a 'defaced' Red Ensign until the familiar Maple Leaf was adopted in 1967. There is nothing worse than seeing a model of the *Bluenose* schooner flying the Maple Leaf – only the replica ship did, but then you would have to fit the auxiliary shaft and screws to be correct!

12: Finishing Up and Inspiration

The last rigging line has been trimmed off. The model is virtually complete and all that remains is to touch up any paint, clean up any debris and cover up any glue marks with a matt or satin varnish. Savour the feeling of accomplishment as you admire your model and show it off to friends, family and fellow model makers. This is a good time to think about what you did right, what you struggled with, and what you would like to improve on your next model. As you contemplate these questions, this is a good time to get some inspiration. Visit a website devoted to model ships, visit a museum, read some fictional novels about life at sea, or purchase some books for your library. Most of all, look at other people's models. It is in this activity that you learn the most and get that spark of joy that propels you to the next one.

I leave you now with a selection of photos of a few models I have built over the years experimenting with different finishes, techniques, and display options. Trying out different types of models keeps the creative spark alive and encourages skill development. This wonderfully varied approach to modelling is embodied by the members of a model ship club in Tokyo, Japan called 'The Rope'. The choice of models and their warm welcome to modellers of all abilities never fails to inspire, and I hope the following small selection from their recent exhibition is as inspirational to you as well.

467

The schooner *Balahoo* (1/64) built from the Caldercraft kit set into a seascape. My goal with this model was to try to portray a ship at sea as realistically as possible. The kit was heavily weathered and the hull planking lines were emphasized by gently bevelling the outside edges of the planks so that a gap appears between each strake. The seascape is papier-mâché painted to match colour photos of the North Atlantic. The figures are 28mm figures designed for ship to ship skirmish wargames made by Old Glory. The sails are paper with twisted wire boltropes as described in the text.

468

The 38-gun frigate *Diana* (1/64) built from the Caldercraft kit. The model is fully painted and built with stub masts and bowsprit to save space. The kit-supplied copper plates were detailed with large dimples to represent the nail heads. These were hammered flat that left a much more realistic representation. Each plate was cleaned and brushed with some green patina solution and washed off before applying to the hull.

469

A view of *Diana*'s waist. The guns are fully rigged and the ship's boats left off to permit a good view of the gundeck.

470

Diana's stern. None of the paintwork on this model was weathered or shaded to get a pristine look to the model. Only the carvings were given a wash of dark brown to bring out the sculpted details.

FINISHING UP AND INSPIRATION

471

The French cutter *Le Cerf* scratch-built to 1/192 scale. The hull is carved from a small piece of wood found in a scrap bin. The decks are individually laid planks of holly. The guns are shaped wooden dowel. The boat was carved from a solid piece of holly and hollowed out. The stern decoration is printed on a piece of paper and painted over. A lot of effort went into shading the drawing to give it a three-dimensional effect in this small scale. The figures and dog are 1/180 railway figures made by Preiser.

472

A view of *Le Cerf*'s mainmast and top. The rigging is a combination of painted wire and fine thread. The sails are painted paper and the rigging blocks are little discs punched from brown paper and glued into the correct places.

473

Royal George (1715). This 1/192 Admiralty style model was scratch-built by Mr Etsuro Tsuboi with half futtock style framing that highlights the sweeping sheer and curves of the hull. (Photo courtesy of Etsuro Tsuboi)

474

Royal William (1719). A stern quarter view showing off the stern galleries and planking of this 1/60 model by Mr Katsuji Tsuchiya. All of the decoration was hand-carved. (Photo courtesy of Katsuji Tsuchiya)

475

Royal William (1719). Mr Katsuji Tsuchiya also built a cross section of the ship that shows all of the interior of the ship and the framing. (Photo courtesy of Katsuji Tsuchiya)

FINISHING UP AND INSPIRATION 169

476
A stern quarter view of *Cutty Sark*. The model uses stub masts which despite clipper ships being defined by towering masts for speed, are not missed on this model. The sense of speed of these tea clippers is conveyed by the shape of the hull and the uncluttered presentation on its plinth highlights the beautiful lines of the hull. (Photo courtesy of Masahiro Ando)

Cutty Sark (1869). This 1/78 scale model built by Mr Masahiro Ando shows the ship at a later time in her career than the model built in Chapter 5. There are differences in decoration and paint work. Of particular note is the excellent coppering of the hull. This was done with individually cut copper plates that have oxidized naturally, and not copper tape. The model began life as a kit by the Italian manufacturer Mantual/Sergal. (Photo courtesy of Masahiro Ando)

478

SS *Beaver* (1835). The Hudson Bay Company steamer was built to 1/64 scale by Mr Kenji Sato. The ship represents the transformation from the age of sail to powered vessels. The model is notable for its finely weathered paintwork that incorporates paint shading and subtle rust and wear and tear effects that captures the feel of a working steamer. (Photo courtesy of Kenji Sato)

479

This close up of *Beaver*'s rigging illustrates how properly shaped blocks and the correct sizes of rigging line come together to show how masts and yards are handled. The viewer really comes to understand how a ship is sailed. (Photo courtesy of Kenji Sato)

FINISHING UP AND INSPIRATION 171

479

480

Higaki-Kaisen. A small Japanese cargo vessel from the seventeenth/eighteenth century by Mr Taketoshi Tanaka. This 1/100 scale model is notable for the sails and its authentic Japanese stitching of the fabric bolts. The inclusion of figures wearing period Japanese dress, in particular the hairstyles, brings the model to life. The lattice work on the hull, called 'Higaki', is a trademark of the ship's owner and illustrates how important in-scale gratings and lattices are. (Photo courtesy of Taketoshi Tanaka)

481

Le Hussard (1848). A view of the forecastle of this 1/64 scale model by Mr Norio Uriu. The photo illustrates in detail how guns were stowed and how much gear filled the deck and bulwarks. Of note is the subtle shading and weathering of the inner bulwarks that bring the model to life. The rigging lines are properly belayed with neat rope coils. (Photo courtesy of Norio Uriu)

482

A view of *Le Hussard*'s stern and there is a great deal of detail work to be taken in. The ship's boat is highly detailed and properly stowed on its davits and retaining straps. Gratings are to scale and the bulwarks are fully detailed. (Photo courtesy of Norio Uriu)

483

Gozabune Taihomaru of the Higo Clan (seventeenth – nineteenth century). Most models from the age of sail are European designs, but ships from this era come from all over the world. Models of ships from Japan, China, and Korea are now more popular as information about them is published in different languages. Mr Taketoshi Tanaka built this 1/62 scale model from scratch using drawings and illustrations from old Japanese texts. It took a great deal of work to research this little ship and draw out his own plans to work from. His work highlights the importance of research in that when done properly, there is no limitation to the types of ships you can build. In today's digital world, being able to instantly translate documents from one language to another removes a major barrier to research. (Photo courtesy of Taketoshi Tanaka)

484

Another view of the *Gozabune*. Although the model is shown being powered by oars, the vessel could be outfitted with a mast on the foredeck. The model's paintwork was designed to represent the Japanese lacquer finish of the actual vessel by using water based lacquer paints. (Photo courtesy of Taketoshi Tanaka)

485

La Belle Poule (1765). A beautiful example of the famous French frigate by Mr Norio Uriu in 1/72 scale. The model was scratch-built using the plans from Jean Boudriot published by ANCRE. (Photo courtesy of Norio Uriu)

486

A close up view of *La Belle Poule*'s bow. In this photo you get a clear sense of how major ship handling items like anchors are stowed, and a sense of how the decoration all must flow together. This ship predated the introduction of copper plating and the absence of sheathing on the ship's bottom shows off the hull planking. The real ship's bottom would have been painted with white paint to protect it from corrosion and worm. (Photo courtesy of Norio Uriu)

FINISHING UP AND INSPIRATION   175

486

487

Star Clipper Sailing Cruise Ship (1992). This was the first clipper type vessel built since 1912 and is used for cruise holidays. This 1/192 model was built by Mr Jun Hida and this photo illustrates how the inclusion of figures brings a model to life. The model is also fully illuminated. (Photo courtesy of Jun Hida)

488

Cumberland (1774). This large-scale 1/60 model in frame by Mr Katsuji Tsuchiya shows in detail all of the timbers that make up the ship. (Photo courtesy of Katsuji Tsuchiya)

Recommended References and Sources

Antscherl, D, *The Fully Framed Model, HMN Swan Class Sloops 1767-1780, Vols I-IV,* (New York, 2004).
Boudriot, J, *The Seventy Four Gun Ship, Vols I-IV,* (Paris, 1986).
Franklin, J, *Navy Board Ship Models 1650-1750* (London, 1989).
Fröchlich, B, *The Art of Ship Modelling* (Nice, 1999).
Goodwin, P, *The Construction and Fitting of the English Man of War 1650-1850* (London, 1992).
Hahn, H M, *Ships of the American Revolution and Their Models* (London, 1988).
Lavery, B, *The Arming and Fitting of English Ships of War 1600-1815* (London, 1987).
Lees, J, *The Masting and Rigging of English Ships of War 1625-1860* (London, 1990).
Longridge, C N, *The Anatomy of Nelson's Ships* (London, 1961).
Longridge, C N, *The Cutty Sark* (New York, 1959).
McNarry, D, *Ship Models in Miniature* (New York, 1975).
Petersson, L, *Rigging Period Ship Models* (London, 2000).
Petersson, L, *Rigging Period Fore-and-Aft Craft* (London, 2007).
Reed, P, *Period Ship Modelmaking* (Barnsley, 2007).
Reed, P, *Building a Miniature Navy Board Model* (Barnsley, 2009).

Vanguard Models
https://vanguardmodels.co.uk/
Kits and distributor of Master-Korabel kits from Russia. Growing range of accessories and fittings.

CAF Models
https://cafmodel.com/
Fully framed ship kits and accessories.

Syren Ship Model Company
https://syrenshipmodelcompany.com/
Kits and semi-kits and a wide array of tools and supplies, including rigging blocks and fittings.

Bluejacket Shipcrafters
http://www.bluejacketinc.com/
Kits and a wide array of supplies including fittings, books, timber, tools, and paints.

Domanoff Workshop
https://shipworkshop.com
Tools such as ropewalks and serving machines.

Scale Warship
https://scalewarship.com/
A growing selection of photo-etch and resin accessories aimed at plastic models of sailing ships.

HiSModel (Historic Ship Models)
www.HiSModel.com
An extremely large range of accessories such as rigging blocks, line, and fittings from guns to wooden decks designed to fit many of the available plastic kits. Of particular note are fabric sail sets sewn by CNC. Their accessories are perfectly suitable for enhancing wooden kits.

Dusek Ship Kits
http://www.dusekshipkits.com/
A large range of kits, including re-releases of kits by Mamoli and other famous brands. Also manufactures a unique range of figures.

Nautical Research Guild
237 South Lincoln Street
Westmont IL, 60559-1917
585-968-8111
https://www.thenrg.org/

Model Ship World
https://modelshipworld.com/

The Rope Ship Model Ship Builder's Club (Tokyo)
https://www.theropetokyo.org/
The Rope holds an annual exhibition of members' models built from kits to scratch. The exhibition is open to the public and warmly welcomes visiting model makers from around the world. They produce a regular newsletter that is translated into English for overseas visitors to keep them in touch with the club.